The Coordination of Inter-Organizational Networks
in the Enterprise Software Industry

INFORMATIONSTECHNOLOGIE UND ÖKONOMIE

Herausgegeben von Christian Becker, Wolfgang Gaul, Armin Heinzl, Martin Schader und Daniel Veit

Band 46

PETER LANG

Frankfurt am Main · Berlin · Bern · Bruxelles · New York · Oxford · Wien

Thomas Kude

The Coordination of Inter-Organizational Networks in the Enterprise Software Industry

The Perspective of Complementors

PETER LANG
Internationaler Verlag der Wissenschaften

Bibliographic Information published by the Deutsche Nationalbibliothek
The Deutsche Nationalbibliothek lists this publication in the Deutsche Nationalbibliografie; detailed bibliographic data is available in the internet at http://dnb.d-nb.de.

Zugl.: Mannheim, Univ., Diss., 2011

D 180
ISSN 1616-086X
ISBN 978-3-631-62097-7

www.peterlang.de

Foreword

The software industry is a key sector that increasingly contributes to the gross national product of modern economies. Enterprise software systems enable efficient and effective processes in other sectors. The development of these enterprise software systems has been following a higher degree of labor division. Large platform vendors establish partnership networks - or software ecosystems - with a large number of complementor organizations that provide niche functionalities. The innovativeness and functional specialization of these smaller niche vendors is crucial for the success of a platform.

Software ecosystems differ from traditional supply networks because there is no exchange of physical goods. The partners offer their solutions separately and the clients decide if and how they integrate the components from different vendors into a functioning system. The interplay of these components depends on the context of their use. As a consequence, software vendors have to coordinate their activity early on in the process of developing software architectures and complementary components.

The partnerships between platform vendors and smaller complementors are unique in terms of the co-existence of competition and cooperation. On the one hand, the success of the overall network has to be ensured. On the other hand, platform vendors may decide to compete with a partner in a certain niche. Other conflicts of interests may result from the rent distribution of the entire ecosystem. Platform vendors aim at establishing comprehensive networks with a large number of niche vendors in order to benefit from network effects. Niche vendors as well draw advantages from participating in a successful network. However, the direct benefits from network effects are much lower. Instead, small and medium-sized complementors may critically depend on their large partner's resources. This suggests that it is crucial for complementor organizations to effectively coordinate their partnerships with platform vendors.

Thomas Kude's dissertation has addressed an exciting and important research gap. It is among the first to examine partnership networks in the enterprise software industry from the perspective of small and medium-sized complementor organizations. The study offers several important results. It provides a theoretical contribution to the Information Systems discipline by improving our understanding of the determinants of coordination mechanisms in the enterprise software industry. Moreover, it contributes to theory development in adjacent disciplines such as organizational science and strategic management by applying and enhancing reference theories in the case of asymmetric partnership networks in the enterprise software industry.

The findings can be applied by small and medium-sized software firms in order to better coordinate their partnerships. Moreover, platform vendors obtain important insights regarding the question of how to balance the trade-off between efficiently coordinating the overall software ecosystem and satisfying particular partners. Altogether, Thomas Kude's dissertation is exceptional in terms of its comprehensive contribution to both theory and practice.

The study was conducted in the context of the research project "CollaBaWü+" (Collaborative Software Development Baden-Württemberg), which was founded by the Ministry of Science, Research and the Arts of Baden-Württemberg (Germany). The project itself was conducted in close cooperation with small and medium-sized enterprise software vendors.

The book targets both practitioners and researchers. Managers of software firms obtain valuable knowledge on the differences between successful and less successful complementor organizations. In particular, owners and managers of small and medium-sized software companies learn about the vital question of what should be taken into account when partnering with large platform vendors. Academic readers are offered a systematic and profound contribution on coordination mechanisms in software ecosystems as well as on theory building in the Information Systems discipline and beyond.

Mannheim, October 2011 Armin Heinzl

Acknowledgments

Developing and writing my doctoral thesis has been an enriching, but also challenging process. I would like to express my gratitude to the many individuals that have supported me during this time and acknowledge their contribution to my work.

First and foremost, I would like to thank my supervisor Professor Dr. Armin Heinzl, who encouraged me to do research in Information Systems at the University of Mannheim. Professor Heinzl has been a great advisor and has always supported me during my time at his chair. He gave me the freedom to develop and pursue my ideas but at the same time guided my research efforts and encouraged me to present our work at conferences and in journals.

During my first two years at the chair, I had been fortunate to have Professor Dr. Jens Dibbern as a colleague. During this time and after, it has been a pleasure to work with and learn from Jens. Discussing ideas and working on research projects with him has always been motivating, insightful, and a lot of fun.

Moreover, I would like to thank Professor Dr. Andrew Burton-Jones for inviting me to a research stay at the University of British Columbia in Vancouver. I appreciated Andrew's support and warm welcome. In addition, I would like to thank the faculty and PhD students at the MIS department for the conversations and comments on my work and for the great time at UBC.

Furthermore, I would like to thank Professor Dr. Irene Bertschek, Professor Dr. Christian Hofmann, Professor Dr. Alexander Mädche, as well as Professor Dr. Michael Woywode for serving as members of my committee.

As a part of my empirical study, I had the opportunity to conduct interviews with numerous industry experts. I very much appreciated the insightful conversations and their time and effort to support me in my research.

In addition, I would like to acknowledge the contribution of the following students who supported me during the process of writing my thesis: Thomas Huber, Hamsa Sankaran, David Zeus, Dominik Münchenbach, and Manuel Draxinger. I further want to thank secretaries Luise Bühler and Ingrid Distelrath as well as the student assistants Nina Jaeger, Melanie Marnet, Olga Oster, Lea Offermann, and Santana Overath for their administrative support.

I have always appreciated and enjoyed the great atmosphere at our chair. Therefore, I would like to thank my wonderful colleagues Sven Scheibmayr, Erik Hemmer, Miroslav Lazic, Lars Klimpke, Sebastian Stuckenberg, Tommi Kramer, Kai Spohrer, Marko Nöhren, and Christoph Schmidt.

Similarly, I would like to thank my former colleagues Jens Arndt, Birte Autzen, Thomas Butter, Sina Deibert, Michael Geisser, Tobias Hildenbrand, Boris Quaing, Jessica Winkler, and Anja Zöller. I particularly thank Jens and Jessica for the conversations and the support in the early phase of my research.

Finally, I wish to thank my closest friends and my family for their unconditional support in all aspects of life. In particular, my deepest gratitude goes to my mom, my dad, and my brother Oliver.

Mannheim, July 2011 Thomas Kude

Contents

List of Figures

List of Tables

List of Abbreviations

BI	Business intelligence
CRM	Customer relationship management
ERP	Enterprise resource planning
IO	Industrial organization
IOS	Inter-organizational information system
IS	Information systems
ISV	Independent software vendor
IT	Information technology
KBV	Knowledge-based view
PC	Personal computer
PLM	Product lifecycle management
RBV	Resource-based view
RDT	Resource dependence theory
SaaS	Software as a service
SCM	Supply chain management
SME	Small and medium-sized enterprise
SOA	Service-oriented architecture
SRM	Supplier relationship management
TCE	Transaction cost economics

1 Introduction

1.1 Problem statement

The coordination of separated activities in the process of developing enterprise software has been an important issue in theory and practice for many decades (Faraj and Sproull, 2000; Kraut and Streeter, 1995; Messerschmitt and Szyperski, 2003). The mechanisms to coordinate enterprise software development processes, however, have been subject to significant changes as a consequence of the changing structure of the enterprise software industry. In the early days of computing, enterprise software was custom-developed in a make-to-order fashion. Later, in the 1970s, standardized, monolithic systems that covered most of the primary business functions in different industries emerged (Cusumano, 2004). During the 1980s, these systems became the state-of-the-art, resulting in an oligopolistic market with a few dominating system vendors like IBM, Oracle or SAP (Campbell-Kelly, 2003).

In the last two decades, however, this trend has been counteracted by a tendency towards disintegration (Bresnahan and Greenstein, 1999; Messerschmitt and Szyperski, 2003; Zenger and Hesterly, 1997). As a result, formerly integrated systems are now more and more characterized by a high degree of modularity (Baldwin and Clark, 1997). From a theoretical point of view, it can be argued that the trend towards disintegrated systems should be reflected in a higher degree of organizational modularity within the industry (Conway, 1968; Hoetker, 2006; Sanchez and Mahoney, 1996; Heinzl and Oberweis, 2007). This is indeed the case. Partnership networks have emerged in which companies work together based on mutually agreed standards (Gao and Iyer, 2008; Ring and Van de Ven, 1992). Two archetypes of organizations can be identified within these partnership networks - hub organizations and spoke organizations. Hub organizations, also referred to as platform leaders or keystones, can be defined as organizations that provide systems' architecture and generic core functionalities (Gawer and

Cusumano, 2002; Iansiti and Levien, 2004; Evans et al., 2006). In contrast, spoke organizations (or niche players) can be defined as smaller software companies that build their solutions on top of and complement platforms offered by hubs (Iansiti and Levien, 2004; Prencipe, 2004). Figure 1.1 shows an idealized hub-and-spoke network (Damsgaard and Truex, 2000; Van de Ven et al., 1979; Evan, 1966).

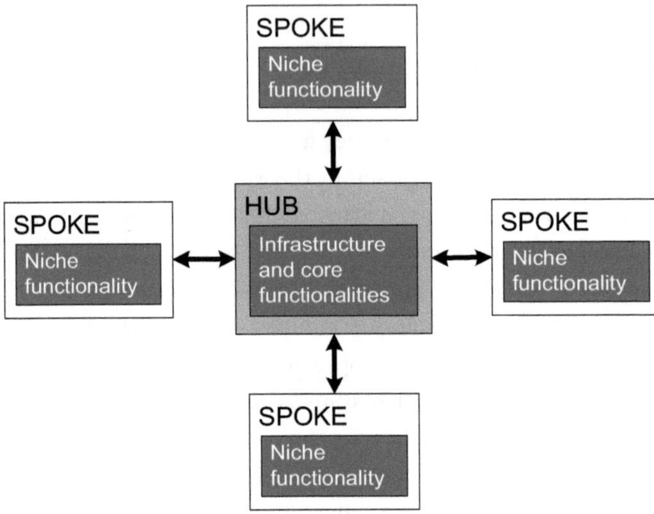

Figure 1.1: Idealized hub-and-spoke network

There has recently been an abundance of research on supply networks in many different industries (e.g., Harland et al., 2001; Pathak et al., 2007). Hub-and-spoke networks in the enterprise software industry differ from these supply networks in that there is no exchange of goods between partners. Instead, both hubs and spokes sell their solutions directly to the market. These new network structures in the enterprise software industry have rarely been addressed in the information systems (IS) literature (Tiwana et al., 2010). A recent exception is a study by Chellappa and Saraf (2010), who used social network analysis to examine the impact of the structural position of an organizational actor in the enterprise software industry on firm performance. Related to this, Gao and Iyer (2008) have drawn on the theory of complementarity (Milgrom and Roberts, 1995) and studied the influence of complementary technology within a software stack model (Grove, 1996) on the success of inter-organizational arrangements.

Even though these studies yield important insights, they disregard some of the special characteristics of enterprise software. In an ideal world, once decided in favor of a certain platform, modularity and standardized interfaces would allow customers to mix-and-match complementary functionality in accordance to their needs (compare Apple's iPhone as an example from the consumer electronics industry). Such a perfect decomposition of systems and organizations, however, is hindered by the obstacles posed by the specific nature of enterprise software. Functionalities and interfaces of most goods are usually clearly defined during the research and development process. However, this is not necessarily the case for enterprise software, which is an intellectual good in the sense that its ability to fulfill certain requirements is limited not by physical attributes but only by human imagination (Lee, 1999). Therefore, the interplay of software components from different vendors is contingent upon the context of use, such as the specific processes of a certain organization. Consequently, there is a need for coordination when developing enterprise software through inter-organizational division of work in order to provide systems of high quality (Adler, 1995; Kraut and Streeter, 1995; Thompson, 1967). Thus, instead of analyzing the link between an organization's structural position or its technological complementarity and the success of inter-organizational arrangements on a high level, it may be fruitful to study the mediating role of the coordination of inter-organizational division of work.

Generally, coordination can be defined as "managing dependencies between activities" (Malone and Crowston, 1994, p. 90). At an individual and team level, the coordination of tasks that are necessary to collaboratively develop IS has been the focus of prior work (Faraj and Sproull, 2000; Kraut and Streeter, 1995). However, when analyzing the coordination of hub-and-spoke networks in the enterprise software industry on an organizational level, the dependencies that need to be managed differ substantially between the roles of hub and spoke.

On the one hand, platform providers depend on the ability to create and exploit two-sided network effects and aim at turning their systems into a de facto standard (Rochet and Tirole, 2003; Shapiro and Varian, 1999). Thus, platform providers may seek to establish large organizational networks by forming partnerships with a multitude of spokes that offer complementary functionalities (Lorenzoni and Baden-Fuller, 1995; Shapiro and Varian, 1999).

On the other hand, the ability of spoke organizations to benefit from network effects is limited. In contrast to hubs, spokes can be assumed to be highly dependent on the resources provided by their larger partner (Bala and Venkatesh, 2007; Pfeffer and Salancik, 1978). Thus, small complementors may strive for effective coordination, thereby rather disregarding efficiency. Also, within large organizations, the coordination of the relationship with a certain partner may take place at various levels. At an organizational, strategic level, the large platform vendor may aim at efficiently coordinating the overall network. However, the actual coordination of specific partnerships may happen in a more pragmatic way at the operative level, that is at a group or individual level.

1.2 Research objectives

Although it is acknowledged that coordination is necessarily a bilateral task, the differences between hub and spoke suggest a specific analysis of the hub and spoke perspective. Previous research has focused on the coordination of inter-organizational networks from the hub organizations' point of view (Iansiti and Levien, 2004; Shapiro and Varian, 1999). In order to efficiently coordinate the overall network, hubs may aim at relational extendability. In other words, they may seek to "redeploy and leverage existing relation-specific assets and routines in other relationships" (Bala and Venkatesh, 2007, p. 343). In contrast, the question of how small organizations that act as complementors (Brandenburger and Nalebuff, 1996) within the hub-and-spoke networks manage dependencies between activities, that is, coordinate their partnership with the hub organizations, remains unanswered. In the face of this lack of research on the coordination of network structures in the enterprise software industry, and specifically on the role of organizations that act as complementors, this research project examines the perspective of spokes within the emerging hub-and-spoke networks and aims at answering the following research questions:

(1) How do small complementor organizations within inter-organizational networks in the enterprise software industry coordinate the partnership with their larger partner?

(2) How can variations in the way how complementors coordinate the partnership with their larger partner be explained?

(3) Taking into consideration the identified contingencies, how should a particular complementor coordinate its partnership with a hub?

Analyzing the determinants of the mechanisms chosen by spoke organizations in the enterprise software industry to coordinate the inter-organizational division of work provides important insights for various stakeholders. First, a contribution to theory in IS is made by addressing the research gap regarding the determinants and implications of coordination mechanisms applied by collaborating firms in the enterprise software industry (Locke and Golden-Biddle, 1997). Second, since this study draws on theories that originate in reference disciplines and applies them to inter-organizational IS development, its findings have implications for theory development in these adjacent disciplines. Third, the question of how to coordinate the partnership with their larger partner is a vital one for small firms that act as complementors. Thus, the results of this study should be relevant for these complementors. Fourth, the findings are of interest for large organizations that foster partnership networks and have to deal with the trade-off to efficiently coordinate the overall network and at the same time satisfy the single partners.

1.3 Research design

The epistemological stance of this study is positivist, assuming that social reality exists independent of human consciousness and cognition (Orlikowski and Baroudi, 1991). Although the object of analysis is clearly determined as the organization that complements other systems within inter-organizational networks, this research endeavor acknowledges that organizational behavior is influenced both by individual action as well as by the network and the industry that forms the organization's environment. Thus, this study adopts a systemic view of the world (von Bertalanffy, 1968). The research project follows a qualitative research design, which is deemed promising in order to answer the question of how organizational networks are coordinated (Yin, 2009).

The research is organized in three stages (see Figure 1.2), beginning with an exploratory phase in which small enterprise software vendors that complement the networks of large platform providers are analyzed. Platform vendors and complementors differ in terms of their resource endowments. As a result, plat-

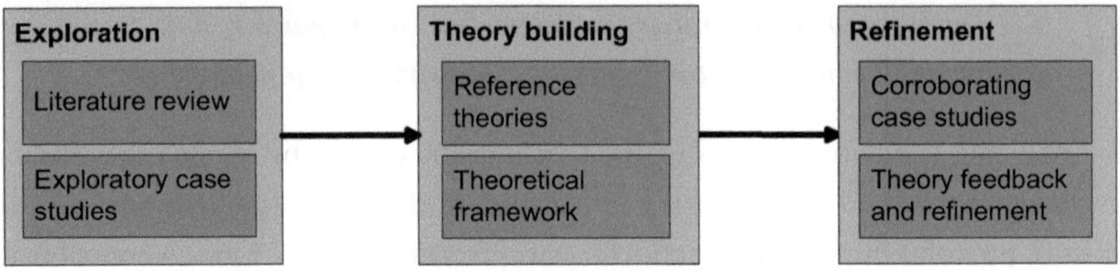

Figure 1.2: Research approach

form vendors depend on a large network of complementors as an important resource, while small complementors depend on the resources of the platform vendor. Hence, it seems reasonable to use a resource-based perspective that stresses resource heterogeneity as the basic frame of the exploratory case studies. With this resource-based theoretical stance in mind, the aim of the case studies is to explore resource complementarity and coordination. Thereby, the conceptualizations of resource complementarity as well as different types of coordination act as preliminary constructs.

Based on the exploratory case studies and existing literature, the second phase of the project develops a framework that is able to explain the type of coordination as well as partnership success. The study hence aims at concretizing the preliminary constructs as well as identifying emergent ones in order to provide a comprehensive but parsimonious explanatory model. As a third step, a second multiple-case study is carried out with the goal of substantiating and further refining the theoretical model. The goal of this study is to develop a mid-range theory that reveals causal relationships which are generalizable to a certain set of phenomena, but does not aim at providing abstract, all-embracing explanations which are valid in every conceivable context (Merton, 1968; Gregor, 2006).

1.4 Study organization

The structure of the thesis basically follows the three phase research design outlined above. Chapter 2 lays the groundwork of the research project by discussing its theoretical foundations and deducing basic constructs central to the research questions. Therefore, an overview of the historical development of the enterprise software industry is given. In addition, the industry's current structure and its archetypical organizational actors are discussed. Next, a review of important literature on the coordination of division of work – both in the field of IS as well as in adjacent disciplines – is presented. Then, based on this literature review, a preliminary framework that guides the exploratory empirical study is proposed.

Chapter 3 gives a well-founded rationale for the chosen research design. Specifically, the epistemological stance of the study is clarified and the chosen qualitative research approach is justified. Moreover, the three phase approach depicted in Figure 1.2 is presented in more detail.

In Chapter 4, two explanatory models that answer this study's research questions are developed based on existing theories and empirical observation. Specifically, the results of an exploratory case study of 17 spoke organizations within two different hub-and-spoke networks are presented.

Subsequently, reflecting the third phase of the study, Chapter 5 discusses the substantiation and refinement of these preliminary models. Therefore, a second multiple-case study of 11 spoke organization was conducted. The empirical results are first presented for each case separately, before a cross-case analysis discusses new themes and theoretical links that have emerged, resulting in a refined mid-range theory of partnership coordination and success.

Chapter 6 gives an in-depth discussion of this study's results as well as its contributions and implications for theory and practice. Moreover, limitations are discussed and opportunities for future research based on this study's findings are suggested. Finally, Chapter 7 summarizes the study.

2 Theoretical foundation

This chapter elaborates on the study's theoretical foundations in order to provide a basis for the empirical examination of the coordination and success of hub-and-spoke partnerships. Although the first phase of empirical research is exploratory in nature, a broad review of existing work is deemed appropriate in order to set the focus of the overall study and discuss basic constructs (Eisenhardt, 1989; Yin, 2009).

Therefore, this chapter provides an understanding of enterprise software and an overview of the historical development of the enterprise software industry that has led to the emergence of the network structures. Moreover, an outline of previous work on inter-organizational networks is given, both in IS literature as well as in adjacent disciplines. After having discussed the need for coordination in the enterprise software industry and existing work on the coordination of distributed tasks, a model of the enterprise software industry that clarifies the assumptions of this study is presented. Then, a summary is given in order to explicitly frame the theoretical foundations of the research.

2.1 Network structures in the enterprise software industry

Generally, the term software refers to "written programs within a particular programming language [...] that are executable after being interpreted by a computer" (Wigand et al., 2003, p. 20). Technically, software consists of data sets, relationships among data items, algorithms and invocations of functions (Brooks, 1987). Enterprise software is a subset of software systems that is claimed to be the "operating system" of an organizations (Chellappa and Saraf, 2010). It aggregates and consolidates information that is scattered throughout the organization into an integrated software system which operates on a shared database (Markus and Tanis, 2000; Hitt et al., 2002; Chellappa and Saraf, 2010; Huang et al., 2009; Heinrich et al., 2010). Today, enterprise software systems installed and used within customer organizations are usually developed by several organizations that work together in what is sometimes referred to as software ecosystems (Adomavicius et al., 2007, 2008; Parker and Van Alstyne, 2008). These software ecosystems jointly provide an enterprise software *system* that aims at fulfilling the customers' requirements (Messerschmitt and Szyperski, 2003).

Two phenomena can be distinguished. On the one hand, enterprise software is embedded in an infrastructure that comprises basic hardware systems like servers and desktop computers, operation systems and database management systems as well as customization services. This infrastructure is often illustrated through a layered stack model (Grove, 1996). Within such a stack model, enterprise software comprises both middleware functionality and business process applications (see Figure 2.1).

On the other hand, enterprise software is not only developed and distributed by well-known organizations such as Oracle, SAP, IBM, or Microsoft, but also by a multitude of smaller organizations that provide specific elements of the overall system. This division of work in the development of enterprise software has substantially increased in recent years (Bresnahan and Greenstein, 1999; Messerschmitt and Szyperski, 2003).

In order to provide an understanding of today's structure of the enterprise software industry, the next section gives an overview of the history of the development, distribution, and use of software in an organizational context.

2.1.1 The emergence of enterprise software systems

The early years of software development were highly influenced by the structure of the hardware industry. In the late 1950s and early 1960s, a few large companies such as IBM, DEC, or Univac offered mainframe computers in a vertically integrated way (Campbell-Kelly, 1995, see Figure 2.2).

Customers of these integrated system manufacturers had three main options to obtain the corresponding operating and application software. Software was either provided by the hardware vendors as part of their sales initiatives, ex-

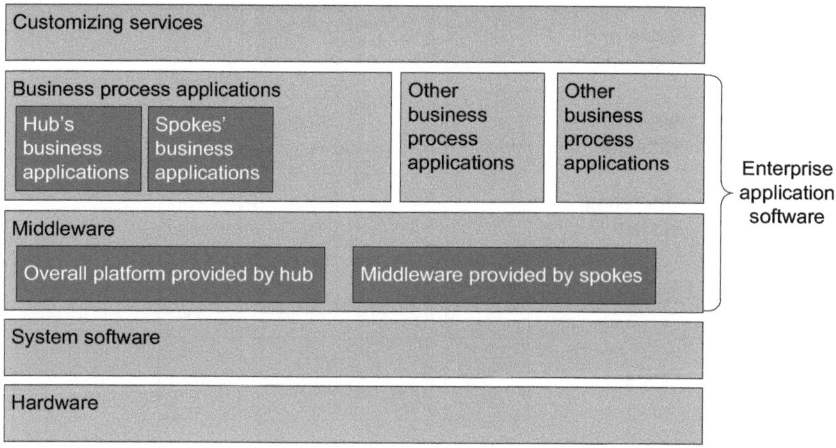

Figure 2.1: Enterprise software in a layered stack model (based on Grove, 1996)

changed freely within communities, or developed in-house by employed programmers. However, as hardware technology became more complex, organizations struggled with internally developing software programs if they were not provided by hardware vendors or available through communities (Campbell-Kelly, 1995). This gave rise to a new market for custom-developed software and specialized software firms that developed these tailored solutions, mainly for repetitive functions such as payroll or accounting (Heinzl, 1996; Haigh, 2002).

In the late 1960s and early 1970s, the software companies started to realize that selling the same software to different customers, instead of developing tailored solutions from scratch for single clients, was a much more cost-effective way to develop software (Cusumano, 2004; Haigh, 2002). Although software products were then sold to a larger number of customers, the diffusion of these products was limited by the small number of existing mainframe computers (Campbell-Kelly, 1995).

This changed in the early 1980s with the widespread use of personal computers (PCs) in an organizational context. IBM was among the first companies to realize the feasibility of using PCs in commercial settings and defined an industry standard (Campbell-Kelly, 1995). However, IBM relied on third-party firms such as Intel and Microsoft to provide core parts of the IBM PC (Bresnahan

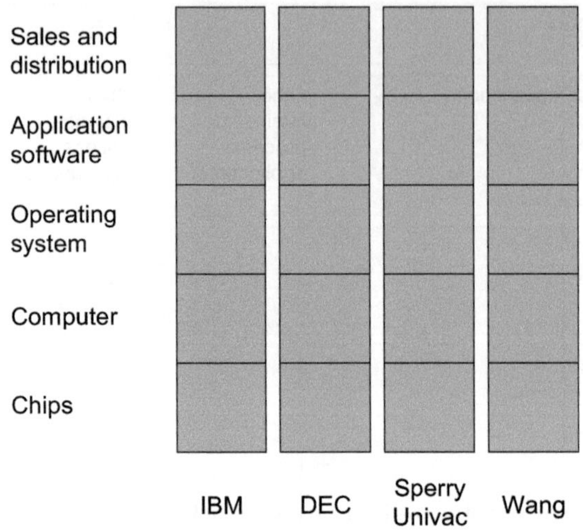

Figure 2.2: Vertical organization of the early IT industry (based on Grove, 1996)

and Greenstein, 1999; Liebowitz and Margolis, 1999). In addition, the IBM PC's open architecture enabled customers to add third-party hardware or software components (Bresnahan and Greenstein, 1999; Baldwin and Clark, 2000).

As a result, the structure of the IT industry moved from a competition between vertically integrated organizations towards a competition on horizontal layers (Figure 2.3). This distinction has been discussed in earlier literature. According to Farrell et al., there are "two very different ways in which an industry can be organized[...]: competing on a final product only (systems), or competing at intermediate stages (components) as well as on final products" (Farrell et al., 1998, p. 144). The former is called system competition, while the latter is referred to as component competition. Thus, the IT industry had moved from system competition to a competition on a component level (Farrell et al., 1998; Garud and Kumaraswamy, 1993).

Around the same time, the new market for enterprise software emerged and formed an additional layer in the software stack (Bresnahan and Greenstein, 1999, see Figure 2.4). Although having existed for almost two decades, enterprise software had its breakthrough with the emergence of client/server architectures in the 1990s. At first, enterprise software was restricted to classical enterprise re-

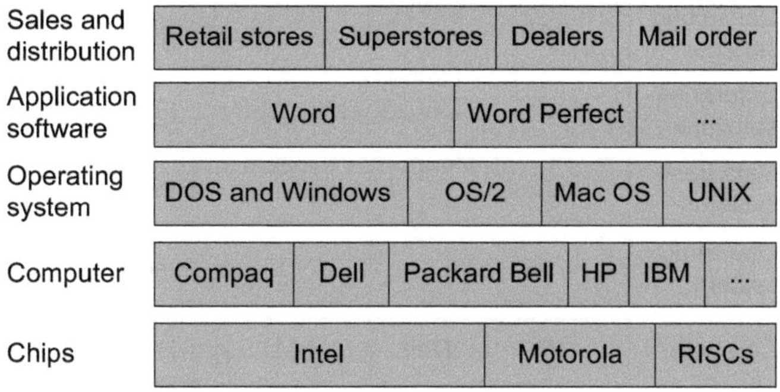

Figure 2.3: Horizontal organization of the IT industry around 1995 (based on Grove, 1996)

source planning (ERP) functionality such as materials management, production management, finance and accounting, or human resources (Buck-Emden and Galimow, 1996; Brehm and Markus, 2000; Brehm et al., 2000). One of the most successful and well-known client/server-based ERP systems was SAP's R/3, which was brought to market in 1992. By the end of the 1990s, additional functionality was added to enterprise software systems, such as customer relationship management (CRM), supply chain management (SCM), supplier relationship management (SRM), product life cycle management (PLM) and business intelligence (BI) solutions (Heinrich et al., 2010; Buck-Emden and Galimow, 1996; Davenport and Brooks, 2004).

Throughout the last decades, the enterprise software industry has developed in a way that is very similar to the evolution of the overall IT industry. Until the 1990s, the major enterprise software vendors such as SAP, Peoplesoft, JD Edwards, Baan or Navision offered monolithic solutions, thus competing in a system competition (Shang and Seddon, 2000; Mabert et al., 2001; Yen et al., 2002). The solutions were proprietary and their compatibility was limited (Buck-Emden and Galimow, 1996). Customers were recommended to rely on the system landscape from a singular vendor instead of mixing and matching different components (Mertens, 2005).

However, as the market for enterprise software consolidated and matured, incumbent firms were looking for new ways to increase the market share of

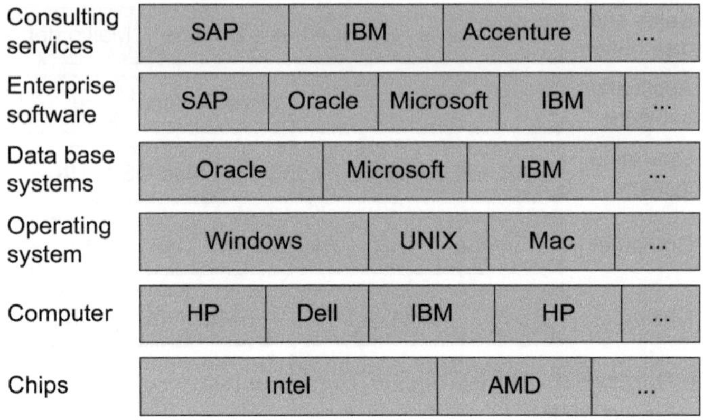

Figure 2.4: Enterprise software as an additional layer in the horizontally organized IT industry (based on Grove, 1996)

their solutions (Vinje and Paemen, 2006; Van Everdingen et al., 2000). The customer base of large, monolithic enterprise software systems is inherently restricted to large organizations with relatively standardized requirements (Shin, 2006; Van Everdingen et al., 2000; Rettig, 2007). Thus, one way to enlarge the market share was to increase the systems' flexibility and offer innovative niche functionality (Iansiti and Levien, 2004; Scheer and Habermann, 2000; Drucker, 1994; Baumol, 2002).

A higher degree of *modularity* is commonly perceived as an enabler of flexible and innovative products that fulfill both the need for standardization and for satisfying varying customer requirements (Mikkola and Gassmann, 2003; Tiwana, 2008a,b; Salvador, 2007; Ro et al., 2007; Langlois, 2002). The concept of modularity has been defined as "building a complex product or process from smaller subsystems that can be designed independently yet function together as a whole" (Baldwin and Clark, 1997, p. 84).

In the last decades, incumbent vendors of enterprise software systems have indeed started to increase the degree of modularity of the formerly monolithic systems by offering different components and industry-specific solutions (Buxmann et al., 2008). In line with theoretical predictions, the increased degree of product-level modularity has been reflected by a higher degree of organizational modularity (Conway, 1968; Hoetker, 2006; Schilling and Steensma, 2001; Evans et al., 2006; Sosa et al., 2004). Specifically, large enterprise software vendors such as SAP, Oracle, IBM, and Microsoft have started to market their software as middleware platforms and have established ecosystems consisting of (mostly smaller) third-party organizations (Evans et al., 2006). These partner organizations provide complementary solutions for the overall system, which is built in a modular way (Messerschmitt and Szyperski, 2003; Baldwin and Clark, 1997). The following section discusses these network structures and its actors in more detail.

2.1.2 Inter-firm networks

The previous discussion on the historical development of the enterprise software industry has shown that incumbent vendors increasingly aim at establishing inter-organizational networks around their platforms. Generally, inter-organizational networks can be considered an intermediate form between markets and hierarchies to govern economic transactions (Thorelli, 1986). Existing literature distinguishes open networks and closed networks as two archetypes of organizational network structures that reside on the continuum between markets and hierarchies (Snow et al., 1992; Farrell et al., 1998).

Leaning more towards a coordination through markets, open networks consist of independent organizations that offer components which are put together ex post in order to form a functioning system. "We call this *open organization* because each system is open to all industry participants" (Farrell et al., 1998, p. 144, emphasis in original). Literature has also referred to this network type as dynamic networks (see Figure 2.5a; Snow et al., 1992; Miles and Snow, 1986), stressing the exchangeability of network actors and the continuous change within the networks.

In contrast, closed network structures are organizational arrangements where "the value chain is closed to outsiders: only firms in the group can contribute an intermediate input" (Farrell et al., 1998, p. 144). Several of these closed networks may compete with each other to sell the collectively produced systems (Thorelli, 1986). Snow et al. (1992) further distinguish between internal networks and stable networks (Figure 2.5). An internal network is formed when companies try to appropriate the advantages of network structures within a company, thus being close to coordination through internal hierarchies (Figure 2.5b). The first enterprise systems that were modular on a product level were developed and marketed by internal networks.

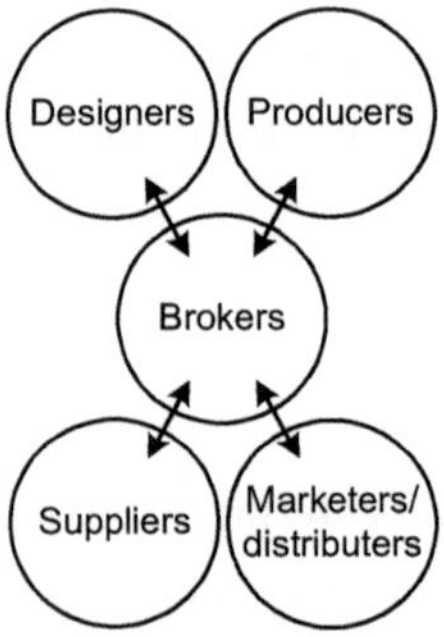

(a) Dynamic network

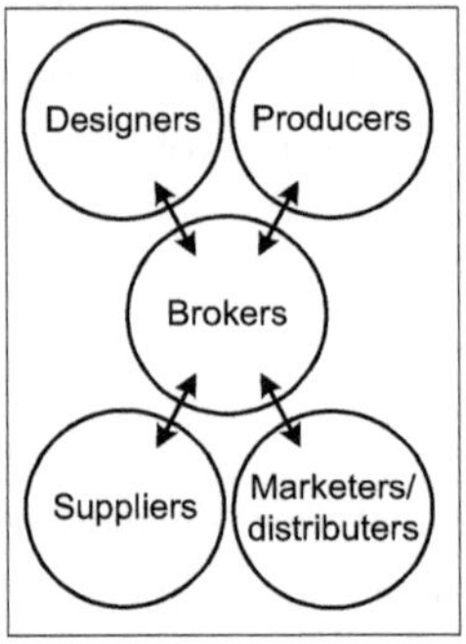

(b) Internal network

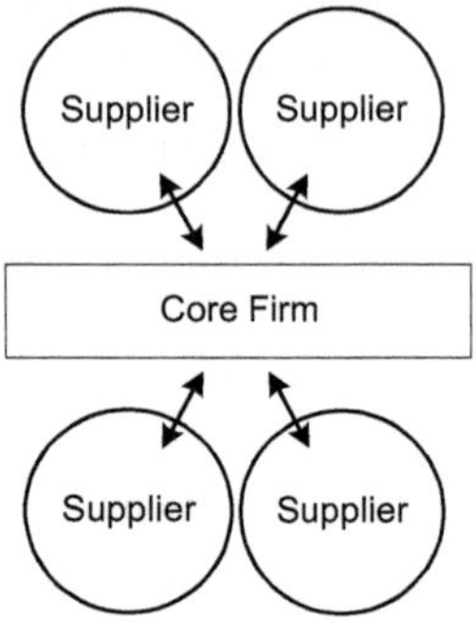

(c) Stable network

Figure 2.5: Network types (based on Snow et al., 1992)

Stable networks can be perceived as an intermediate form between internal and dynamic networks (Figure 2.5c). In stable networks, assets are owned by different firms, but dedicated to a specific business (Snow et al., 1992). This specific business is often defined by a large core firm, around which a set of vendors is nestled (Snow et al., 1992). Hence, the hub-and-spoke networks (see Figure 1.1, Jarillo, 1988) that compete in today's enterprise software industry can be considered stable networks. A large number of independent organizations complement the platform of a focal firm, that is, are dedicated to a specific business.

In establishing these stable networks, large vendors like SAP, IBM, Microsoft and Oracle aim at finding the optimal trade-off between openness and control as depicted in Figure 2.6. On the one hand, these companies try to remain the platform leader and keep control over core parts of the overall systems in order to appropriate a major part of the revenues (Shapiro and Varian, 1999). On the other hand, the incumbent enterprise software vendors aim at benefiting from the positive feedback loop initiated by two-sided network effects in making the system more attractive for both customers and additional complementors (Rochet and Tirole, 2003; Shapiro and Varian, 1999; Katz and Shapiro, 1985).

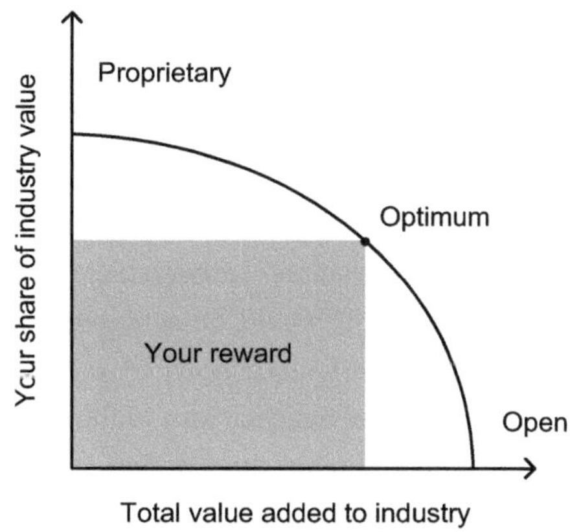

Figure 2.6: Openness versus control (Shapiro and Varian, 1999, p. 198)

Consequently, platform vendors have allowed for a certain degree of mixing and matching of different complementary solutions by establishing partner networks (Messerschmitt and Szyperski, 2003). However, the core part of the system remains proprietary and controlled by the respective vendor. The networks are usually closed in the sense that partners that want to build solutions based on a certain system have to apply for certification of products and/or personnel by the platform vendor (Alvaro et al., 2005; Stafford and Wallnau, 2001; Vitharana et al., 2003). In doing so, the incumbent system vendors try to tie complementors to their own platform and ensure the (exclusive) availability of a large number of innovative niche functionalities (Arndt et al., 2008).

According to a different perspective on network structures that traces back to the general systems theory, the resulting networks in the enterprise software industry can be considered as loosely-coupled systems. The general systems theory is based on the observations that "similar foundational conceptions appear in all branches of science, irrespective of whether inanimate things, living organisms, or social phenomena are the objects of study" (von Bertalanffy, 1950, p. 135 f.). In general, three organizational arrangements are distinguished depending on the degree of integration and specialization (Brusoni et al., 2001). The first situation in which goods are produced within vertically integrated organizations without any kind of inter-organizational collaboration is referred to as a tightly-coupled system (Brusoni et al., 2001). Consequently, the degree of specializations is low within tightly-coupled systems. Thus, tightly-coupled systems reflect the scenario of an internal network structure or the lack of networks.

The second situation, an extreme case where highly specialized firms interact solely through market transaction is referred to as decoupled systems (Brusoni et al., 2001). In such decoupled systems, integration "would not require any conscious managerial effort because it would be achieved just by respecting the technological and organizational interfaces defined by the modular architecture" (Brusoni et al., 2001, p. 615). As per Sanchez and Mahoney (1996), a decoupled system is a situation where a modular product design is reflected by a modular organizational design. Thus, decoupled systems are comparable to open, dynamic networks.

The third situation, a loosely-coupled system, is characterized by both integration and specialization and therefore resides in between the two extreme cases (Orton and Weick, 1990). A loosely-coupled network is constituted by different actors with different specializations that together form a system (Simon, 1962). Thus, the stable hub-and-spoke networks in today's enterprise software industry can be perceived as loosely-coupled system.

Loosely-coupled systems are assumed to have several advantage over both tightly-coupled and decoupled systems. For example, as a result of the disaggregation of systems into modular subsystems, flaws within subsystems do not necessarily propagate to other subsystems. Moreover, the design of a complex system is considered less problematic if hierarchical subsystems are formed to reduce complexity within the subsystems (Simon, 1962). Loosely-coupled systems can thus outperform both tightly-coupled systems as well as decoupled systems in handling complexity (Simon, 1962).

Tightly-coupled systems are often too complex to be comprehended by the limited cognitive capabilities of individuals. Decoupled systems have the problem that the market mechanism may fail to coordinate the interplay within the system. In contrast, loosely-coupled system are neither coordinated through pure market mechanisms like in decoupled systems, nor through rigid hierarchies like in tightly-coupled systems. Instead, they have a focal firm that acts as a systems integrator and that helps ensure coordination in a loosely-coupled scenario (Brusoni et al., 2001). The following section discusses existing work on the coordination of these inter-firm networks.

2.1.3 The coordination of inter-firm networks

Activities that are carried out based on the division of work, such as the provisioning of enterprise systems through partnership networks, need to be coordinated in order to reach the goal of assembling a functioning system (Adler, 1995; Kraut and Streeter, 1995; Thompson, 1967; Malone and Crowston, 1994; Kieser and Walgenbach, 2007). Table 2.1 summarizes definitions in previous literature of the notion of coordination. In this study, coordination is understood as "managing dependencies between activities" (Malone and Crowston, 1994, p. 90).

Since coordination efforts result from the need to manage interdependent activities, the necessary coordination effort is subject to the type of dependency that exists between distributed tasks. Thompson (1967) identified three types of dependencies that determine the coordination effort: pooled, sequential, and reciprocal interdependence. Pooled interdependence means that involved actors either contribute their task output to or take their task input from a shared pool of resources. The interdependence in this setting and thus the coordination and communication effort is rather low. In the case of sequential interdependency, the output of one actor's task is the input for the task of another actor. In order to ensure a smooth flow of resources, the involved actors must agree when and how the resource transfer happens. Lastly, in case of reciprocal interdependency, the task output of one actor is the task input of another actor and vice versa. That is, the involved parties interact in a continuous cycle, until a desired end state is reached. This type of interaction is the most intense one because in case of difficulties at any stage of the process, all actors are affected.

Previous research has studied the interdependencies of activities in the case of software development (Staudenmayer, 1997). Software developers that work in a distributed setting were found to face two types of interdependencies. First, coordination needs may arise from dependencies in software architectures. Second, dependencies may exist because of shared artifacts, because particular tools are

Definition	Source
The operation of complex systems made up of components	NSF-IRIS (1989)
The emergent behavior of collections of individuals whose actions are based on complex decision processes	NSF-IRIS (1989)
Information processing within a system of communicating entities with distinct information states	NSF-IRIS (1989)
The joint efforts of independent communicating actors towards mutually defined goals	NSF-IRIS (1989)
Networks of human action and commitments that are enabled by computer and communications technologies	NSF-IRIS (1989)
Activities required to maintain consistency within a work product or to manage dependencies within the workflow	Curtis (1989)
The additional information processing performed when multiple, connected actors pursue goals that a single actor pursuing the same goals would not perform	Malone (1988)
Managing dependencies between activities	Malone and Crowston (1994)

Table 2.1: Definitions of coordination in previous literature (based on Malone and Crowston, 1990, 1994)

required for a particular task, or because of relationships between the software and the documentation associated with it (Staudenmayer, 1997).

In the context of partnerships between enterprise software firms, coordination needs result from interdependencies both in software development tasks, as well as in marketing complementary products. In particular, a perfect decomposition of systems and organizations into modular sub-systems is hindered by the obstacles that result from the specific characteristics of the enterprise software systems. Specifically, these obstacles result from the fact that enterprise software possesses the characteristics of information goods and of intellectual goods.

The term information good refers to "anything that can be digitalized - encoded as a stream of bits" (Shapiro and Varian, 1999, p. 3). Information goods are assumed to possess three types of idiosyncrasies (Shapiro and Varian, 1999). First, information goods are subject to the so-called first-copy effect, that is, while the costs to develop information goods can be considerably high, the marginal costs of producing an extra unit (e.g., through copying on a DVD) can be assumed to be close to zero. Second, information goods possess the characteristic of non-rivalry, that is, the product is not exhausted through consumption.

Third, and most important in the context of this study, information goods are experience goods. Generally, there are two ways for a potential customer to assess the quality of a product (Nelson, 1970). One way is through experience after purchase of the good, and the other way is for customers to search and evaluate the quality of a good before purchasing it. A customer's decision of how to asses the quality of a product was found to depend on the costs of searching before the act of purchasing in relation to the price of the good (Nelson, 1970). For example, the cost for assessing the quality of a certain issue of a newspaper will most likely be higher than its price (Shapiro and Varian, 1999; Nelson, 1970). Interestingly, the same may hold true for expensive goods. The quality of appliances, for instance, is very hard to evaluate without actually using them (Nelson, 1970). The same concept may be assumed for enterprise software, the quality of which is very complex to determine, because its quality is a function of both utility and maintainability (Boehm et al., 1978).

Moreover, enterprise software can be considered an intellectual good rather than an industrial good. The functionalities and interfaces of industrial goods are usually clearly defined during the development phase. In contrast, the ability of intellectual goods to fulfill certain requirements is not limited by physical attributes (Lee, 1999). In other words, intellectual goods can be used "in virtually unlimited ways to solve problems or organize information" (Curley and Pyburn, 1982, p. 33).

Although the use of an information system is constrained by its functional affordances (Markus and Silver, 2008; Orlikowski and Gash, 1994; Griffith, 1999; Hutchby, 2001b,a), its actual shaping and use is subject to the user's interpretation (Grint and Woolgar, 1997; Pentland, 1992). It has been proposed to view *technology as text*, implying that technology, and thus information systems, are open to interpretation. Hence, different users could have different *readings* of a technology, that is, attach different interpretations and meanings to the same technology (Grint and Woolgar, 1997; Pentland, 1992). This process of interpretation and sense-making is particularly true in the case of enterprise software, where the interplay of software components from different vendors is dependent on the context of use, such as the specific processes of a certain organization.

As a consequence of these characteristics of enterprise software, there is a continuous need for coordination when developing and marketing enterprise software through inter-organizational division of work in order to provide systems which (1) have a high quality that is (2) acknowledged by potential customers (Adler, 1995; Kraut and Streeter, 1995; Thompson, 1967; Malone and Crowston, 1994). One of the most influential discussions on the mechanisms to coordinate division of labor is the work by March and Simon, who argue that two archetypes of coordination exist: coordination by plan and coordination by feedback (March and Simon, 1958).

According to this classification, coordination is either achieved through a pre-established plan, or through the transmission of new information in a changing environment. Which type is more appropriate in a specific situation depends on the situation's stability. "The more stable and predictable the situation, the greater the reliance on coordination by plan; the more variable and unpredictable the situation, the greater the reliance on coordination by feedback" (March and Simon, 1958, p. 160).

Van de Ven et al. adopted this distinction and argued that coordination by plan is equivalent to impersonal coordination: Coordination by plan is "exemplified by such integration mechanisms as the use of pre-established plans, schedules, forecasts, formalized rules, policies and procedures, and standardized information and communication systems. The common element of each of these exemplary mechanisms is that a codified blueprint of action is impersonally specified" (Van de Ven et al., 1976, p. 323). In contrast, coordination by feedback involves personal relationships between individuals or within groups (Van de Ven et al., 1976). In a similar way, Kraut and Streeter (1995) categorized techniques for coordinating distributed software development based on whether they are impersonal versus interpersonal and formal versus informal. Table 2.2 gives an overview over the identified techniques.

	Impersonal	Interpersonal
Formal	- Project documents and memos - Project milestones and delivery schedules - Modification request and error tracking procedures - Data dictionaries	- Status review meetings - Design review meetings - Code inspection
Informal		- Group meetings - Collocation of requirements and development staff

Table 2.2: Coordination techniques for software development (based on Kraut and Streeter, 1995)

The distinction between personal and impersonal as well as formal and informal coordination is also addressed by Mintzberg (1979), who argues for mutual adjustment, direct supervision, and standardization as three types of coordination. Direct supervision – the issuing of instructions and monitoring of actions of others – can be assumed not to be applicable in the context of relationships between legally and economically independent organizations that is in the focus of this study. In contrast, mutual adjustment and standardization are coordination mechanisms potentially used within the enterprise software industry.

As discussed previously, organizations like SAP, Oracle, IBM, or Microsoft have established loosely-coupled partnership networks that consist of a vast number of mostly small and medium-sized organizations that act as complementors. Previous research has found that while complementors benefit from a one-to-one relationship with a platform vendor, platform vendors mostly draw advantages from a one-to-many relationship with the network as a whole (Ozcan and Eisenhardt, 2009; Lorenzoni and Lipparini, 1999; Kude et al., 2008). As a consequence, platform vendors were found to aim at relational extendability, that is, they try to re-use existing relation-specific assets and routines in other relationships (Bala and Venkatesh, 2007). Hence, incumbent firms can be assumed to generally prefer standardization (e.g., coordination by plan) as a mechanism to coordinate the network of spokes rather than a costly mutual adjustment with single complementors (Chesbrough and Teece, 1996).

Following Mintzberg (1979), standardization can be achieved on the level of processes, outputs, or skills. In the context of inter-organizational enterprise software development, all three types of standardization are common. The standardization of processes and skills is often achieved through a certification from the collaborating party (Alvaro et al., 2005; Stafford and Wallnau, 2001; Vitharana et al., 2003). Huang et al. (2009) describe the certification process for the case of SAP's partnership network, where independent software vendors (ISVs) develop solutions that are certified by SAP and labeled "powered by SAP Netweaver" or "xApps", or obtain a certification for an interface of their solution. As a first step of the certification process, ISVs submit a formal application. Then, ISVs go through development, documentation, and testing phases to ensure compliance with SAP's standards. Third, the ISV and SAP sign a formal contract and ISVs pay the applicable fees. SAP then allows ISVs to use a certification logo and lists the solution on its web portal (Huang et al., 2009). A similar process of certification has been reported in other partnership networks (Huber et al., 2010).

In addition, coordination through standardized outputs is also applied in the enterprise software industry by means of standardized system architectures and corresponding interfaces that all components have to comply with (Henderson and Clark, 1990; Vitharana et al., 2003). The establishment of software platforms that are based on service-oriented architecture (SOA), such as SAP's Netweaver or IBM's Websphere, can be perceived as a means to standardize outputs (Stal, 2002; Erl, 2005; Papazoglou and Georgakopoulos, 2003; Ren et al., 2008).

2.1.4 The role of complementors

The above discussion on the emergence of stable networks in the enterprise software industry has implicitly taken the perspective of the focal firms, that is of incumbent vendors like SAP, IBM, Oracle, or Microsoft that have established inter-organizational networks around their platforms. Indeed, the discussion of these platform leaders is the basis of this study, since they define the basic parameters of the emerging inter-firm networks. The focus on platform leaders is also reflected in existing literature, which has predominantly studied the role of incumbent firms (e.g. Cusumano, 2004; Morris and Ferguson, 1993). The role of the focal firm is commonly perceived as being advantageous. "Companies that control proprietary architectural standards have an advantage over other vendors" (Morris and Ferguson, 1993, p. 88). While it may indeed be advantageous to control a platform instead of providing components for another firm's platform, the reality is that the majority of small and medium-sized software companies lack the resources to act as a platform leader.

In systems that are more and more modular and assembled by component parts, component manufacturers are of utmost importance. "Traditional rules of competitive strategy focus on competitors, suppliers, and customers. In the information economy, companies selling complementary components, or *complementors* are equally important" (Shapiro and Varian, 1999, p.10, emphasis in original). Yet, the role of organizations that act as complementors has rarely been discussed in previous research. The goal of this study is to help closing this gap.

The efforts of platform vendors to foster loosely-coupled networks and to coordinate the overall network with the help of certification and standardization of architectures and interfaces may be assumed to be in the interest of complementors to some extent. Specifically, complementors may benefit from these standardization efforts because standardization allows them to participate in inter-firm partnership networks in spite of the discussed characteristics of enterprise software. In particular, standardized architectures and interfaces may reduce the costs of developing compatible, complementary solutions. Moreover, the certification label issued by the platform vendors may reduce the difficulties faced by small and medium-sized enterprises in being an unknown entity in a market of experience-based goods (Kude et al., 2012).

However, as discussed above, complementors particularly benefit from the one-to-one relationship with the hub organization (Kude et al., 2008). The benefit resulting from this partnership may be higher if small complementors coordinate the partnership through mutual adjustment, that is, through a higher degree of organizational coupling and of communication between peers (Mintzberg, 1979; Brusoni, 2005).

From an organizational perspective, the reason for a higher degree of coupling can be seen in the synergistic specificity of a certain partnership, that is, the "degree to which a system achieves greater functionality by its components being specific to one another" (Schilling, 2000, p. 316). Thus, a closer cooperation between firms can be understood as an optimization of the components of a system working in a particular configuration, resulting in combinations that "achieve a functionality unobtainable through combinations of more independent components" (Schilling, 2000, p. 315 f.).

Taking into account this tension between coordination through standardization and through mutual adjustment, that is, between loose and tight coupling, the question arises as to what determines the type of coordination chosen by complementor organizations. In order to answer this question, the following section looks at related work on inter-organizational arrangements, both in the IS literature as well as in adjacent disciplines. Based on the previous discussion and on existing literature, a model of hub-and-spoke networks in the enterprise software industry is developed with the goal of specifying this study's research questions and providing an understanding of the study's assumptions.

2.2 Previous work on inter-organizational networks

Although there is a considerable amount of extant literature on inter-firm alliances both in IS as well as in adjacent disciplines, the specific question of how complementors in the enterprise software industry coordinate hub-and-spoke partnerships has been mostly neglected so far.

Previous work in the IS field that considered the special characteristics of enterprise software has either studied how network structure may lead to partnership success, or has focused on the motives of organizations to enter partnership networks. The question of how complementors may successfully coordinate these partnerships, once established, has not been addressed. The following section first presents related work on inter-organizational arrangements in the field of IS in order to clearly identify the research gap that this study addresses. Second, reference theories that this study draws on are selected and discussed. In doing so, the discussion lays the ground for the subsequent empirical analysis.

2.2.1 Existing work in the field of information systems

Many researchers in the field of IS have touched upon the topics of enterprise software and inter-firm division of work. Yet, most of this work has either focused on customization efforts, adoption, and use of enterprise software systems (e.g. Robey et al., 2002; Scott and Vessey, 2002; Burton-Jones and Gallivan, 2007), or has studied IT-enabled inter-firm supply chain relationships (e.g. Bharadwaj et al., 2007; Malhotra et al., 2007; Malhotra and El Sawy, 2005). The inter-firm networks that are in the focus of this study differ substantially from IT-enabled supply chain relationships. While the hub-and-spoke networks in the software industry focus on filling holes in the product lines, supply chain networks are typically formed for manufacturing processes (Huang et al., 2009). As a result, the payoff structures also differ significantly. In one case, the payoff results from additional sales, while in the other case, suppliers receive payments for manufacturing (Huang et al., 2009).

As discussed above, the higher degree of both technological and organizational modularity in developing enterprise systems has resulted in an increasing flexibility of these systems. Therefore, customer-specific requirements are more and more anticipated by organizations in the enterprise software industry. Consequently, there has been an increasing interest in the IS field in inter-organizational arrangements within the enterprise software industry.

Two major streams of inquiry can be distinguished. First, previous work studied the antecedents of partnership formation, both from the platform vendors' perspective as well as from the complementors' point of view. Second, previous work has studied the structural properties of inter-firm networks in the IS industry as determinants of partnership success both at a network as well as an inter-firm level. The following discussion gives an overview of the results of these studies.

2.2.1.1 Partnership motives

A recent stream of IS literature on inter-organizational arrangements in the enterprise software industry has studied the antecedents of partnership formation from the perspective of platform vendors as well as complementors.

Arndt et al. (2009) took a resource-based perspective and found that platform vendors form partnerships in order to fill gaps in their own portfolio of resources and capabilities. More specifically, based on Hagedoorn (1993), it is argued that platform vendors form partnership networks in order to gain access to three types of dynamic capabilities that incumbent firms are assumed to lack and that small complementors are assumed to possess (Ahuja, 2000). First, complementors are assumed to have the capability to innovate at a modular level as opposed to the architectural innovations of the hub organization (Henderson and Clark, 1990). These modular innovations have the potential to ensure that the overall system keeps up with recent technological and organizational developments.

The complementors' ability to provide niche functionality for the existing platform is proposed as a second motivator for platform vendors to establish partnership networks (Arndt et al., 2009; Prencipe, 2004). Third, platform vendors are proposed to foster partnership networks in order to obtain address to the spoke organizations' capability to access novel markets (Arndt et al., 2009). Incumbent firms, whose traditional customers are large organizations, are assumed to have difficulties in addressing niche markets and may therefore benefit from partnering with small complementors.

In a case study of two large platform vendors, Arndt et al. (2009) found that the three proposed motivators to establish partnership networks indeed play an important role. Moreover, the study shows that the partnership formation pattern can be perceived as a process structure in which different capabilities of spokes play different roles over time (Arndt et al., 2009; D'Aunno and Zuckerman, 1987). The capability to provide niche functionality was found to be crucial at the outset of a potential partnership, while the capabilities to innovate and to access novel markets become prevalent over time as the partnership evolves into a closer collaboration (Arndt et al., 2009).

In a comparable study, (Kude et al., 2012) took the perspective of complementors and asked why these firms decide to enter partnerships with platform vendors. This study also takes a resource-based perspective and argues that complementors participate in the inter-firm networks established by platform vendors in order to get access to the hub organization's technological, commercial, and social capital (Ahuja, 2000; Kude et al., 2012; Arndt et al., 2009). In the context of inter-firm partnerships in the enterprise software industry, technological capital refers to the platform vendor's capability to provide comprehensive enterprise systems and its capability to innovate the overall system's architecture (Hagedoorn, 1993; Henderson and Clark, 1990). The hub's commercial capital refers to a complementor's opportunity to benefit from an incumbent firm's access to broad and global markets. Social capital means that small enterprise software vendors may tap into the hub's reputation by entering a partnership (Ahuja, 2000).

The study took a qualitative approach with the goal of substantiating and refining the proposed explanatory model. The empirical results show that the hub's commercial and social capital are generally attractive for smaller software firms. In contrast, the hub's technological capital was found to be a double-edged sword for small software firms. On the one hand, the hub's capability to provide the technological base of the spoke organizations' solutions was indeed found to act as a motivator to partner with the hub. On the other hand, the influence of the hub's capability to innovate systems on the spoke's motivation to partner was found to be ambiguous. In some cases, the hub's innovativeness was found to be advantageous for spokes because it enables innovations on the component level. On the other hand, architectural innovations are a potential threat to complementors because they could render core parts of the complementors' solutions obsolete (Kude et al., 2012).

The study of Huang et al. (2009) aimed at answering the same research question of what induces complementor organizations in the enterprise software industry to participate in partnership networks. As a basis of their analysis, the authors assumed that the general advantage of partnering with an incumbent vendor lies in these organizations' ability to access broad markets and in the benefits reaped by teaming up with a prestigious industry leader. Yet, based on the observation that entering a partnership with a platform provider is not costless for small ISVs, the authors argued that firms may refrain from partnering. In addition to the fees for partnering, the study identified appropriation issues resulting from the potential competition between the partners' products (Huang et al., 2009).

Based on these assertions, the study proposed that ISVs may be more likely to partner the more their innovations are protected by intellectual property rights, the more they possess specialized downstream capability, and the less the products offered by a focal ISV and its potential partner overlap in terms of their functionality (Huang et al., 2009). Moreover, the study proposed an interaction effect between the degree of intellectual property protection and downstream capability which are assumed to act as substitutes. That is, the positive effect of innovation protection was hypothesized to be lower when an ISV owns strong downstream capabilities. In contrast to the studies presented above, Huang et al. took a quantitative approach based on longitudinal data on the history of partnering of 1208 ISVs that complement SAP's enterprise software solution. The empirical findings confirmed the proposed theoretical links.

In another study, Mathiassen and Vainio (2007) proposed a sense-and-response framework to understand and actively manage the dynamic capabilities of small software firms. Among other results, the authors concluded that small software firms should cultivate external relationships. Thereby, the study stressed the need for accessing knowledge that resides outside the firm. Yet, the focus was on gaining knowledge through interacting with customers. Moreover, while it has been argued that small software firms often depend on "one or a few large powerful players" (Mathiassen and Vainio, 2007), the question if and under which circumstances these powerful players may be a source of valuable resources and capabilities was not addressed.

2.2.1.2 Structural properties and success

While the studies presented above analyzed the antecedents of entering a partnerships between a platform vendor and a complementor, another stream of literature within the field of IS focuses on the structural characteristics of these partnerships and their influence on partnership success.

Gao and Iyer analyzed the influence of product complementarities on the success of inter-firm arrangements in the software industry. Specifically, the authors studied the success of mergers and acquisitions (Gao and Iyer, 2006), as well as inter-firm partnerships (Gao and Iyer, 2008). In both cases, the complementarity between the functionalities offered by the products of collaborating organizations were theorized to influence the success of these arrangements. Based on the definition of complementarity as the superadditive value of combining activities (Milgrom and Roberts, 1995), the authors studied product complementarity in terms of the relative vertical distance of companies within a software stack model as depicted in Figure 2.1. Complementarity between the products of potential partners is assumed to be high, if the distance between the layers in the software stack model on which the firms operate is high. In other words, the closer the firms are in the software stack model, the lower is their complementarity (Gao and Iyer, 2006, 2008).

Through a quantitative analysis of the stack distance and the success of 193 mergers and acquisitions (Gao and Iyer, 2006) and 103 alliances (Gao and Iyer, 2008) in the software industry – with success measured by means of changes in stock prices – the authors found that the success of mergers and acquisitions is higher if the firms that join forces reside on adjacent layers in the stack model (Gao and Iyer, 2006). In contrast, inter-firm partnerships were found to be particularly successful if the layers that actors reside on overlap to a great extent (Gao and Iyer, 2008).

The studies on partnerships in the enterprise software industry presented so far focus on the *dyadic* relationship between a platform vendor and a certain organization that complements this particular platform. Another set of studies analyzed the structure of partnership *networks* and its influence on success. Based on the assumption that software firms form partnerships to access complementary resources and ensure interoperability, Iyer et al. (2006) performed a longitudinal analysis of the network of alliances and partnerships of 509 firms in the packaged software industry. By applying social network analysis (Nohria and Eccles, 1992), the authors found that the topological structure of these inter-firm arrangements exhibits the characteristics of a "small world network", which means that linkages are characterized by a high degree of clustering and short path lengths between the actors (Watts, 2004). Drawing on these observations, the study concludes with a number of recommendations to manage software ecosystems. Among other insights, the authors advice actors to explicitly identify and keep track of their own role within the network and the roles played by partners and competitors (Iyer et al., 2006).

Similarly, Chellappa and Saraf (2010) studied the structure and success of inter-firm networks in the enterprise software industry by applying social network analysis. The authors argue that the enterprise software industry substantially differs from other industries in that partnership formation is mainly triggered by demand-side instead of supply-side considerations, that is, by the customers' need for interoperability. Yet, through participating in these partnerships, firms are assumed to "gain access to social and technical resources through their ties with *both* directly and indirectly connected partners" (Chellappa and Saraf, 2010, p. 3, emphasis in original).

By analyzing a total number of 69 enterprise software firms and their partnerships between 1999 and 2003, the study found that there was no state of equilibrium which would result in dominant technical standards throughout the industry. Therefore, in order to ensure interoperability, firms were found not only to partner with organizations that provide complementary solutions, but also with those that compete in certain parts of the solution portfolio. The results also show that a prominent structural position, that is, a position where firms are linked directly and indirectly to a great number of other vendors, is positively linked to firm performance. This was found to be especially true for small software firms (Chellappa and Saraf, 2010).

2.2.1.3 Summary

The preceding discussion shows that although most of the research on enterprise software in the field of information systems has predominantly focused on the adoption and use of these systems, there has been a recent increase in interest in inter-firm partnerships within the enterprise software industry. Previous work on these partnerships has either focused on the motivation of firms to participate in the partnerships or on structural characteristics and their influence on partnership success. These extant studies neglect the intensity of a partnership and instead treat partnering as a binary variable, that is, firms either do partner or they do not.

The question of how partnerships in the enterprise software industry are coordinated and managed has so far been mostly disregarded. This study aims at filling this gap. In order to provide a basis for addressing this paucity of research, the following section presents existing work from adjacent fields that act as reference theories for this study.

2.2.2 Theories of the firm as reference theories

Considering the identified research gaps in the IS literature, it seems reasonable to consult existing work from adjacent fields as reference theories in order to address partnership coordination in inter-firm networks. Generally, inter-organizational networks can be considered to be an intermediate form between coordination through markets and the internalization of activities (Thorelli, 1986). As discussed above, the different types of inter-firm networks reside on a continuum between market and hierarchy. While dynamic, open networks lean more towards market structures, internal networks are closer to hierarchies. Stable, loosely-coupled networks are an intermediate form between dynamic and internal networks.

The discussion in the sections 2.1.3 and 2.1.4 has shown that in the case of hub-and-spoke networks in the enterprise software industry, hub organizations can be assumed to aim at establishing loosely-coupled networks by applying standardization as the main coordination mechanism. Instead, it has been argued that in some cases, spokes may strive for a tighter coupling with their larger partner.

The term "theory of the firm" describes a set of theories that address the questions of why firms exist as opposed to coordinating the work of economic actors through markets (Seth and Thomas, 1994). In other words, these theories deal with the questions why some transactions are carried out by tightly-coupled organizational actors, whereas others are performed via more loosely-coupled structures. Consequently, the theories that are subsumed under the term "theory of the firm" can be expected to be promising reference theories for answering the research questions of this study.

Following the comprehensive taxonomy provided by Dibbern (2004), the term "theory of the firm" can be understood to subsume a number of different streams such as neoclassical economics, industrial organization (IO), behavioralism, new institutional economics, and dynamic theories. Earlier work within the realm of neoclassical economics (e.g., Marshall, 2009; Cournot, 1838) and IO (e.g. Bain, 1956; Porter, 1985) treat the firm as a black box and assume homogeneity among rational organizational actors. Considering the assumed differences in resource endowments of hubs and spokes, these lenses seem to be less promising for answering this study's research questions.

Institutional theory (DiMaggio and Powell, 1983; Meyer and Rowan, 1977) and power/politics theory (Pfeffer, 1981; Tushman, 1977) as important behavioral theories relieved the assumption of a the firm as a black box and studied decision processes within the firm, based on the assumption that decision makers are "boundedly rational" (Simon, 1957, 1947; Cyert and March, 1992). Institutional theory analyzes how organizational actors respond to influences from their environment. In particular, institutional theory aims at explaining homogeneous behavior of organizations. The goal of this study is to explain variances in the behavior of spoke organizations. Consequently, institutional theory is not considered as a reference theory.

Power/politics theory focuses on the role of power and politics in organizational decision making. Power can be perceived as the counterpart of dependence (Emerson, 1962). Since spoke organizations can be assumed to depend on their larger partner, power/politics theory can provide important insights when addressing this study's research question.

The theories subsumed under the stream "new institutional economics" – most notably transaction cost economics (TCE, Williamson, 1979, 1981; Coase, 1937), agency theory (Jensen, 2003; Berle and Means, 1932), and the theory of incomplete contracts (Hart and Moore, 1988) – also relax the assumption of neoclassical theories and deal with the function of the firm. In particular, new institutional economics refers to efficiency criteria when addressing the question of why some transactions are carried out over the market, whereas others are kept in-house. Thus, new institutional economics is a promising lens to analyze this study's research questions. Yet, the above discussion on previous work on inter-firm networks in the enterprise software industry has shown that hub-and-spoke partnerships in the enterprise software industry are not only driven by efficiency considerations, but also by the opportunity to obtain access to complementary resources.

Consequently, as presented above, previous work on inter-firm arrangements has mostly drawn on the resource-based view of the firm (RBV, Penrose, 1959; Wernerfelt, 1984; Barney, 1991), which is a dynamic theory in that it stresses idiosyncrasies and heterogeneity of firms that may change over time (Dibbern, 2004). While the classical resource-based view of the firm aims at identifying internal resources that lead to sustainable competitive advantage, other studies extended the resource-based perspective to inter-organizational arrangements (Eisenhardt and Schoonhoven, 1996; Ahuja, 2000).

These extensions appear to be particularly useful for answering this study's research question because they also draw on the theories that have been identified above as appropriate lenses. The relational view of competitive advantage suggests that sustainable competitive advantage may result from a close collaboration of different organizations (Dyer and Singh, 1998). It is based on the RBV but also draws on arguments from TCE, thus considering potential adverse implications of tight coupling. Hence, the relational view of competitive advantage can be expected to be an appropriate lens for analyzing the coordination of hub-and-spoke partnerships.

While the relational view of competitive advantage draws on dynamic theories and on new institutional economics, the resource-dependence theory (RDT) (Pfeffer and Salancik, 1978; Casciaro and Piskorski, 2005) integrates a power/politics view with a resource-based perspective. The RDT fits in the context of this study because it explicitly considers an organization's dependence on external resources. As discussed above, platform vendors depend on a large network of complementors as an important resource, while small complementors depend on the resources of the platform vendor. Therefore, the RDT is promising for addressing the implications of asymmetric resource dependency on partnership coordination and success.

The following sections briefly introduces the RBV of the firm as well as important derivatives. Subsequently, the relational view of competitive advantage and the resource dependence theory (RDT) are presented.

2.2.2.1 Firm resources and capabilities

The resource-based view of competitive advantage. Firms strive for the generation of competitive advantages (Teece et al., 1997). An organization is said to have a competitive advantage "when it is implementing a value creating strategy not simultaneously being implemented by any current or potential competitor" (Barney, 1991, p. 102). The notion of competitive advantage contradicts the assumptions of neoclassical microeconomic models, which assume perfect competition on all markets and treat companies as black boxes that transform input factors into output factors according to a well-defined production function (Cournot, 1838). In contrast, strategic considerations aim at achieving super-normal returns (Porter, 1985).

Proponents of the market-based perspective assume imperfect markets for end products, which can be capitalized by organizations to obtain super-normal returns. Consequently, competitive advantages result from a skilled choice of product-market combinations, taking into account different market forces (Porter, 1985). The market-oriented perspective is thus built on the structure-conduct-performance model, which posits that the structure of an industry influences the behavior of organizations, which in turn influences organizational performance (Bain, 1956; Conner, 1991). Such an external perspective implicitly assumes that firms within a certain industry are equal regarding the resources they possess (Barney, 1991). Heterogeneity among firms is assumed to be possible in the short run only, because resources would be offered on perfect markets at market prices that reflect their actual value (Barney, 1991).

In contrast, the RBV understands firms as collections of resources and relaxes the assumption of perfect markets for input factors (Penrose, 1959; Wernerfelt, 1984; Barney, 1991). It is assumed that firms are heterogeneous in terms of the resources they possess (Barney, 1991; Wernerfelt, 1984; Peteraf, 1993; Wade and Hulland, 2004). The RBV does not neglect the importance of an organization's environment. Instead, it is argued that in order to develop competitive advantage, firms need to possess relevant resources (Astley and Fombrun, 1983). The structure of the industry surrounding a firm, in turn, is considered to determine which resources are relevant (Amit and Schoemaker, 1993).

In accordance with existing work, this study adopts a definition of resources that includes both tangible and intangible factors (Daft, 1995). Thus, resources are defined as "all assets, capabilities, organizational processes, firm attributes, information, knowledge, etc. controlled by a firm that enable the firm to conceive and implement strategies that improve its efficiency and effectiveness" (Barney, 1991, p. 101). To enable the generation and maintenance of competitive advantages, previous work argued that resources need to be valuable, rare, not perfectly imitable and not substitutable (Barney, 1991).

Resources are *valuable* if the strategies implemented with the help of these resources improve the firm's effectiveness or efficiency, that is, enable the firm to either neutralize its weaknesses or exploit its strengths (Barney, 1991). Because competitive advantages enable companies to implement a strategy not simultaneously implemented by competitors, resources need to be *rare* in order to lead to a competitive advantage.

In addition to the properties of being valuable and rare, only those resources that are neither imitable nor substitutable enable the generation of sustainable competitive advantage (Dierickx and Cool, 1989; Barney, 1991; Mata et al., 1995). Previous research lists several characteristics that determine the imitability of a resource. First, the existence of resources that are valuable and rare is assumed to be subject to historical conditions (Barney, 1991). Due to *time compression diseconomies*, resources that are accumulated over a long period of time cannot be build up by competitors in the short run through investing a larger amount of money. Moreover, referring to synergies between existing, firm-specific resources, *asset mass efficiencies* and the *interconnectedness of asset stocks* are assumed to increase the non-imitability of resources (Dierickx and Cool, 1989). In other words, in contrast to a market-oriented perspective, the RBV explicitly takes into account the history of organizational actors and the related path dependencies (Liebowitz and Margolis, 1995).

A second determinant of the imitability of a resource is the *causal ambiguity* of the origin and foundations of competitive advantages (Barney, 1991; Dierickx and Cool, 1989). That is, if the causal relationship between the existence of certain resources and the success of a strategy remains unclear, then the particular resource combination and the resulting competitive advantage are hard to imitate.

Third, previous literature mentions the *social complexity* of strategic resources as a determinant of their imitability (Barney, 1991). For instance, well-established inter-personal relationships or organizational culture may be causal for a competitive advantage. Also, building up a positive reputation can be considered a complex social process. While social complexity decreases the imitability of resources, previous work found that technological complexity is per se imitable, because competitors can potentially acquire the skills and tools necessary to build complex technological systems (Mata et al., 1995). Therefore, technological complexity alone does not contribute to sustainable competitive advantage. However, the social processes associated with the exploitation of a certain (complex) technology may contribute to a resource's non-imitability (Barney, 1991).

Even if resources are valuable, rare, and not imitable, a resource may still not lead to sustainable competitive advantage if the resource can be substituted by another resource (Barney, 1991; Dierickx and Cool, 1989). Two resources or bundles of resources can be considered "strategically equivalent" if they can be exploited independent from each other in order to implement the same strategy (Barney, 1991, p. 111).

Dynamic capabilities and the knowledge-based view of the firm. The RBV has been the basis for several extensions that further developed the idea of heterogeneity between firms and resulting competitive advantage. Previous research introduced the concept of dynamic capabilities as an answer to critiques that the RBV fails to consider the inherent dynamics of resources (e.g., Black and Boal, 1994). Capabilities have been defined as "a firm's capacity to deploy *Resources*, usually in combination, using organizational processes, to effect a desired end" (Amit and Schoemaker, 1993, p. 35, emphasis in original). *Dynamic capabilities* are processes and organizational knowledge that enable firms to change these resources and capabilities in order to react to changing environmental conditions (Teece et al., 1997). This ability is particularly relevant in dynamic contexts, such as enterprise software development (Ethiraj et al., 2005; Miles et al., 2005).

In the light of the above discussion on sustainable competitive advantages, dynamic capabilities can be assumed to be socially complex and causally ambiguous. Also, dynamic capabilities usually involve a combination of resources and competences, resulting in firm-specific asset-interconnectedness (Dierickx and Cool, 1989). Hence, dynamic capabilities may provide firms with a long-term advantage over their competitors, especially in dynamic domains.

The knowledge-based view (KBV) of the firm treats knowledge as the core resource of firms (Grant, 1996b; Nonaka and Takeuchi, 1995; Spender, 1996; Poppo and Zenger, 1998). While the RBV perceives knowledge as one resource among others and does not distinguish between different types of knowledge, the KBV differentiates between explicit knowledge and tacit knowledge (Nonaka and Takeuchi, 1995).

Explicit knowledge (or codified knowledge) can be made explicit and transmitted in formal, systematic language (Nonaka and Takeuchi, 1995). In contrast, tacit knowledge is difficult to formalize and communicate. Following Nonaka, tacit knowledge is "deeply rooted in action, commitment, and involvement in a specific context" (Nonaka, 1994, p. 16). Tacit knowledge can hence be assumed to be particularly difficult to imitate because of its inherent social complexity and causal ambiguity. Therefore, from a resource-based perspective, tacit knowledge is likely to be a source of competitive advantage (Madhok 1997).

Firm resources and inter-firm arrangements. The original RBV as presented above focuses on singular companies and internal resources. Consequently, firms are advised to identify and develop resources *within* the organization and generate competitive advantages based on these assets (Prahalad and Hamel, 1990; Grant, 1991). However, the practical relevance of inter-organizational arrangements (Gomes-Casseres, 1996; Richardson, 1972) raised questions of whether a firm's resources and capabilities may also reside outside the firm. That is, the question was raised whether the resource-based perspective can be transfered to the case of organizational structures that span the boundaries of single firms.

Indeed, existing literature on strategic alliances has stressed that the access to resources and capabilities, such as technological know-how, are important reasons for firms to enter inter-organizational arrangements, thus implicitly taking a resource-based perspective (Hagedoorn, 1993; Mariti and Smiley, 1983; Harrigan, 1988).

Later work analyzed inter-firm partnerships explicitly from a resource-based perspective (Eisenhardt and Schoonhoven, 1996; Ahuja, 2000). It has been argued that firms enter inter-organizational arrangements if they both have a need to close own resource gaps, and the opportunity to form partnerships. This coexistence of needs and opportunities for an alliance has been referred to as a "duality of inducements and opportunities" (Ahuja, 2000). Previous findings suggest that firms have an inducement to form partnerships if they find themselves in "strategic vulnerable positions", which is especially the case if firms operate in difficult competitive environments or pursue high-risk strategies (Eisenhardt and Schoonhoven, 1996). In addition to the inducement to form a partnership, firms also have to find opportunities to do so. In particular, firms have to be attractive for potential partners in the sense that they have to offer resources and capabilities that a potential partner lacks (Ahuja, 2000; Baum et al., 2000).

Extant research has also studied the role of small and medium-sized enterprises (SMEs) in strategic alliances (e.g. Baum et al., 2000; Jensen, 2003; Lee et al., 2001; Lu and Beamish, 2001; Rothaermel, 2001). In accordance with the findings discussed above, these studies stress the importance of alliances for SMEs, since they often act in dynamic or competitive environments, that is, they can be considered to be in strategic vulnerable positions. Moreover, because of their inherent resource limitations, SMEs can be assumed to have a particular need for external resources to fill their own resource gaps.

Thus, SMEs have a high inducement to form alliances, especially with large and incumbent companies. Yet, following the idea of the duality of inducements and opportunities of partnership formation, SMEs may have difficulties in finding alliance partners due to their low resource stock. Despite the seemingly low attractiveness of SMEs, partnerships with small firms can be observed in many different industries (Baum et al., 2000; Lee et al., 2001). According to Ahuja (2000), the reason for this may be seen in the innovativeness of SMEs and in important inventions that mark a technological breakthrough (Dosi, 1988; Schumpeter, 1934). Innovations were found to both increase the inducements and opportunities of SMEs to partner. "[L]arge firms need the technology developed by small firms, and small firms need the financial muscle and distribution power of the large firms" (Miles et al., 2005, p. 46).

2.2.2.2 The relational view of competitive advantage

The discussion above shows that the RBV which has originally focused on singular organizations can generally be transferred to inter-organizational arrangements. According to the RBV, firms may generate competitive advantages by cultivating resources that are valuable, rare, and non-substitutable. These competitive advantages were found to be sustainable only if they are not imitable. This is particularly the case if resources are specific to the respective organization (Barney, 1991; Dierickx and Cool, 1989).

In addition to these firm-specific resources, the relational view as proposed by Dyer and Singh holds that "idiosyncratic inter-firm linkages" (Dyer and Singh,

1998, p. 661) may be a source of competitive advantages, also referred to as *relational rents.* In other words, "a firm's critical resources may span firm boundaries and may be embedded in inter-firm routines and processes" (Dyer and Singh, 1998, p. 661). Thus, relational rents emerge from intensive collaboration. Inter-firm collaboration is proposed to particularly result in the generation of relational rents, if partners are willing to invest in *inter-firm relation-specific assets.* Hence, the RBV's concept of a resource's specificity is transferred to inter-organizational arrangements. However, resources that lead to competitive advantages are not firm-specific, but relation-specific.

Specifically, *inter-firm knowledge sharing routines* and *complementary resource endowments* are proposed as inter-firm relation-specific assets that lead to relational rents. Inter-firm knowledge sharing routines have been defined as "a regular pattern of inter-firm interactions that permits the transfer, recombination, or creation of specialized knowledge" (Dyer and Singh, 1998, p. 665). It is important to stress that these routines and processes go beyond a pure information exchange (Grant, 1996a). In fact, competitive advantages particularly result from the exchange of tacit, implicit knowledge (Reber, 1989). From a technological and organizational point of view, a simple transfer of data and facts can be realized, and thus imitated, fairly easily. In contrast, the exchange of implicit knowledge requires the establishment of capabilities and resources that have been termed as "absorptive capacity" in literature. Absorptive capacity has been defined as "the ability of a firm to recognize the value of new, external information, assimilate it, and apply it to commercial ends" (Cohen and Levinthal, 1990, p. 128).

In addition, partners' endowments with complementary resources are generally regarded as a source of relational rents. Complementary resource endowments have been defined as "distinctive resources of alliance partners that collectively generate greater rents than the sum of those obtained from the individual endowments of each partner" (Dyer and Singh, 1998, p. 666 f.). However, investments in partner-specific resources may not only lead to relational rents, but also to significant transaction costs.

By referring to the transaction costs that may result from the investments in partner-specific resources, the relational view of competitive advantage draws on findings from new institutional economics, and particularly TCE. The arguments of TCE are build on the insight that firms exists because there is a cost of using the price mechanism (Coase, 1937). Williamson (1975; 1981; 1985; 1990) extended Coase's explanation in several ways. First, market costs were substituted by transaction costs, which are defined as the "comparative costs of planning, adapting, and monitoring task completion under alternative governance structures" (Williamson, 1981, p. 552 f.). Thus, transaction costs can occur both within and across the boundaries of a firm.

Second, Williamson argued that economic actors are boundedly rational (Simon, 1957) and that contracts may be incomplete (Williamson, 1981). Moreover, it is assumed that some actors behave opportunistically, which means that they take advantage of opportunities at the expense of others (Williamson, 1981). Accordingly, transaction costs arise because of the need to safeguard against the potential opportunistic behavior of exchange partners, for instance by putting more effort into finding the right contractual partner, on specifying the details of the contract, or on monitoring and coordinating the exchange partner.

Third, Williamson (1979, 1981) elaborated on the contextual conditions under which transaction costs are lower in-house as opposed to a market transaction. Four types of contingencies that characterize a transaction or exchange relationship were identified: asset specificity, site specificity, frequency, and uncertainty. It is argued that in the presence of these four factors, opportunistic behavior and hence transaction costs can be more efficiently prevented by the internal authority system.

In the case of inter-firm partnerships, it can be assumed that companies that invest heavily in partner-specific assets are locked into this particular partnership because partner-specific assets are of low use in other inter-firm arrangements. This, in turn, increases the partner's propensity to behave opportunistically, anticipating the lock-in situation that collaborators are faced with (Dyer and Singh, 1998). Moreover, efforts to establish knowledge-sharing routines may be misused unilaterally by "free-riding" and aiming at "out-learning" the partner (Baum et al., 2000; Duschek, 2004; Khanna et al., 1998). Existing literature on alliances often assumes that partners aim at accessing and internalizing external knowledge through cooperations (Hamel, 1991). "The resource-based logic suggests that competitive advantage of alliances is based on the effective integration of the partner firm's valuable resources" (Das and Teng, 2000a, p. 47 f.). Such a perspective does not perceive inter-organizational partnerships as a trustful cooperation but as a "competitive collaboration" (Hamel, 1991) or "co-opetition" (Brandenburger and Nalebuff, 1996).

In contrast, the relational view of competitive advantage takes a more "optimistic" perspective and stresses that the establishment of effective governance mechanisms may lead to relational rents through a reduction in transaction costs and incentivization of partners to invest in relation-specific assets (Dyer and Singh, 1998). Two general classes of governance mechanisms can be distinguished: *third-party enforcement* and *self-enforcing agreements* (Dyer and Singh, 1998).

Third-party enforcement describes the conclusion of a formal contract to avoid opportunistic behavior which is enforced by a third party. Self-enforcing agreements, in contrast, are safeguards against opportunism that do not rely on third-party enforcement (Dyer and Singh, 1998). Incentive-compatible formal agreements and informal safeguards like trust and reputation can be distinguished (Dyer and Singh, 1998).

Informal governance is considered to have certain advantages over formal agreements. A direct consequence of the assumption that human actors are boundedly rational is that formal contracts are necessarily incomplete (Hart and Moore, 1988). Moreover, informal governance structures can be assumed to be harder to imitate than formal contracts, and thus be more likely to result in competitive advantages (Barney, 1991). In addition, informal governance mechanisms like reputation and trust are assumed to incentivize partners to exchange knowledge and combine complementary resources (Dyer and Singh, 1998).

However, the development of trust between organizations may be difficult. First, trust can be assumed to develop over a longer period of successful collaboration, potentially resulting in the need to rely on formal governance at the outset of a partnership (Dyer and Singh, 1998). Second, firms may face a "paradox of trust" in that while trust indeed results in norms and expectations about appropriate behavior, the perception of the inherent risks may be lowered, leading to an increased threat of opportunism (Granovetter, 1985; Dyer and Singh, 1998).

Following the RBV, only those resources that are not imitable have the potential to result in sustainable competitive advantages. The same holds true for the special case of inter-organizational corporations. If the link between a focal firm and a collaborator can be easily imitated by competing dyadic arrangements, then this relationship does not have the potential to result in sustainable competitive advantage.

Generally, the resource properties that have been proposed by the RBV to lead to sustainable competitive advantages can be transferred to the case of inter-firm arrangements. The reasons why trust is established throughout the collaboration of certain partners may be subject to causal ambiguity. Moreover, certain aspects of collaboration, such as trust or absorptive capacity, may evolve over time and therefore be hard to imitate in the short run due to time compression diseconomies (Dyer and Singh, 1998). In addition, Dyer and Singh suggest reasons for non-imitability that are specific to the context of inter-firm arrangements. *Asset stock interconnectedness* describes the situation where resources are mutually dependent across firm boundaries, that is, their full value evolves only if combined. In a similar vein, *resource indivisibility* refers to the situation where resources that are spread across organizations cannot be separated without loosing their value. In addition, *partner scarcity* and the *institutional environment* of a certain partnership may hinder its imitation by other dyads of organizations (Dyer and Singh, 1998).

Summing up, in contrast to the RBV and its derivatives which focus on singular firms, the object of analysis of the relational view is linkages between firms. On the one hand, the RBV and the relational view can be perceived as complementary given that most organizations develop resources and capabilities internally *and* form partnerships to generate competitive advantages. However, the RBV advises companies to avoid a spill-over of knowledge to third parties, while the relational view proposes to systematically share knowledge with partners in order to generate relational rents (Dyer and Singh, 1998). The contribution of the relational view lies in the fact that firms may develop competitive advantages by establishing unique inter-organizational relationships. In order to so, however, adequate governance mechanisms have to be in place.

2.2.2.3 The resource dependence theory

While the relational view considers linkages between firms as resources that may lead to competitive advantage, the resource dependence theory (RDT) stresses inter-firm dependencies within partnership arrangements (Pfeffer and Salancik,

1978; Cool and Henderson, 1998; Harpaz and Meshoulam, 1997; Inkpen and Beamish, 1997). The RDT studies power relations that result from firms being dependent on resources they do not control (Yamagishi et al., 1988; Yamaguchi, 1996; Markovsky et al., 1988). Power is perceived as the counterpart of dependence, since "the power of A over B is equal to, and based upon, the dependence of B upon A" (Emerson, 1962, p. 33). Power, in turn, is defined as "the potential (or capacity) of an actor to influence the behavior of another actor" (Tushman, 1977, p. 207).

The degree of a firm's dependence on a resource, and thus its dependence on the organization that possesses the resource, is influenced by several factors. First, the higher the *importance* of the respective resource, the higher the dependence is suggested to be. Second, the lower the number of *alternatives* for a particular resource, the higher the dependence on external organizations. Third, the greater the degree of *discretion* that a firm has in the deployment of a resource, the greater another firm's dependence on it (Medcof, 2001).

From the perspective of the RDT, linkages between firms are understood as "a set of power relations based on the exchange of resources" (Ulrich and Barney, 1984, p. 472). Organizations are assumed to strive for improving their position by decreasing the dependence on other firms, or by increasing other firms' dependence on their resources and thus increasing the power over these firms (Ulrich and Barney, 1984). Firms may hence be mutually dependent, that is, power relations between firms may have a reciprocal character. The power over each other may be balanced, but could also be distributed asymmetrically among organizational actors (Casciaro and Piskorski, 2005; Oliver, 1990).

According to previous literature, firms can follow two strategies to increase their power over other organizations. First, through a strategy of growth, firms may be able to lower their dependence on external resources. For instance, firms may use mergers or acquisitions to eliminate external dependencies. Moreover, a diversification strategy of entering new product-market combinations (Ansoff, 1965) may reduce the importance of formerly vital resources (Pfeffer and Salancik, 1978).

Second, previous literature suggests informal coordination mechanisms to improve the distribution of power, even if a direct control over resources may not be feasible. "There are many informal mechanisms and semiformal interorganizational linkages that can be employed to coordinate the respective interests of various social actors" (Pfeffer and Salancik, 1978, p. 143). Existing work mentions a wide range of informal coordination mechanisms that may be used to this end by firms, such as the establishment of norms and expectations, the formation of joint ventures, a reciprocal placement of board members ("board interlock"), or the formation of inter-organizational institutions (Pfeffer and Salancik, 1978).

These strategies that aim at gaining (partial) control over external resources have been referred to as "constraint absorption mechanisms" (Pfeffer and Salancik, 1978; Casciaro and Piskorski, 2005). Casciaro and Piskorski argue that constraint absorption is particularly likely if the mutual dependence between organizational actors is high and the power relation between partners is balanced. If, however, power is asymmetrically distributed among partners, then constraint absorption is argued to be unlikely due to the powerful partner's goal to maintain the status quo (Casciaro and Piskorski, 2005).

2.2.2.4 Summary

The previous sections have discussed the RBV, its extensions to inter-firm arrangements, the relational view of competitive advantage and the resource dependence theory. Generally, the resource-based perspective provides an appropriate framework for studying inter-firm partnerships in the enterprise software industry, since both platform vendors as well as complementors were found to participate in partnerships with the goal of accessing external resources and capabilities. Moreover, the differences between the role of platform vendors and complementors suggest a resource-based perspective which stresses firm heterogeneity.

The relational view of competitive advantages gives a rationale of why firms form close partnerships in spite of the threat of opportunism. Instead, the RDT suggests that firms may be more successful if external dependencies can be reduced. Both approaches may be transferable to the case of enterprise software. However, in order to answer the question of how spoke organizations coordinate a partnership with a platform vendor, the idiosyncrasies of the enterprise software industry need to be accounted for. Therefore, the following section presents a model of hub-and-spoke networks in the enterprise software industry that forms the basis of this study's empirical inquiry and makes the idiosyncrasies of the enterprise software domain explicit.

2.3 A model of hub-and-spoke networks in the enterprise software industry

This section provides a model of the analyzed networks in the enterprise software industry in order to provide a basis for the study's empirical exploration. Specifically, an explicit formulation of the model's assumption and the resulting implications and limitations is necessary to increase the external validity of the study.

In accordance with Wand et al. (1999), a model comprises the *things* that the relevant part of the world is made up of and its respective properties, as well as the *relationships* that link these things to each other. The relevant part of the world in the context of this study consists of organizations that develop and market components of an enterprise software system. Specifically, two types of actors can be distinguished. First, actors can take the role of a *platform leader* or *hub*. Hubs are characterized as organizations that provide a software platform that other actors can use as an architectural base and build solutions on. Second, organizations can play the role of a *complementor* or *spoke*. Spokes build solutions on the platforms provided by hub organizations and extend the overall system with specific niche functionality. If hubs and spokes are *linked* to each other, a *formal certification* of the spoke's solution or its resources by the hub exists.

Apart from these roles that organizations can play and the relationship that exist between these actors, the model makes additional assumptions. A hub-and-spoke network is assumed to consist of exactly one hub and a sufficiently large number of spokes that are small enough so that a power imbalance between the hub and a singular spoke exists. It has to be noted that this assumption restricts the model to a subset of the partnerships that can be observed in the enterprise software industry. Large platform vendors also form partnerships with each other (e.g. IBM and SAP). However, the power imbalance resulting from partnerships between *large* platform vendors and *small* complementors is at the core of this study and justifies the delimitation.

Power imbalance is assumed to result from the assertion that only the network as a whole brings benefits to a hub as a result of network effects, while the hub's benefit from a singular relationship to a certain spoke is marginal. Spokes, in contrast, are assumed to particularly benefit from the one-to-one relationship with a certain hub (Kude and Dibbern, 2009). As a result of these properties of hub-and-spoke networks, it is assumed, in accordance with existing work, that platform vendors aim at coordinating the overall network with the help of formal governance mechanisms, specifically through standardization of outputs (i.e., standardization of architectures and interfaces), standardization of processes and skills (i.e., through certification of partners), and investments in network-specific resources as opposed to spoke-specific ones (Kude et al., 2008; Huber et al., 2010).

The enterprise software industry is assumed to exhibit the characteristics of both system and component competition (Farrell et al., 1998). Specifically, hub-and-spoke *systems*, that is, certain platforms together with the respective compatible extensions, compete for customers. Moreover, within a hub-and-spoke network, component competition may exist to a certain extent, that is, hubs may partner with several spokes whose products have overlapping functionality. Also, the solutions offered by spokes may partly overlap with functionality that is part of the hub's platform.

In addition, participating in a partner network established by a certain platform vendor, that is, having a solution certified by an incumbent firm, is assumed to be costly for complementors. As a result, complementors have to carefully consider the trade-off between partnership and certification fees as well as other expenses that occur throughout the partnership, and the benefits resulting from these partnerships. Figure 2.7 depicts this study's model of a hub-and-spoke network in the enterprise software industry.

2.4 Summary

This chapter presented the historical evolution of the development of enterprise software that led to the emergence of inter-organizational networks within the

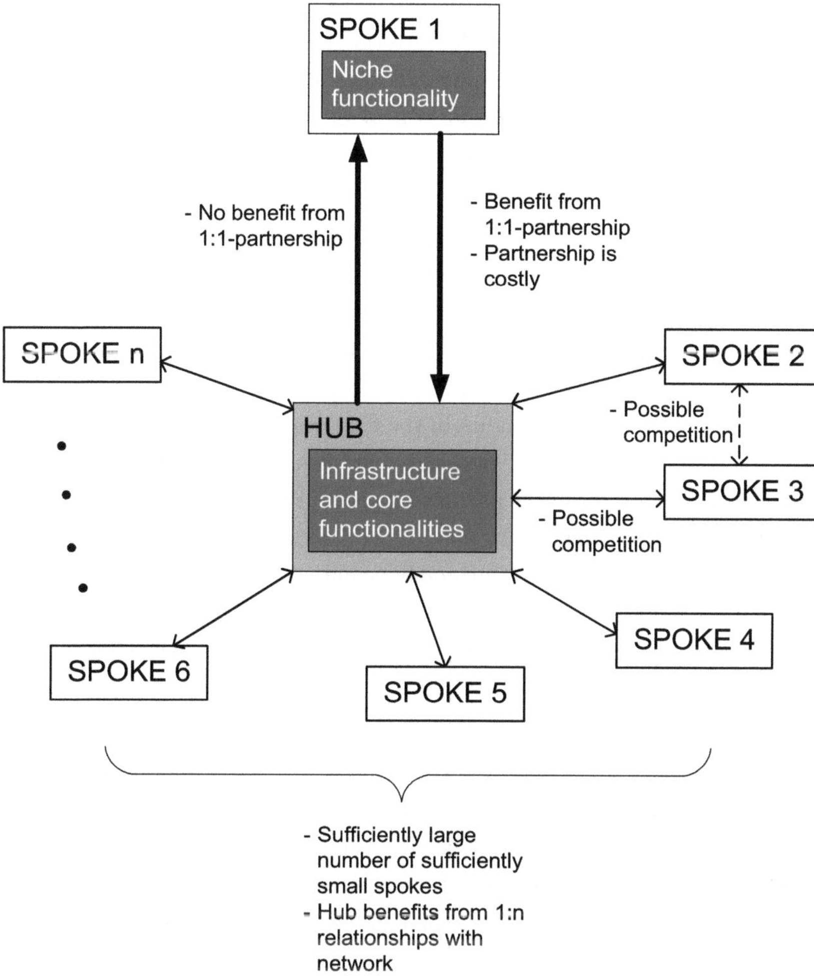

Figure 2.7: A model of hub-and-spoke networks in the enterprise software industry

industry. In particular, a specific structure became dominant that consists of a central actor that provides the overall platform and basic functionality, together with a number of small and medium-sized organizations that develop complementary functionality based on the focal firm's platform. These networks were found to compete amongst each other in a system competition. In addition, organizations that act as complementors may also compete on a component level.

Inter-firm networks have the potential to increase the flexibility of the overall systems and reduce post-implementation effort by anticipating customer requirements. Researchers in the field of information systems have recently acknowledged the growing importance of these inter-organizational structures in the enterprise software industry. By taking into account the idiosyncrasies of enterprise software, these recent studies in the field of IS made significant theoretical and practical contributions. Specifically, previous work empirically analyzed why platform vendors establish partnership networks and why complementors participate in these networks. Moreover, previous work in the field of IS has analyzed structural properties of partnerships and networks and the implications of topology for partnership and network success. Even though the studies provide important insights, the previous discussion identified a gap regarding the coordination of these partnerships when explaining and predicting partnership success.

Therefore, this chapter reviewed work on the coordination of division of work. The general concepts of mutual adjustment and standardization have been identified as relevant coordination mechanisms. Analyzing the coordination through mutual adjustment from an organizational perspective, the relational view of competitive advantage provides a rationale of why firms enter close partnerships that are coordinated informally through peer-level communication. The relational view builds on the resource-based view of the firm and argues that firms may create competitive advantages by forming close partnerships with other organizations that provide complementary resources.

On a network level, the principles of modularity and loose coupling were found to describe a common way to design complex products. While the relational view advocates close relationships between organizations that jointly create a product, modularity refers to the concept of building a system from smaller subsystems that can be designed independently but function together. As discussed

Construct	Conceptualization
Resource complementarity	Alliance partners' dissimilar but compatible resources and capabilities that collectively generate greater rents than the sum of those obtained from the individual endowments of each partner (based on Das and Teng, 2000b; Dyer and Singh, 1998; Ahuja, 2000).
Degree of organizational coupling	The degree to which an organization ties itself to another organization in a way that increases its responsiveness to the other organization and decreases its distinctiveness. (based on Dyer and Singh, 1998).

Table 2.3: Conceptualization of central constructs

above, modularity results in what has been referred to as loosely-coupled systems. Drawing on the resource-dependence theory, such a loose coupling may be in the interest of complementors to reduce the dependence on the large partner's resources. Moreover, a certain degree of standardization was found to be indispensable in order to enable a loosely-coupled and modular system (Brunsson, 2000).

In accordance with the recommendations of literature on qualitative case studies (e.g. Yin, 2009), the review of broad theoretical concepts as summarized above is used to guide the exploratory case studies. The complementarity between partners' resources and the degree of organizational coupling between partners – as a representation of the type of coordination – act as general constructs that form a basic framework for the empirical study. Table 2.3 gives the definition of these basic constructs according to the literature presented above.

In line with the findings from literature discussed above, a positive relationship between complementarity and organizational coupling is assumed (Dyer and Singh, 1998; Schilling, 2000; Schilling and Steensma, 2001). That is, the higher the complementarity between a platform vendor's and a complementor's resources, the more the complementor is proposed to tie its business to the platform vendor in order to reap the benefits that result from resource complementarity. In other words, the higher the complementarity, the higher the degree of organizational coupling that complementors aim at. Figure 2.8 depicts this proposed relationship that acts as a tentative proposition and basic frame of the following exploratory study.

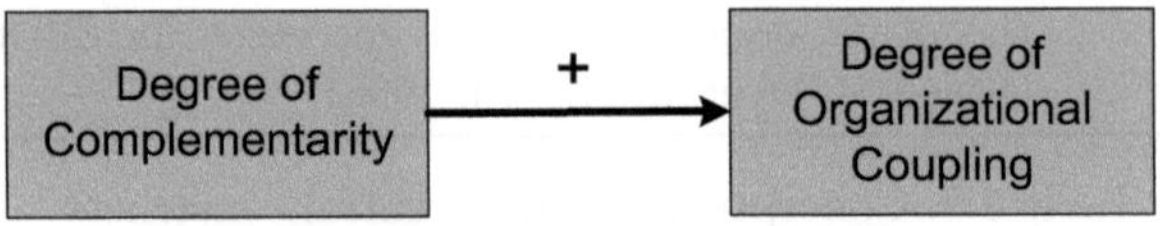

Figure 2.8: Preliminary research framework

3 Research design

The goal of this study is to build a mid-range theory that explains how complementors in the enterprise software industry (successfully) coordinate the relationship with platform vendors and that is accessible to theory testing (Gregor, 2006). In order to reach this goal, a careful selection and rigorous application of an appropriate and instrumental research design is crucial. Therefore, this chapter presents the selection and implementation of a qualitative multiple-case study as a research strategy. The epistemological stance of the study, the research process, as well as the data collection and analysis procedure are discussed in detail. In particular, this chapter elaborates on the successive procedure of first, conducting an exploratory case study based on the general frame presented in Chapter 2 and second, carrying out a second case study in order to substantiate and refine the developed mid-range theory.

3.1 Selection of a research strategy

As discussed in Chapter 2, there has be a paucity of previous research on the coordination of inter-firm networks in the enterprise software industry. The goal of this study is to fill this gap and build an explanatory model that answers the research question of how complementors coordinate the partnership with platform vendors and how coordination leads to partnership success. In order to do so, case study research (Yin, 2009; Eisenhardt, 1989; Benbasat et al., 1987; Lee, 1989), a method which has been widely used in IS research (Orlikowski and Baroudi, 1991; Alavi and Carlson, 1992; Vessey et al., 2002; Dibbern et al., 2008), appears to be instrumental.

The case study method is one of a multitude of research strategies commonly used in social sciences and distinguished in the respective literature (Creswell, 1998; Kerlinger and Lee, 2000; McGrath, 1981; Stone, 1978; Yin, 2009; Siggelkow,

2007). As an example, the taxonomy of Stone (1978) includes laboratory experiments, simulations, field experiments, field studies, sample surveys, and case studies. Extant literature agrees that research settings differ in several dimensions, and that there is no one method that is appropriate and superior in all possible situations (Scandura and Williams, 2000; McGrath, 1981). Consequently, a particular research endeavor has to be carefully analyzed in order to select an appropriate research method. In order to make a justified selection, the dimensions identified in literature can be used to evaluate the appropriateness of different approaches in certain contingencies. One set of dimensions identified in existing work distinguishes research settings according to the following three dimensions (Scandura and Williams, 2000; McGrath, 1981).

First, the *realism or naturalness* of a research setting describes the degree to which the context of a certain study is perceived to be real to its participants. These research settings are assumed to particularly suit situations in which multiple aspects are studied that are linked in a way that has so far been undiscovered (Stone, 1978). This study analyzes the partnership behavior of organizations, a situation that can be assumed to be hard to replicate in an unnatural setting, such as a laboratory experiment.

Second, research scenarios can be distinguished in terms of the *control an investigator has over the participants.* If the research aims at confirming hypothesized relationships between variables, the independent variable has to be manipulated and measures for the independent and dependent variables have to be defined. In order to do so, a high degree of control over these variables is indispensable (Stone, 1978). The goal of this study is to develop a mid-range theory on the coordination of inter-firm partnerships. Thus, manipulating clearly defined variables can be considered to be a secondary goal.

Third, research settings may be distinguished by referring to the degree to which research findings are *generalizable* to other contexts. While basic research can be assumed to aim at a fundamental understanding of characteristics of the studied entities and their interrelations, applied research tries to apply findings in different contexts (Kerlinger and Lee, 2000). While this study does aim at providing results that are generalizable and transferable to related contexts, the main goal is to shed light on fundamental relationships between relevant concepts.

The characteristics of this study's research setting fit particularly well with the case study research approach. A case study is an in-depth investigation of units of interest. The phenomenon of interest is studied in a natural setting, and no control is exercised over the participants, which means that variables cannot be manipulated by the researcher (Stone, 1978). When carrying out a case study, particular attention must be paid to the fact that case studies are less systematic than other research methods and may be exposed to certain biases. These disadvantages of case study research implies a reduced statistical generalizability of its results. Instead, results are transferred to a broader set of phenomena by means of analytical generalization, that is, by replicating the analysis and comparing the results in related settings (Yin, 2009). Case studies allow for the examination of complex settings in a flexible way within their natural environment and are therefore considered appropriate for the goal of theory-building (Stone, 1978).

In a similar vein, Yin (2009) suggests three dimensions to support the selection of an appropriate research design. The respective occurrences regarding the three dimensions indicate which method is the most adequate. The *form of the posed research question*, the required degree of *control over the behavioral events*, and the *focus on contemporary events* versus historical ones determine the appropriateness of certain strategies (see table 3.1). This study poses the questions of *how* complementors coordinate inter-firm partnerships. Controlling the behavior of organizations in real-world settings can be assumed to be unfeasible. In addition, the study focuses on contemporary partnerships instead of historical ones. Hence, an evaluation of the criteria proposed by Yin (2009) as well suggests the case study method as an appropriate approach to answer this study's research questions.

3.2 Specification of the case study strategy

After having selected the case study method as a suitable approach to build a mid-range theory that answers the posed research questions, this section provides details on the specific design of the conducted empirical analysis. Several design options exist regarding the specification of a case study strategy.

Strategy	Form of research question	Requires control of behavioral events?	Focuses on contemporary events?
Experiment	how, why?	yes	yes
Survey	who, what, where, how many, how much?	no	yes
Archival analysis	who, what, where, how many, how much?	no	yes/no
History	how, many?	no	no
Case study	how, many?	no	yes

Table 3.1: Relevant situations for different research strategies (Yin, 2009, p. 8)

First of all, case study research can be based on different epistemological positions. Moreover, the study's unit of analysis must be made explicit. In addition, case studies can be exploratory in nature or they can confirm or disconfirm hypotheses deduced from literature. Also, when following a case study approach, singular cases can be the focus of analysis, but case studies can also analyze multiple cases (Stake, 2006). In the latter case, the replication logic is of importance. Finally, it has to be decided whether the empirical study relies on the analysis of quantitative data or on evidence that is qualitative in nature. The following discussion specifies the research strategy chosen in this study and justifies the respective design decisions.

Case studies can be positivist, interpretive, and critical (Myers and Avison, 1997). Positivists assume that reality is independent of the observer and can be objectively perceived through human sensation (Orlikowski and Baroudi, 1991; Friedman, 1999). Advocates of a positivist epistemology assume that fixed relationships between entities exist at the outset that can be deduced and formulated in nomological hypotheses with the help of measurable properties (Straub et al., 2004; Dube and Pare, 2003).

In contrast, interpretive research is based on the general ontological assumption that reality can only be grasped through social construction by the investigator by means of language, consciousness, and shared meanings (Orlikowski and

Baroudi, 1991). The goal of interpretive research is to discover the meaning that social actors ascribe to certain behavior (Miles and Huberman, 1994). Instead of describing and testing unidirectional, causal relationships between variables, interpretive research aims at an in-depth understanding of a phenomenon (Orlikowski and Baroudi, 1991).

As a third epistemological stance, critical research assumes that social reality is a result of history and is produced and reproduced by human actors. Critical research aims to overcome the impediments to change social reality that result from social, political, and cultural domination by providing social critique (Myers and Avison, 1997; Hirschheim, 1985).

The goal of this study is to develop and refine a mid-range theory that explains partnership behavior. In order to do so, the study mainly relies on interviews of individuals within the organization (see Section 3.3). Thus, the researcher has to interpret and ascribe meaning to the statements of these actors and reflect on them, while taking into account the respective context. In spite of this acknowledged need for interpreting the individual actors' utterances in order to extract determinants and implications of organizational behavior to some extent, the epistemological stance of this work is a positivist one, referring to the assumption that organizational behavior can be explained objectively and independent of the researchers' preconceptions (Orlikowski and Baroudi, 1991). The study aims at developing an explanatory model that is accessible to statistical tests and generalizable to related settings. In order to do so, the constructs within the model have to be clearly defined so that they can be measured independent of the observer.

Implicitly defined by the research question of how complementors coordinate inter-firm partnerships, the unit of analysis of this study is at the level of organizations that act as complementors in the inter-firm networks within the enterprise software industry. Yin (2009) differentiates between holistic case studies that have a clearly specified, single unit of analysis, as well as embedded case studies that have multiple units of analysis which are usually hierarchical. This study examines partnership behavior on an organizational level, that is, it draws on a holistic unit of analysis. However, it is acknowledged that the network in which an inter-firm partnership is embedded and the personal relationships that go beyond formal agreements may influence organizational links. Thus, the study takes a systemic perspective on inter-organizational partnerships in the enterprise software industry that has a clear focus on the organizational level, but still allows for inter-network comparisons (von Bertalanffy, 1968).

Existing literature generally assumes that case study research can be either exploratory or confirmatory in nature (Pare, 2004; Katz, 1953; Yin, 2009). Following Kerlinger and Lee, it is argued that "exploratory studies have three purposes: to discover significant variables [...], to discover relations among these variables, and to lay the groundwork for later, more systemic and rigorous testing of hypotheses" (Kerlinger and Lee, 2000, p. 586). In other words, the goal of exploratory research is to build theory (Eisenhardt, 1989; Eisenhardt and Graebner, 2007).

On the one hand, in accordance with existing work, it is argued that it is unfeasible and even impossible to explore the field without preconceptions about entities and relationships in mind (Yin, 2009; Eisenhardt, 1989; Miles and Huberman, 1994). On the other hand, it is important to note that although these preconceptions are necessary to guide and structure exploratory research, it is crucial to recognize that these a priori assertions are tentative in nature (Eisenhardt, 1989). This insight has been stressed by Katz (1953), who suggests that "researchers do have hypotheses in mind, but these are not precisely formulated" (Katz, 1953, p. 77).

While exploratory case studies have the goal of building theory, confirmatory ones aim at corroborating an explanatory model that has either been deduced from existing literature or built inductively through (exploratory) empirical research (Cavaye, 1996).

Generally, case study research is assumed to have an iterative character in which a redesign of the approach should occur throughout the data collection process (Yin, 2009). Such a redesign may "involve the selection of alternative cases or changes in the case study (i.e., data collection) protocol" (Yin, 2009, p. 58). Drawing on this insight that case study research is inherently a cyclic endeavor, this study follows a two-staged approach.

In a first phase, an exploratory case study is conducted that has a basic frame and a general working hypothesis in mind. This basic frame is a resource-oriented perspective and proposes that a higher degree of complementarity leads to a higher degree of organizational coupling (see Section 2.4). This basic and abstract proposition leaves enough room to explore new variables and relationships, but is adequate for guiding exploratory research. Based on the explanatory model developed in this exploratory phase, a second phase of case study research is carried out with the goal of substantiating and refining the model and making the developed theory amenable to theory testing and statistical generalization. The two-staged research approach is shown in Figure 1.2 in Chapter 1.

In order to increase the analytical generalizability of the findings, this study applies a multiple-case approach in both the exploratory and the refinement phases. Yin (2009) discusses the replication logic of multiple-case studies and distinguishes literal as well as theoretical replication. While a literal replication logic refer to the selection of cases in a way that similar results can be expected, a theoretical replication logic predicts different results. The exploratory phase is based on a rather broad theoretical framework that aims at developing a theoretical model. In terms of this abstract theoretical frame, similar results can be expected a priori when analyzing several organizations that have entered partnerships with a platform vendor (see Section 3.3 for details). After having elaborated on this preliminary model through the insights gained from the exploratory phase, a theoretical replication logic is applied by deliberately varying the explanatory model's independent variables.

Although mostly subsumed under the category of qualitative research, case studies can also draw results from a quantitative data analysis. While quantitative research relies on the use of numbers or measurements (Kerlinger and Lee, 2000), the goal of qualitative studies is "to obtain a rich set of data surrounding the specific research issue, as well as capturing the contextual complexity" (Benbasat et al., 1987, p. 374). The use of qualitative data is deemed particularly suitable in studies that aim at developing theory and that study research subjects in their natural setting (Creswell, 1998).

Extant literature suggests a multitude of possible sources of qualitative data such as expert interviews, observation of behavior, documents, physical artifacts, and audio-visual materials (Stone, 1978; Yin, 2009; Creswell, 1998). The use of multiple data sources is suggested to allow for triangulation and hence increase the validity of the data (Patton, 2002; Yin, 2009; Gibbert et al., 2008). Moreover, it is not uncommon in case study research to enrich qualitative findings with a quantitative analysis (e.g., Dibbern et al., 2008). For example, previous work suggests "coding text and then counting the frequency of different code occurrences as a means of identifying key areas for further investigation" (Crabtree and Miller, 1992, p. 95) as one of several ways to analyze data that is in text form.

In order to build a theory that answers the research question of how complementors coordinate the partnership with a dominant platform vendor, a qualitative approach appears to be well-suited (Golden-Biddle and Locke, 2007). The first, exploratory phase of this study relies solely on qualitative data analysis. The second phase aims at corroborating and refining the developed model by using qualitative data that is enriched with an evaluation of the value of the identified constructs. It is assumed that congruence between the qualitative analysis and the evaluation of constructs increases the validity of the study's findings. The following section discusses how data was collected and analyzed in the exploratory and refinement phases of this study.

3.3 Data collection and analysis procedure

In the preceding section, the case study approach has been selected as an appropriate method to answer this study's research question by building an explanatory model. Moreover, the design of the case study conducted in this work has been specified. A two-staged approach has been selected, consisting of first, a multiple-case study that is exploratory in nature, and a second multiple-case study that aims at substantiating and refining the proposed model. This section sheds light on the procedure of collecting empirical data and analyzing it in both phases.

In line with the goal of theory building, the exploratory phase focused on an in-depth analysis of the partnership networks of two core companies. The refinement phase added additional spoke organizations in order to substantiate and refine the findings of the first phase. The two selected core firms are globally acting organizations that offer software platforms on which partners can build complementary solutions and therefore represent hub organizations in the sense of the model depicted in Figure 2.7. Both hub organizations are sufficiently large and have built an extensive network of mostly much smaller partners so that an asymmetry exists in terms of the value derived from the access to resources through a singular partnership (Gulati and Sytch, 2007). Considering the oligopolistic structure of today's enterprise software industry as discussed in Chapter 2, focusing on the networks of two important platform vendors seems a feasible approach.

The two hub organizations under consideration historically focus on different core businesses. This can be illustrated based on the software stack model shown in Figure 2.1. HUB A has its traditional core competency in delivering enterprise applications and therefore has had its main activity in the application layer. Although this is still mostly the case today, the recent versions of HUB A's enterprise software system are based on SOA technology rather than on a standardized, monolithic system. Thus, while still having its core competency of enterprise applications, today HUB A occupies both the application and the middleware layer. In contrast, HUB B formerly covered the whole information systems stack as depicted in Figure 2.1. During the 1990s, however, HUB B made the strategic decision not to offer enterprise applications anymore and instead focus on infrastructure and middleware solutions as well as implementation and consulting services. Both selected hub organizations have fostered partnerships with a multitude of smaller ISVs that build their solutions on the hub organizations' platform and reside both on the application as well as on the middleware layer.

Out of the networks established by these two platform vendors, organizations that act as complementors were selected for the multiple-case studies to build and substantiate an explanatory model. While the description of the respective cases and interview partners are presented in detail in Chapter 4 and 5 respectively, the discussion that follows gives an overview of the general approach to the selection of data sources, the collection of empirical evidence, and the analysis of the collected data.

Both phases relied on expert interviews and document analysis as the two major sources of evidence (Yin, 2009). Therefore, the main focus was on interviewing knowledgeable members of the complementor organizations. Since spoke organizations are generally fairly small (on average, the case companies employ around 20 individuals), it is a justifiable assumption that one key individual per case is sufficient to provide information about partnership coordination and success. In fact, the small size of the analyzed organizations allowed for interviewing experts that had a comprehensive picture of the organization.

The spoke organizations that took part in the two multiple-case studies were selected purposefully (Patton, 2002). First, it was ensured that each of them represented an independent legal entity and none of them was a subsidiary of a larger organization. Second, each spoke is a solution provider that builds its system on top of the respective hub's platform and hence extends the overall system in a certain way. Third, each of the spoke organizations is a certified partner of the respective hub. The selected case companies were first approached by telephone and then supplied with additional information on the general topic and aim of the study as well as a rough interview guideline (see Chapter 4 and 5 for details). Contact information was retrieved from the information about the partnership network on the hubs' websites.

For the exploratory phase of the study that aimed at gaining an in-depth understanding of important constructs and their interrelations in the respective context, on-site visits and personal conversations with interviewees were considered desirable. Consequently, the cases for the exploratory phase were selected out of those complementors that could be reached within a reasonable time and without exceeding a reasonable traveling budget. In order to be able to obtain more generalizable results through enlarging the data set (e.g., to overcome a potential bias that may result from geographical proximity to the hub organizations' headquarters), some of the interviews for the refinement phase were also carried out via telephone. This was considered a feasible approach because the purpose of the second phase was to substantiate and refine theoretical links already discovered in the first phase's in-depth analysis.

Both in the exploratory and in the refinement phase, the conversations with experts had the form of a semi-structured interview (Yin, 2009; Stone, 1978). Semi-structured interviews are based on a predetermined set of questions that broadly guide the conversation, giving the interviewee the chance to speak freely. Moreover, the interviewer can move away from the structure by adjusting the questions and get into detail whenever interesting issues emerge (Stone, 1978). Yin (2009) describes semi-structured interviews as focused interviews, "in which a respondent is interviewed for a short period of time - an hour for example. In such cases, the interviews may still remain open-ended and assume a conversational manner, but you are more likely to be following a certain set of questions derived from the case study protocol" (Yin, 2009, p. 107).

The interview guidelines for this study's two-staged approach (see Appendix 1) are driven by theory. The interviews of the exploratory phase were guided by the basic theoretical frame discussed in Section 2.4, while the conversations in the refinement phase corresponded to the explanatory model developed in Chapter 4. Inherent in the two-staged approach and in line with its purpose, the expert interviews became more structured when moving from the first to the second stage of the empirical analysis. The first round of interviews was guided by a rather broad and abstract frame and had the explicit goal of discovering constructs and their interrelations through an exploratory, in-depth case analysis. Consequently, the interviews of the exploratory phase were more open. Instead, the second multiple-case study had the goal of substantiating and refining an explanatory model devised in the first phase and were therefore based on a more structured interview guideline. Yet, in order to be open to emerging variables and links, the interviews remained semi-structured instead of having the form of a questionnaire.

In order to allow for triangulation and thus increase the internal validity of the study, publicly available documents such as the companies' websites were analyzed with the goal of complementing the expert interviews. As an example, the spoke organizations' marketing activities and the usage of the larger partner's brand name on the spokes' websites were examined in order to substantiate the comments of the interview partners on resource complementarity.

After having discussed this study's approach to case selection and data col lection, the general way to analyze data as well as build and refine a theoretical model is outlined shortly. The specific data analysis procedures of the corresponding phase are presented in Chapter 4 and 5 respectively. Once the interviews are transcribed, the initial step in analyzing qualitative data "involves identifying, coding, categorizing, classifying, and labeling the primary patterns in the data. This essentially means analyzing the core *content* of interviews" (Patton, 2002, p. 463, emphasis in original).

With the help of the software tool NVivo, the core content of the interviews was analyzed by assigning codes to text passages. "Codes are tags or labels for assigning units of meaning to the descriptive or inferential information compiled during a study. Codes usually are attached to 'chunks' of varying size – words, phrases, sentences, or whole paragraphs" (Miles and Huberman, 1994, p. 56). The data analysis procedure of this study's exploratory phase started out with two codes which represent the initial constructs identified and (tentatively) defined in Section 2.4 – *complementarity* and *organizational coupling.* In an iterative process, the interview transcripts were carefully analyzed in order to generate and define new codes, drop existing ones, and identify potential links between the theorized concepts. This re-coding procedure was done until a coherent mid-range theory emerged, that is, until eventually the explanatory model that resulted from linking the identified constructs was able to explain all cases without further adjustments (Miles and Huberman, 1994; Patton, 2002).

The second phase of the empirical analysis generally followed the same pattern. However, the goal was not to build a theoretical framework, but to substantiate and refine an existing one. Thus, the analysis of the interview transcripts began based on the final set of codes resulting from the exploratory phase. Besides corroborating the proposed theoretical relationship through contextually enriched case data, an evaluation of the defined constructs and their interrelations was performed by estimating the level of the emerging constructs across the analyzed cases in order to further increase the validity of the findings (Miles and Huberman, 1994; Sherif et al., 2006).

3.4 Summary

This chapter has described the research strategy that this study follows in order to reach the goal of answering its research questions by means of an explanatory model. Therefore, a justified selection of the case study method has been made. Subsequently, the specific case study approach followed in this study has been discussed. While keeping in mind the need to interpret utterances of individual actors in order to draw conclusions on organizational behavior, the general epistemological perspective is a positivist one. That is, the goal of this study is to develop an explanatory model that consists of objectively measurable constructs that are linked to each other. These links are expressed by propositions.

In order to reach this goal, the case study research follows a two-staged approach that consists of an exploratory phase and a refinement phase that aims at substantiating and, if necessary, revising the explanatory model. Both phases rely on a multiple-case study that analyzes complementors with the help of theory-driven, semi-structured interviews and document analysis. The exploratory phase follows a literal replication approach, since – based on its broad theoretical frame – similar results can be expected. In contrast, the second phase deliberately analyzes cases that can be expected to differ in the variables that emerge in the exploratory phase.

The following two chapters present the results of this study's empirical research. First, Chapter 4 presents the exploratory phase of this study and, based on the results and on existing literature, develops two explanatory models that answer the study's research question. Chapter 5 presents the results from the refinement phase. Both chapters start with a description of the analyzed cases and the data collection procedure.

4 Empirical exploration and theory development

The previous chapters have elaborated on foundations of this study and discussed its methodological approach. A two-staged procedure was selected that consists of an exploratory case study, followed by a refinement phase. This chapter presents the study's exploratory phase which has the goal to develop a model that is able to explain how complementors coordinate the partnership with the larger hub and how these coordination efforts lead to partnership success. The exploratory phase is guided by the basic theoretical framework formulated in Section 2.4 and draws upon a multiple-case study as well as existing literature. The following sections first present the detailed description of the cases as well as the data collection and analysis procedure. Next, the development of the explanatory model is presented.

4.1 Data selection and analysis

As described in Section 3.3, this study focuses on the partnership networks of two hub organizations (HUB A and HUB B) that have fostered networks of organizations that complement their respective platform. Out of these networks of spoke organizations, 17 companies were selected that participate in a partnership with one of the two hubs, eight of them with HUB A and nine with HUB B. Table 4.1 gives a description of the case companies' core businesses.

As described in Chapter 3, data was collected through expert interviews within each spoke's organization as well as by gathering secondary material on the case companies. Since the research question of this study is concerned with issues of strategic relevance, executives of the partner firms were selected as interview partners whenever possible. In six of the 17 cases, the CEO (or equivalent) participated in the study. Four case companies had a dedicated role of establishing and managing the partnership with the hub company. Consequently, these partnership managers were selected as experts. In the other cases, professionals like the head of software or product development that were considered to have a good understanding of the companies' partnerships were selected.

Case company	Hub	Core business
MACHINE	A	Integration between the hub's system and various machines such as vending machines or intelligent refrigerators
CAD	A	Integration between the hub's system and a CAD system of a different vendor
GROUP	A	Integration between the hub's system and a groupware system of a different vendor
MOBILE	A	Providing systems for automatic, mobile data recording, used for example in inventory management
MEDIA	A	Full-range supplier of IT systems and services for newspaper publishing companies
ARCHIVE	A	Integration between the hub's system and various archiving systems
PRINT	A	Integration between the hub's system and various enterprise output systems, such as high-volume printers
PIM	A	Providing a product information management system for cross-media publishing
PROCURE	B	Development of groupware and e-procurement solutions
FINANCE	B	Provision of groupware components and workflow applications, especially for the financial services industry
EMAIL	B	Provision of document and email archiving, IT security, and groupware solutions

Case company	Hub	Core business
PROJECT	B	Development of applications based on the hub's groupware system, for example project and knowledge management systems
ERP	B	Development of enterprise resource planning software
DECISION	B	Providing a decision support system for credit approval processes in the financial services industry based on the hub's groupware system
PORTAL	B	Providing solutions for archiving, groupware, CRM and portals
CONTENT	B	Providing applications for content management, enterprise portals, groupware, and ERP systems
WORKFLOW	B	Providing e-business, groupware, and portals solutions

Table 4.1: Analyzed case companies – exploratory phase

In two of the larger case companies (MEDIA and PIM) more than one interview was necessary in order to gain a comprehensive picture. In two other spoke organizations (MACHINE and ARCHIVE) the interviews were completed in follow-up meetings. Overall, the data set consists of 22 expert interviews within the 17 spoke organizations. Table 4.2 provides a summary of the conducted interviews within the case companies.

All interviews were held face-to-face and took place on-site, except for one (PRINT) which was carried out via telephone, meeting the interviewee's preferences. The interviews were held in German and had an average duration of one hour. As discussed above, the conversations were semi-structured and based on an interview guideline that reflected the preliminary theoretical framework and also included general questions about the interviewee and the respective company (see Appendix 1.1).

Case company	Hub	Number of interviews	Interviewee(s)
MACHINE	A	2	Founder and CEO
CAD	A	1	Partnership manager
GROUP	A	1	Head of product development
MOBILE	A	1	Head of sales, marketing, and partnership management
MEDIA	A	3	Head of product development Head of industry solution Head of marketing
ARCHIVE	A	2	Partnership manager
PRINT	A	1	Head of software development
PIM	A	2	Founder and CEO Sales director
PROCURE	B	1	Head of IT
FINANCE	B	1	Founder and CEO
EMAIL	B	1	Head of software development
PROJECT	B	1	Partnership manager
ERP	B	1	Director of software development
DECISION	B	1	Founder and CEO
PORTAL	B	1	Co-founder and director
CONTENT	B	1	Owner and director
WORKFLOW	B	1	Sales director
Total		22	

Table 4.2: Interviewees and number of interviews – exploratory phase

To allow for triangulation and increase the internal validity of the study, publicly available documents like the companies' Internet pages were analyzed to complement the expert interviews (Yin, 2009). All interviews were tape-recorded and transcribed, except for one case (MOBILE), where the expert felt uncomfortable with recording of the interview. Instead, comprehensive notes were taken during and right after the conversation. In total, the interview protocols resulted in more than 80,000 words and more than 160 pages of qualitative data.

As discussed above, the data was analyzed by assigning codes to text passages in an iterative process of sense-making. This cyclic approach started out with the two tentatively defined constructs *complementarity* and *organizational coupling* (Yin, 2009; Eisenhardt, 1989). By re-iterating the interview transcripts in an exploratory manner, this basic link was substantiated and extended to a comprehensive but parsimonious explanatory framework with broadly defined constructs (Patton, 2002; Miles and Huberman, 1994).

In the first round of analysis, all statements of interview partners that appeared relevant to the study's research questions were either related to one of the two initial constructs or labeled with new, emerging concepts. In a second step, similar or closely related concepts were merged in order to reduce the total number of constructs. This process resulted in a total number of 530 text passages that were assigned to ten constructs. Then, based on the researcher's comprehensive picture on the case studies as well as on existing literature, links between the identified constructs were proposed. Subsequently, these constructs and links were refined through more iterations of the case studies until the partnership behavior of all analyzed cases could eventually be explained (Miles and Huberman, 1994; Patton, 2002).

4.2 Results

Two explanatory models resulted from this iterative process. The model in Figure 4.1 explains how complementors coordinate the partnership with a larger hub organization, that is, whether these spokes choose a tight coupling as opposed to a looser one. In addition, the model depicted in Figure 4.2 proposes an answer to the research question of how coordination efforts may lead to partnership success.

Table 4.3 gives definitions of the identified constructs that are based on previous work presented in Chapter 2.

It should be stressed that it was not feasible to simultaneously explain partnership behavior and partnership success through resource complementarity. The model in Figure 4.1 explains partnership behavior by proposing antecedents of the degree of organizational coupling. A possible way of explaining and predicting partnership success would be to propose that a higher "fit" between the constructs in Figure 4.1 increased partnership success (Venkatraman, 1989). However, if the model in Figure 4.1 indeed explains partnership behavior of spokes, then the "fit" between the constructs in the model is always high. Consequently, such a model would either be unable to explain low levels of partnership success, or the proposed antecedents of the degree of organizational coupling would be refuted.

The developed explanatory models solve this issue by introducing *perceived* complementarity – as opposed to *actual* complementarity – as the core antecedent of organizational coupling (Figure 4.1). Instead, the actual degree of complementarity interacts with the degree of organizational coupling in explaining partnership success (Figure 4.2).

In the following section, the discovered theoretical links are discussed by referring to the exploratory study. Moreover, as suggested by Dube and Pare (2003), the emerging concepts are compared with extant literature that provided guidance for the formulation of the propositions and the preliminary definitions of constructs. The discussion begins with the preliminary constructs (complementarity and coordination) and the relationship between them as discussed in Section 2.4, first shedding light on inter-organizational resource complementarity.

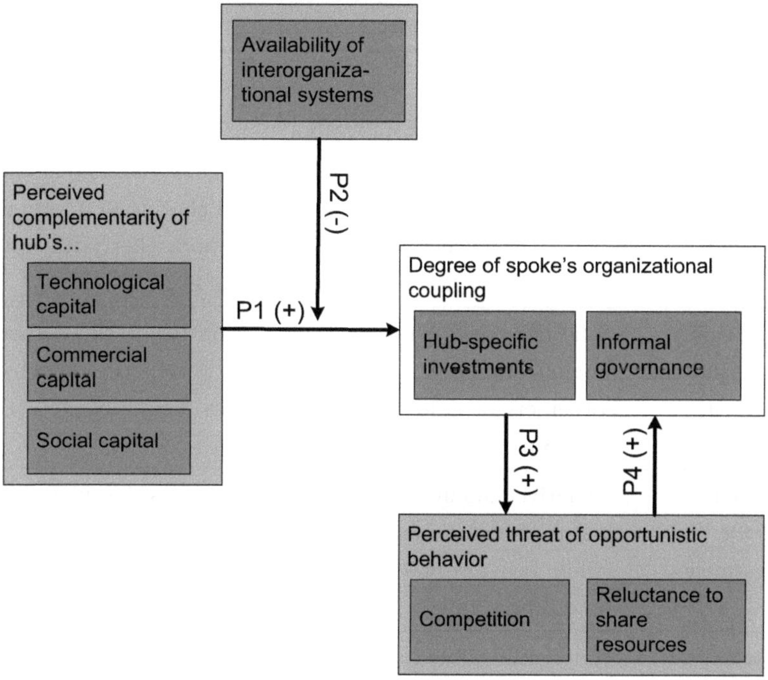

Figure 4.1: Explanatory model of the degree of spoke's organizational coupling

Construct	Conceptualization
Resource complementarity	Partners' dissimilar but compatible technological, commercial and social capital that collectively generates greater rents than the sum of those obtained from the individual endowments of each partner (Milgrom and Roberts, 1995; Das and Teng, 2000b; Dyer and Singh, 1998; Ahuja, 2000).
Technological capital	The capability to provide and innovate systems (Hagedoorn, 1993).
Commercial capital	The capability to manufacture and market products, as well as assets such as manufacturing facilities and service and distribution networks (Ahuja, 2000).

Construct	Conceptualization
Social capital	The capability to create and uphold reputation as well as beneficial network positions (Ahuja, 2000; Gulati, 1999).
Inter-organizational information systems	Software solutions that transcend organizational boundaries and facilitate the dissemination and sharing of information and knowledge throughout the network (Lertpittayapoom et al., 2007; Premkumar, 2000; Saraf et al., 2007).
Degree of organizational coupling	The degree to which an organization ties itself to another organization in a way that increases its responsiveness to the other organization and decreases its distinctiveness (Dyer and Singh, 1998).
Relation-specific investments	Relative amount of investments into assets that increase the value of a particular relationship with another organization while being of lower usefulness in other relationships (Dyer and Singh, 1998).
Informal vs. formal governance mechanisms	Implicit, flexible governance mechanisms like mutual adjustment based on socialization and trust, as opposed to explicit, rigid ones like plans and standards (Adler, 1995; Das and Teng, 2000a).
Opportunistic Behavior	Taking advantage of opportunities at the expense of others (Williamson, 1981).
Competition	Addressing a partner's market by capitalizing on knowledge spillover resulting from close cooperation (Lavie, 2006).
Reluctance to share resources	Reluctance to grant access to technological, commercial and social capital to a partner (Lavie, 2006).
Partnership success	The extent to which the benefits resulting from the access to complementary technological, commercial and social capital exceed the costs of organizational coupling (Kale et al., 2001; Zajac and Olsen, 1993).

Table 4.3: Definition of constructs

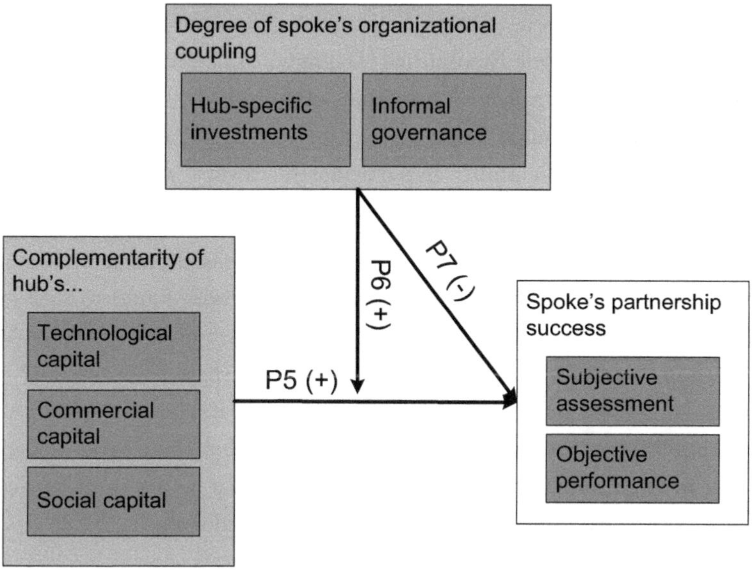

Figure 4.2: Explanatory model of the spoke's partnership success

4.2.1 Complementarity of resources and capabilities

In order to better understand the notion of complementarity in the context of partnership networks in the enterprise software industry, it is instructive to analyze the reasons why spokes enter partnerships (Dexter and Nault, 2006; Dyer et al., 2004). Previous research has predominantly drawn on the RBV for understanding why organizations participate in cooperative relationships (Das and Teng, 2000a; Ireland et al., 2002). By viewing firms as bundles of resources, it has been argued that the main reason why firms partner is to gain access to resources that they currently do not possess, but which the partner is offering (Eisenhardt and Schoonhoven, 1996).

Organizations form partnerships in order to access external resources which they perceive to be complementary, that is, which are dissimilar from and compatible with their own resources and which are assumed to collectively generate greater rents than the sum of those obtained from the individual endowments of each partner (Colombo et al., 2006; Das and Teng, 2000a; Dyer and Singh,

1998; Milgrom and Roberts, 1995). In particular, firms are proposed to strive for complementary dynamic capabilities. Dynamic capabilities refer to the ability of using resources in a way that enables organizations to not only react to changes in their environment but to a certain extent shape their environment (Teece et al., 1997). This ability is particularly relevant in dynamic contexts, such as the development of enterprise software systems (Miles et al., 2005).

Generally, the empirical findings support a resource-based perspective on interfirm arrangements since the analyzed complementors were found to seek access to external resources and dynamic capabilities that they do not possess (Ahuja, 2000; Teece et al., 1997). In line with existing work, these resources and capabilities can be divided into technological, commercial, and social capital (Ahuja, 2000). The following discussion sheds more light on what these types of capabilities mean in the context of hub-and-spoke partnership networks by presenting the findings of the exploratory case studies (see also Kude et al., 2012) .

4.2.1.1 Access to a hub's technological capital

The analyzed case companies were found to partner with hub organizations in order to access technological capital, that is the capability to provide and innovate systems (Hagedoorn, 1993). By partnering with an incumbent vendor and building their systems on top of a hub's platform, the spokes tried to ensure the availability of a comprehensive enterprise system, which was deemed necessary to sell their own niche solutions. In particular, accessing technology-related know-how that resides within the hub organization was found to be one of the primary motives for spokes to participate in hub-and-spoke partnerships. The cases of WORKFLOW and MACHINE are presented subsequently to illustrate these findings.

WORKFLOW provides e-business, groupware, and portal solutions based on the middleware offered by HUB B. WORKFLOW was established 15 years ago and decided to enter a partnership with HUB B two years after being founded. According to WORKFLOW's sales director, HUB B "fits very well because of its broad and comprehensive product portfolio." The company collaborates with employees of HUB B in specific projects in order to benefit from their know-how. The sales director said that WORKFLOW had accumulated a large body of knowledge that is specific to HUB B's solutions over the years, but admitted that for some larger projects, collaborating with HUB B is a reasonable approach. S/he[1] explained that while WORKFLOW focuses on specific niches, HUB B's personnel have a more comprehensive understanding of HUB B's platform and know where the knowledge resides inside HUB B.

MACHINE became a partner of HUB A soon after being founded in 2005. The company complements the enterprise software provided by HUB A by offering software tools that connect HUB A's platform to various kinds of machinery, such as vending machines and wind turbines. According to its founder and CEO, MACHINE began to partner with HUB A because its solutions completely depend on the availability of HUB A's platform. More specifically, the interviewee explained that MACHINE entered the partnership with HUB A because it provides access to expert knowledge that resides within HUB A's research division. Thus, the main reason for partnering with HUB A was the access to technological know-how.

The analyzed spoke organizations also partnered with a hub in order to obtain access to its technological capability to *innovate* systems. The sales director of WORKFLOW described that his company depends on constant platform innovations to develop innovative complementary solutions based on new features of the overall system. WORKFLOW's sales director captured this in a nutshell when s/he said that "HUB B is innovative and this is something that we need."

4.2.1.2 Access to a hub's commercial capital

Commercial capital can be defined as an organization's manufacturing and marketing capabilities, its manufacturing facilities, as well as its service and distribution networks (Ahuja, 2000; Teece, 1986; Mitchell, 1989). In the case of the enterprise software industry, manufacturing assets and capabilities are of minor importance. This is because once developed, the marginal cost for producing additional entities of the software product – for example by copying data on DVDs – is close to zero (Shapiro and Varian, 1999). This is reinforced by the emergence of new deployment models such as software as a service (SaaS; Sääksjärvi et al.,

[1]The gender of interview partners is not revealed for reasons of anonymity. Interviewees were both male and female.

2005). Consequently, the following discussion focuses on the hubs' marketing capabilities as well as its service and distribution networks as motivators for spoke organizations to enter partnerships.

The crucial role of the hub's commercial capital in the motivation to participate in partnerships is well-illustrated by the case of GROUP. GROUP was founded in 1980 as an engineering office, but started to develop complementary software for HUB A's platform in 2003. GROUP offers a tool that connects HUB A's enterprise system to a third-party vendor's groupware solution. GROUP's head of product development reported that after starting its software business, the company struggled to market its product. Specifically, its plan to sell the tool on a global scale initially failed due to the fact that GROUP is a local and rather small company. According to the head of product development, "one important aspect [of the partnership] is that together with the hub, we try to find new customers on a global scale, for example in the U.S. and in Southeast Asia."

PIM, another partner of HUB A, develops a product information management solution that allows customers to manage a large amount of product data and publish it in various ways such as websites, product brochures, and catalogs. Although customers could use PIM's system in combination with any enterprise software solution, PIM decided to focus on and enter a partnership with HUB A. The CEO of PIM described the motive for this step as follows: "Ideally, through a partnership with an established player, a company obtains a very good market access through using the channel of the large organization. That's a very important aspect."

According to PIM's CEO, a crucial part of these marketing benefits are personal recommendations by hub employees: "In the best case, the partner's sales staff says to the customer: If you need a product management system, you should choose the one from [PIM]. That's a great solution, and it is certified." In addition, the sales director of PIM explained that product information management is a relatively new topic and not yet established in the market. Therefore, PIM had trouble convincing customers about the advantages of a product information management system. The sales director said that the "strategic goal of the partnership is to sensitize the market for the product information management topic with the help of [HUB A]."

4.2.1.3 Access to a hub's social capital

Social capital provides information and reputation benefits to firms that are well-connected (Ahuja, 2000; Gulati, 1995, 1999). In the context of this study, social capital is understood as the hub's popular brand name and high-profile in the market. By tapping into the reputation of a large and well-established platform vendor, complementors may benefit from a hub-and-spoke partnership.

The case of EMAIL is a good example of a complementor that participates in a partnership with a well-known enterprise software vendor in order to to benefit from the partner's reputation. EMAIL provides document and email archiving, IT security, and groupware solutions based on HUB B's platform. The company was founded in 2002 and entered a formal partnership with HUB B three years later. When asked about the reasons to build their solutions on HUB B's platform and enter a formal partnership, EMAIL's head of software development stated that customers know that HUB B and its products have been around for many years and will be around in the future. Since EMAIL's products complement HUB B's solutions, customers trust that buying EMAIL's software is not going to be a false investment. "We benefit from [HUB B]'s reputation because our company is not very well known yet," the head of software development said. "With [HUB B]'s logo we signal trustworthiness to our customers. Partnering with a large and well-known company is beneficial for us because of the high degree of familiarity." A look at EMAIL's website corroborated the importance of HUB B's brand name for the spoke as described by the head of software development, since the partnership is mentioned prominently on the home page as well as in various other contexts.

MACHINE was also found to partner with HUB A in order to tap into its reputation in the market. Due to its specific product portfolio, MACHINE's customers are almost exclusively large, global organizations. When approaching potential customers, the CEO of MACHINE experienced several times that "large corporations would not talk to a small software vendor like [MACHINE]. In these situations, the partnership with [HUB A] and its reputation and brand name were a door opener for us."

4.2.2 Complementarity and coordination

As discussed above, in order to benefit from external resources, hub and spoke organizations within the enterprise software industry must coordinate the inter-organizational linkages in order to be successful. It has been argued in Section 2.3 that due to the asymmetry between a platform vendor and a singular complementor, platform vendors can be expected to aim at a standardized and formal coordination of the large number of links with smaller complementors and invest in network-specific as opposed to partner-specific resources and capabilities.

In contrast, spoke organizations were found to participate in hub-and-spoke networks because of the potential benefits resulting from the one-to-one relationship with the platform vendor. More specifically, the case analysis showed that spokes are motivated to partner because hub organizations provide the architecture and basic business applications that the spokes' solutions are based upon (e.g., SAP's Netweaver or IBM's Websphere). In a similar way, by partnering with a hub organization, spokes aim at accessing the hub's capability to address broad markets and marketing channels. Moreover, by participating in hub-and-spoke networks, complementor organizations were found to aim at tapping into the hub's reputation.

In accordance with the literature discussed in Section 2.2.2, the empirical findings suggest that the variance in coordination mechanisms applied by the spokes can be modeled by incorporating the degree of organizational coupling that spokes strive for (Orton and Weick, 1990). In other words, the way how spokes coordinate the partnership is reflected in Figure 4.1 through the degree of organizational coupling. The degree of organizational coupling appears to manifest itself in two ways: first, through investing in hub-specific assets and second, by aiming at informal rather than formal governance mechanisms.

The empirical findings suggest that in order to actually access and appropriate the complementary resources that the platform vendor potentially offers, spoke organizations may strive for a higher degree of organizational coupling, that is, spokes may aim at tying the business closer to a platform vendor. It is important to stress that the behavior of the spokes in terms of the aspired degree of organizational coupling depends on the actors' assessment of the complementarity between the hub's and spoke's resources and capabilities. Such an assessment of complementarity does not necessarily reflect the actual complementarity of resources and capabilities. Therefore, the degree of *perceived* complementarity of a hub's and a spoke's technological, commercial, and social capabilities is suggested to increase the degree of organizational coupling.

Subsequently, the suggested link between perceived resource complementarity and the organizational coupling that complementors strive for (i.e., the amount of relation-specific investments and an informal rather than formal governance) is illustrated by presenting the findings from the conducted case studies and referring to existing literature.

4.2.2.1 Relation-specific investments

The exploratory analysis suggests that spokes differ in the degree of organizational coupling with the respective hub in terms of partner-specific investments. While some complementors tie their business only loosely to their larger partner and invest only a small share of their total expenditures specific to the hub, others invest heavily in hub-specific resources.

Regarding the assets that are generally deemed necessary in order to develop and market software products, the individuals that are involved in the production and marketing process were found to be very important, rendering software production a people business (De Marco and Lister 1987). More specifically, the knowledge of the involved individuals plays a pivotal role in producing and marketing software (Robillard 1999). This is reinforced in the enterprise software industry, where knowledge about both software development and business processes is needed. Indeed, the empirical data suggests that in the context of enterprise software development, the majority of the relation-specific investments refer to investments in relation-specific knowledge creation (DeMarco and Lister, 1987; Grant, 1996b; Robillard, 1999).

FINANCE is an example of a complementor whose partnership with a platform vendor is rather loose. Founded in 1979, FINANCE originally focused on services and training for HUB B's groupware solution. In 2002, FINANCE decided to develop complementary solutions based on HUB B's platform, focusing primarily on groupware and workflow solutions specific to the financial services industry.

Although having a clear focus on the partnership with HUB B, FINANCE's investments in resources and capabilities specific to HUB B and its platform are very limited. The founder and CEO of FINANCE stated that there are no other investments apart from the certification fees. However, the interviewee acknowledged that FINANCE is dependent on HUB B to a certain extent. FINANCE plans to reduce this dependence on a singular platform by focusing on more than one system in the future. Interestingly, the founder and CEO was of the opinion that solution and process know-how can be transferred to other platforms, that is, the know-how is considered not to be partner-specific. Consequently, the interview partner argued that FINANCE is able to have similar partnerships with several partners, because "the time and effort to build up partnerships is not very high." Interestingly, s/he added that "neither are the benefits resulting from the partnerships."

A different example is EMAIL. EMAIL's head of software development stated that "if we used different platforms, it would be much more difficult for us to gain experience and accumulate knowledge." When asked about investments specific to HUB B that EMAIL performs, the interviewee mentioned certification fees and a large amount of expenditures for partner-specific training and knowledge accumulation – technological know-how in particular. EMAIL's head of software development argued that "it would be impossible to train our employees on different platforms. It is a huge amount of know-how and a big effort to gather information, that's why it is reasonable to focus on [HUB B]'s platform."

PIM, the vendor of product management solutions introduced above, also invests in resources and capabilities that are specific to its parter HUB A. The founder and CEO stated that partner-specific investments for technological capabilities are moderate. PIM's products have to be integrated with HUB A's platform. Therefore, hub-specific knowledge is required to some extent. However, the interviewee explained that PIM's products comply with a service-oriented architecture and are developed as a Java application, which makes interface management relatively straightforward. Similarly, certification fees are deemed to be moderate from the CEO's point of view because PIM tries to benefit from promotions that support first movers when it comes to certifying complementary solutions for new platform releases. In contrast, both the sales director as well as the CEO argue that partner-specific investments in capabilities, know-how, and information concerning sales and distribution are very high. The CEO states that "the management of such a partnership from a sales and marketing perspective is very complex and extensive. In order to actually sell your product, a formal partnership is not enough. It is necessary to keep up with recent developments about chances and risks in all relevant markets. That's a huge effort and to some extend we depend on the partnership with [HUB A] because of the knowledge we have accumulated concerning sales and distribution."

Thus, in order to participate in a partnership with a platform leader, complementors may have to invest in hub-specific knowledge accumulation regarding the functioning of the hub's platform and its interfaces. In the course of the partnership, continuous investments in hub-specific technological and market-related knowledge accumulation may be necessary to keep up with new developments in the dynamic enterprise software industry and actually benefit from the partnership with a hub. Empirical results of the exploratory case study show that the degree of partner-specific investment differs widely among different complementors. Before dealing with the reasons for these inconsistencies, the next section discusses organizational coupling in terms of using informal governance mechanisms.

4.2.2.2 Informal governance mechanisms

The exploratory case studies suggest that complementors differ in terms of the type of governance they strive for in the partnership with a platform vendor. While some complementors rely on formal and standardized governance mechanisms institutionalized by the hub organization (see Section 2.1.3), others aim at establishing informal governance mechanisms such as mutual adjustment based on socialization and trust (Adler, 1995; Dyer and Singh, 1998; Kraut and Streeter, 1995). In order to benefit from informal governance based on trust, spokes may have to put effort and invest in the creation of partner-specific absorptive capacity (Cohen and Levinthal, 1990). Thus, informal governance and the spokes' investment into partner-specific absorptive capacity can be perceived as a special case of hub-specific investments. However, the level of informal governance goes beyond investments in absorptive capacity because it also comprises a complementor's decision to either rely on the formal coordination that platform vendors aim at, or to try to establish more informal governance mechanisms. Subsequently, the empirical findings regarding this decision are presented.

DECISION is an example for a complementor that governs the partnership with a platform vendor in a formal way. DECISION was founded in 1996 and is a service provider for HUB B's groupware solution. DECISION offers development, administration, and training in the context of HUB B's groupware system. In particular, DECISION provides a decision support tool that complements HUB B's platform. As regards partnership governance, the founder and CEO stated that the relationship with HUB B is rather impersonal and very formal. "We only had personal contact with [HUB B]'s employees during the certification process in order to clarify formal details." Generally, the communication with HUB B is anonymous and impersonal, consisting mainly of information that HUB B sends to its partners in the form of newsletters and the partner section on HUB B's website. According to DECISION's CEO, personal, "unofficial" contacts based on trust with HUB B personnel might be possible. However, as the founder and CEO explained, a higher effort would be necessary by DECISION that is not perceived to be justified.

Instead, WORKFLOW aims at a more informal governance of its partnership with HUB B. WORKFLOW's sales director explained that the informal contacts with HUB B are partly rooted in the fact that some of WORKFLOW's employees are former HUB B personnel, resulting in a social network of acquaintances within HUB B. These relationships were also responsible for establishing the partnership with HUB B. WORKFLOW has informal and personal contacts to HUB B's employees both in technical and sales areas. "The most successful projects are those where we work with [HUB B] employees that we know on a personal level," the sales director said. These contacts are based on trust and loyalty. According to the interviewee, WORKFLOW receives a lot of information in a formal way, but it is much more important to know people within the partner organization and thus be able "to read between the lines." Interestingly, the interview partner added that the fact that HUB B's personnel switch roles within the organization on a regular base may be both a challenge and an advantage. On the one hand, WORKFLOW has to deal with different contact persons and put a lot of effort into establishing informal governance. On the other hand, the organizational shifts help WORKFLOW foster a social network within many different parts of

HUB B's organization. Thus, while DECISION mostly relies on the formal governance mechanisms established by HUB B, WORKFLOW aims at establishing a more informal governance that is based on personal contacts and trust.

Similarly, MACHINE tries to govern its partnership with HUB A in an informal way. MACHINE's CEO states that the knowledge transfer between HUB A and MACHINE is not a standardized procedure of hub-and-spoke partnerships, but instead results from the personal contacts between MACHINE's and HUB A's personnel. The CEO specifically mentioned HUB A's research area, stating that "we have very good personal contacts to the research division. If we have a technological problem, we ask [HUB A]'s people if they can help us. It's as if you ask a colleague within [MACHINE]." The tight coupling with HUB A's research division is also illustrated by the fact that HUB A's vice president for research is a member of MACHINE's advisory board, a committee that meets regularly and discusses new opportunities for MACHINE. The interviewee emphasizes that the personal and trustworthy relationships with HUB A's staff have emerged over a period of several years and are still growing.

Thus, similar to hub-specific investments, the analyzed complementors differ substantially in terms of the governance mechanisms they aim at within the hub-and-spoke partnerships. The next section discusses the theoretical link between perceived resource complementarity and the organizational coupling that complementors aim at.

4.2.2.3 Perceived complementarity and organizational coupling

The empirical findings so far suggest that complementors participate in hub-and-spoke networks in order to get access to resources and capabilities they perceive to be complementary. Moreover, while platform vendors try to standardize the coordination of the numerous linkages to complementors, the empirical results suggest that the organizational coupling that spokes strive for varies greatly. Spokes differ in the extent to which they invest in partner-specific assets and the extent to which they aim at an informal partnership governance as opposed to the formal governance mechanisms established by the platform vendors. A comprehensive analysis of the case companies suggests a theoretical link between the complementarity of a hub's and a spoke's resources and capabilities as perceived by the spoke and the degree to which a spoke ties its business to its larger partner.

This is very well illustrated by the case of PIM. Both the CEO as well as the sales director stressed that PIM extensively benefits from HUB A's sales and distribution capabilities as well as its brand name. Therefore, PIM invests heavily in resources and capabilities that are specific to the platform vendor in the field of sales and distribution, for instance by participating in sales initiatives and accumulating market-related knowledge. In a similar way, PIM aims at establishing personal relationships with HUB A's personnel in the area of sales and distribution in order to tap into the partner's commercial capital and reputation. PIM's founder and CEO stated that "the sales people we know personally at [HUB A] would tell the customer that our product is great and works well."

PIM formed a partnership with HUB A in order to get access to the hub's commercial and social capital. Thus the level of partner-specific investments and informal partnership governance in the field of sales and distribution were found to be high. In addition to commercial and social capital, MACHINE also benefits from technological know-how that resides within HUB A's organization. Talking about the benefits of informal governance mechanisms, the founder and CEO of MACHINE stressed that there are a lot of trainings to attend and information to gather on HUB A's partner websites, newsletters, and forums. "But we obtain the useful knowledge through personal contacts. [HUB A]'s employees and ours know each other and if there is a problem, our people call their peers at [HUB A] and say: We have a problem, could you please help us?" The interviewee also adds that MACHINE tries to establish and maintain close personal contacts with HUB A's research staff in order to be a preferred partner when it comes to new projects in the field of research and development.

In contrast, as discussed above, FINANCE does not invest heavily into resources that are specific to its partner HUB B. In addition, FINANCE mostly relies on the formal governance mechanisms established by HUB B. The founder and CEO explained that "the communication with our contact person within [HUB B] is not very intense." FINANCE is hence only loosely coupled with its partner HUB B. This may be explained by the low level of perceived complementarity between FINANCE's resources and capabilities and the ones within HUB B. For instance, FINANCE's founder and CEO described that HUB B and

FINANCE address different markets and therefore investing in hub-specific resources and capabilities, and particularly hub-specific absorptive capacity, would be unjustified. "It would be helpful to have a closer corporation if there was a win-win situation. In principle, the idea is appealing, but [HUB B] and [FINANCE] work in different markets."

If the perceived synergies with the hub's complementary capabilities are high, spokes may increase the degree of organizational coupling by increasing their responsiveness to the hub organization while at the same time decreasing their distinctiveness in order to actually benefit from these complementarities (Dyer and Singh, 1998; Schilling, 2000). In particular, in order to gain access to external tacit knowledge, spokes may have to put effort and invest in the creation of partner-specific absorptive capacity (Cohen and Levinthal, 1990).

For instance, partnering with a hub may provide the spoke with immediate access to explicit information on technological issues. However, in order to gain a competitive advantage by leveraging resource endowments that are perceived to be complementary, spokes may aim at accessing know-how within the hub that is not amenable to codification, e.g. because it resides within the experience and long-time collaboration of certain individuals (Yli-Renko et al., 2001). In other words, spokes may rely on informal governance mechanisms based on trust and thereby establish a "privileged information exchange" (Malhotra et al., 2007, p. 264). The following proposition is suggested based on the previous discussion.

> *Proposition 1: The higher the degree of complementarity between the partners' technological, commercial, and social capital as perceived by the spoke, the higher is the spoke's organizational coupling with a certain hub organization.*

4.2.3 Inter-organizational information systems

Inter-organizational information systems (IOS) are software solutions that transcend organizational boundaries and are shared by two or more organizations (Barrett and Konsynski, 1982; Liu and Chen, 2008; Cash and Konsynski, 1985; Diao and Ma, 2008; Gregor and Johnston, 2001; Hong, 2002). The results of previous research show that investments in IOS may lead to a higher degree of organizational modularity and loose coupling within an industry (Sahaym et al.,

2007; Brews and Tucci, 2004; Brynjolfsson et al., 1994; Hitt and Brynjolfsson, 1997; Hitt, 1999).

In the context of hub-and-spoke partnership networks, such an IOS established by the core firm may facilitate the dissemination and sharing of information and knowledge throughout the network (Lertpittayapoom et al., 2007; Premkumar, 2000; Saraf et al., 2007). These IOS can be perceived as standards for knowledge-sharing, and may therefore – similar to standards on the product-level – facilitate the creation of a more modular organizational network (Schilling and Steensma, 2001). In other words, if the hub provides the required information and knowledge in an easily accessible way, then spokes may refrain from engaging in tightly coupled partnerships. The examples of WORKFLOW, MACHINE, and MEDIA illustrate the role of IOS in hub-and-spoke partnerships.

The case companies reported that IOS established by the respective hub may help access valuable knowledge. In particular, the interviewees stated that in those areas where knowledge is transferred through appropriate IOS, the need for a tighter coupling is reduced. The sales director of WORKFLOW reported that information systems established by HUB B are used by WORKFLOW's employees to answer technical questions. In contrast, for sales and distribution purposes, WORKFLOW mainly relies on personal contacts. While being helpful in some situations, the information systems are, according to WORKFLOW's sales director, "extremely huge, which makes it difficult to work with them [the systems]."

The same is true for MACHINE, whose founder and CEO explained that "the information systems offered by [HUB A] are very good and comprehensive." As for WORKFLOW, MACHINE's employees use the systems predominantly to obtain information on technical issues. The CEO of MACHINE also had a critical perspective on the IOS established by the hub. "The knowledge data bases are good, but the main problem is that there is too much information. That's a typical Internet phenomenon."

MEDIA, a spoke that develops complementary functionality specific to the media and newspaper industry based on HUB A's platform, also uses IOS offered by its partner. MEDIA's head of product development explained that IOS established and maintained by HUB A are used heavily by MEDIA's staff to obtain information in the area of systems development. Generally, MEDIA is satisfied with HUB A's offerings of IOS. "In my opinion, [HUB A] invests in the right systems. They try to establish platforms that enable communication", the head of product development commented.

Taken together, IOS may provide the spokes with knowledge and information that would otherwise be available only through information exchange on a personal, informal level (Schmidt and Simonee, 1996). Moreover, as outlined above, in order to benefit from the hub organization's complementary resources and capabilities, spokes may have to invest heavily in partner-specific knowledge accumulation. Information systems that offer hub-specific information in an easily accessible and well-structured way may reduce the amount of hub-specific investments that are necessary in order to benefit from the hub's complementary resources (Gosain et al., 2004). Therefore, the availability of IOS is suggested to moderate the proposed link between complementarity and organizational coupling.

> *Proposition 2: The higher the availability of adequate information and knowledge through an IOS, the weaker is the proposed positive effect of the perceived degree of complementarity on the degree of organizational coupling.*

4.2.4 Organizational coupling and opportunistic behavior

A higher degree of the spokes' organizational coupling through more hub-specific investments and a more informal partnership governance may increase the perceived threat of the hub behaving opportunistically. Spoke organizations that invest heavily in their relationship with a hub cannot easily switch to other platform vendors without losing the majority of their up-front, hub-specific investments and being forced to re-invest in a new platform. This lock-in situation may increase the hub's propensity to behave opportunistically by taking advantage of opportunities at the spokes' expense (Lavie, 2006, 2007; Williamson, 1981; Hill, 1990).

In particular, hubs may capitalize on the knowledge that is transferred in the course of the partnership and (partially) compete with its partner (Brandenburger and Nalebuff, 1996; Lavie, 2006). Moreover, hubs may be reluctant to share resources with a specific spoke and may thus decrease the complementor's possibilities of value creation.

Subsequently, both the leakage of knowledge as well as the reluctance to share resources are discussed with the help of this study's exploratory findings and existing literature. Moreover, implications of the perceived threat of opportunistic behavior on the degree of organizational coupling aimed at by spokes are elaborated.

4.2.4.1 Competition

The high degree of investments in relation-specific assets by the spoke together with the informal personal relationships may induce the hub to change its product-market-combination and compete with the spoke in its field of operation (Brandenburger and Nalebuff, 1996; Bengtsson and Kock, 1999; Beck et al., 2008; Abdallah and Wadhwa, 2009). Specifically, the hub may behave opportunistically and capitalize on its dominant position by absorbing the spokes' critical knowledge and applying it to commercial ends itself (Lavie, 2006). Platform vendors may hence decide to include functionalities provided by a partner into their own solutions.

As discussed above, FINANCE, the partner of HUB B that provides complementary groupware and workflow solutions for the financial services industry, has tied its business in a rather loose fashion to HUB B. In particular, FINANCE has invested only modestly in resources and capabilities that are specific to HUB B and its platform. In accordance with the predictions that can be made based on TCE (Williamson, 1981), the threat of opportunistic behavior on part of HUB B is perceived to be rather low for FINANCE. Even though the CEO of FINANCE acknowledged that there might be situations of competition between HUB B and its partners, s/he is "not worried about [HUB B] entering our market by including our functionalities into its platform. They could have done that years ago if they were interested." According to the interviewee, HUB B is "interested in its middleware platform and does not care too much about what its partners put on top." Moreover, the CEO of FINANCE said that "our solutions are too specific and the market is too small to be interesting for HUB B."

The situation is different for PIM. As discussed above, PIM has invested heavily in resources and capabilities that are specific to HUB A, particularly in the area of sales and distribution. Hence, according to the CEO, PIM has become dependent on HUB A, resulting in a high threat of opportunistic behavior on part of the hub. If the partnership with HUB A ceases to exist in the near future, PIM would need a lot of time and effort to reach a similar level of partner-specific knowledge and personal relationships with another hub.

A comparable risk of opportunistic behavior can be observed for HUB A's partner MEDIA that tied its business closely to HUB A through partner-specific investments. Since both MEDIA and HUB A provide functionality for the media and newspaper industry, new releases of HUB A's industry solution may overlap with functionality provided by MEDIA.

Thus, the empirical findings suggest that if hub-specific investments are high, the threat perceived by the spokes that the larger partner may behave opportunistically and capitalize on knowledge leakage increases.

4.2.4.2 Reluctance to share resources

As discussed above, platform vendors may act opportunistically in that they enter their partners' markets and compete with organizations that offer products complementary to their own platform. A second type of opportunistic behavior – given the high amount of hub-specific investments performed by some spokes and the resulting power imbalance – is when hubs are reluctant to share resources with the spokes (Williamson, 1981; Lavie, 2006; Gawer and Henderson, 2007).

This is well illustrated by the case of MEDIA. MEDIA invested heavily in resources and capabilities that are specific to HUB A, thereby focusing their business completely on complementary solutions and services that are based on HUB A's platform. Interestingly, MEDIA is not satisfied with the information flow between HUB A's and MEDIA's employees regarding both technological as well as commercial aspects. The head of industry solutions complained that HUB A regularly changes its product and marketing strategy in the area of enterprise software for the media industry without considering or informing MEDIA. "There are a lot of cumbersome and lengthy discussions with [HUB A]'s staff about the strategic direction of their products and services. They want our opinion on their product road map, but we don't get any feedback about what's going on." As a consequence, MEDIA struggles in developing new solutions and discussing system landscapes with customers because information about future releases of HUB A's platform is often unavailable.

Similarly, the partnership manager of PROJECT, a developer of complementary applications such as customer relationship management software, was rather disappointed by the limited access to HUB B's commercial capital. "Our expectations concerning marketing advantages might have been too high." Specifically, PRODUCT's partnership manager complained that HUB B does not put enough effort into promoting the groupware platform on which PROJECT's solutions are based. Moreover, the interviewee mentioned a lack of pragmatic support for marketing campaigns. According to PROJECT's product manager, HUB B does not offer satisfying slide shows or brochures as help to approach potential customers. Interestingly, the interviewee is convinced that from a technological point of view, HUB B's platform is better than similar products from competitors. Yet, given the hub-specific investments, s/he would expect better support in sales and distribution.

Taken together, if complementors aim at a higher degree of organizational coupling, then the perceived threat of platform vendors behaving opportunistically as perceived by the spokes. In particular, platform vendors may enter the market of their partners and compete with the spokes in certain areas. Moreover, hubs may be reluctant to fulfill the spokes' expectations regarding the resources and capabilities they are allowed access to through the hub-spoke partnership. This is summarized by the following proposition.

Proposition 3: The higher the organizational coupling between a spoke and a hub, the higher is the threat of opportunistic behavior by the hub as perceived by the spoke.

4.2.4.3 Implications of the threat of opportunism

It could be expected that spokes try to reduce their dependence on a dominant partner as a result of the perceived threat of opportunistic behavior (Williamson, 1981, 1979). However, instead of loosening the partnership with the hub organization when facing the threat of opportunistic behavior, spokes were found to tie their business even closer to the hub. In particular, spokes were found to rely on informal governance mechanisms, thus striving for relational specificity (Bala and Venkatesh, 2007; Dyer, 1997; Subramani and Venkatraman, 2003). Informal governance mechanisms may allow spokes to reinforce the existence of synergies in spite of the hub's potential reluctance to share resources with a specific spoke. Furthermore, informal relationships with decision makers of the hub organization that are based on trust may relieve the threat of obsolescence if architectural innovations overlap with the spoke organizations' functionality (Casciaro and Piskorski, 2005). The cases of ARCHIVE and MEDIA illustrate these findings.

The partnership manager of ARCHIVE, a provider of archiving functionality that complement HUB A's system, explained that due to the long-lasting collaboration between HUB A's and ARCHIVE's employees and the personal relationships, it is often HUB A's staff that "warn" ARCHIVE in advance if new developments might overlap with ARCHIVE's functionality. Through being forewarned that complementary solutions may become obsolete, ARCHIVE has more time to innovate on a modular level and come up with new solutions or functionalities that address new niches. Moreover, according to ARCHIVE's partnership manager, HUB A's staff actively provide ARCHIVE with hints which market segments are promising and will not be addressed by the hub in the near future (Uzzi, 1997).

As another example, MEDIA tries to get access to information related to strategic decision of HUB A that influence the future development of its own media solutions. However, although personal and informal contacts between MEDIA's employees and hub personnel have been established for this purpose, these links are of no great help for the spoke when it comes to anticipating future releases of HUB A's software, as explained by MEDIA's head of marketing.

Summing up, the empirical data suggests that in the face of high threat of opportunistic behavior, spoke organizations try to increase organizational coupling with the hub. Hence, the following proposition is put forth.

> *Proposition 4: The higher the perceived threat of opportunistic behavior by the hub, the closer the spoke ties its business to this hub.*

4.2.5 Partnership success

For a hub-and-spoke partnership to be successful from the spoke's point of view, the benefits resulting from the relationship in terms of gaining access to the hub's complementary technological, commercial, and social capital should outweigh the costs associated with organizational coupling (Kale et al., 2001; Mohr and Spekman, 1994; Zajac and Olsen, 1993). Following existing literature, partnership success can be understood as both the objective firm performance as well as a subjective assessment of the partnership (Hansen and Wernerfelt, 1989; Claro et al., 2003). The following section discusses the antecedents of partnership success from the spokes' perspective.

4.2.5.1 Complementarity and partnership success

Complementary resources and capabilities collectively generate greater rents than the sum of those obtained from individual endowments (Das and Teng, 2000b; Dyer and Singh, 1998; Ahuja, 2000). Although it can be assumed that dominant platform vendors appropriate a significant share of the generated value (Lavie, 2007; Gulati and Singh, 1998; Subramani and Venkatraman, 2003), both the results from previous work as well as the empirical data suggest that the access to external technological, commercial, and social capital increases partnership success from a complementor's perspective.

Spokes may benefit from the hub's *technological capital* because the enterprise software offered by small complementors is usually dedicated to a very specific fraction of the customer's business processes. Therefore, spoke organizations depend on the availability of a complementary system that covers the core functionalities of an enterprise software system. Providing such comprehensive systems is one of the core competencies of hub organizations (Campbell-Kelly, 2003).

This capability to provide integrated systems stems from a profound understanding of various underlying technological disciplines and their interrelations, an understanding of the entire system behavior, the ability to design the entire system and its key components of the system, and the ability to assemble component interfaces (Prencipe, 2004). In fact, the capability to provide such an integrated system served as the foundation of the success story of large providers of ERP systems. These providers were the first to enable a seamless integration of entire information flows within an organization (Davenport, 1998).

Today, the system landscapes of customer organizations are largely dominated by solutions of incumbent enterprise software vendors (Mertens, 2005). Therefore, the spokes' business has a critical dependency on the interoperability of their solutions with that of a large system provider (Mertens, 2005). In order to achieve this interoperability, small companies require an in-depth knowledge about the functionalities and interfaces of these systems (Brusoni and Prencipe, 2001; Brusoni, 2005). Small vendors can facilitate their access to this knowledge by partnering with a large system provider.

In addition, the hub's *commercial capital* may increase partnership success from the spokes' perspective. Since spokes may be unable to make large investments in marketing activities and distribution networks, partnering with a global player may provide the opportunity to make the spokes' innovative products available to a great number of potential customers (Ahuja, 2000; Eisenhardt and Schoonhoven, 1996; Hagedoorn, 1993; Rao and Klein, 1994).

The scope of the hub organization's marketing support may range from a simple communication of the partnerships or recommendation of the partner and its solutions to a joint and comprehensive market addressing. One specific example of external marketing support that has been discussed in literature is the entry into the international market by small software companies (Winkler et al., 2009; Licht et al., 2009). In this context, partnerships with established firms were found to be of great importance (Winkler et al., 2009; Coviello and Munro, 1997; Moen et al., 2004; Mohr and Spekman, 1994; Ruokonen et al., 2008; Varis et al., 2005).

In addition, spoke organizations may benefit from their partnership with a hub organization that defines markets and strategies of the partnership network (Gawer and Cusumano, 2002). This is because the spokes may gain access to market-related information that would otherwise be impossible to obtain.

Moreover, complementor organizations may benefit from the hub's *social capital*. Spokes often face the challenge that they are unknown in the market and that customers are doubtful about the quality and reliability of their products and services. Signaling trustworthiness is of special importance in the enterprise software industry, since the quality of software and the knowledge and experience of business processes is difficult to assess in advance (see Section 2.1.3, Akerlof, 1970; Vitharana et al., 2003). The market reputation of large system providers may help small vendors overcome this problem. A partnership with a large vendor and an official certification of the complementor's resources or products by the hub organization may help small companies increase the level of trust in their solutions and their sustainability (Sanders and Boivie, 2004; Vitharana et al., 2003). Mentioning the partnership with the famous brand name of the global hub organization may hence improve the customers' perception of the small spoke companies.

The case of CAD illustrates these insights. CAD is a partner of HUB A that provides solutions to integrate HUB A's enterprise software system with a third-party provider of software solutions for computer-aided design. Through the partnership with HUB A, CAD gets access to complimentary technological, commercial, and social capital. CAD benefits from the access to technological know-how because its core business is the complex integration of HUB A's system and third-party software. For this task, CAD needs up-to-date knowledge about the functioning of HUB A's software, which it can access through the partnership. Moreover, CAD heavily benefits from using HUB A's marketing channel and being on HUB A's price list, that is, CAD's solutions are sold by HUB A's sales staff. In addition, the partnership manager explained that "thanks to [HUB A]'s reputation, we convinced several customers that we could not have convinced otherwise." As a result of these advantages, the partnership with HUB A can be considered successful for CAD, as reported by the partnership manager.

In contrast, the partnership between HUB A and PRINT was seen as rather unsuccessful by PRINT's head of software development. The reason for this can be seen in the lower degree of complementarity between PRINT's resources and capabilities and HUB A's technological, commercial, and social capital. PRINT's and HUB A's solutions communicate via standardized interfaces, so that PRINT's need for technological knowledge regarding the overall platform is limited. While PRINT does benefit to some extent from HUB A's reputation when approaching customers, PRINT's head of software development stated that the strategic goals of PRINT and HUB A do not match.

Similarly, MEDIA reported that the partnership could be optimized. In particular, MEDIA was hoping to obtain information on HUB A's product strategy through the partnership, but was rather disappointed. Still, MEDIA's head of product development said that the partnership is "generally successful." According to the interviewees, the reason for this is the benefit resulting from the hub's reputation and its resources and capabilities for marketing software solutions.

Based on these empirical findings and on existing literature, it is proposed that the actual degree of complementarity between hub's and spoke's resources and capabilities (as opposed to the complementarity perceived by spokes) influences partnership success in the following way.

> *Proposition 5: The higher the actual degree of complementarity between the partners' technological, commercial, and social capital, the more successful the partnership is from the spoke's perspective.*

4.2.5.2 Organizational coupling and partnership success

The discussion above showed that if spoke organizations perceive the complementarity of their own resources and the hub's technological, commercial, and social capital to be high, then the spokes try to tie their businesses closer to the hub organization with the goal of benefiting from the hub's resources. In line with existing literature, a higher degree of organizational coupling can be expected to increase the benefits resulting from complementary resource endowments (Dyer and Singh, 1998). Indeed, the empirical analysis of the case studies suggests that the benefits resulting from the actual complementarity between hub's and spoke's resources increase with a higher degree of organizational coupling between hub and spoke. This is illustrated by the cases of CAD, MEDIA, and PRINT.

The success of CAD's partnership with HUB A can be ascribed to resource complementarity, but also to the high degree of organizational coupling that CAD has established. For example, CAD benefits from HUB A's technological capital particularly through informal contacts with software developers within the partner organization. "It's a big advantage to know developers within [HUB A]. If we have a certain requirement, we can just call and ask if it's possible," commented CAD's partnership manager. Interestingly, the interviewee explained that CAD faces the risk of obsolescence if HUB A decides to enter CAD's market. "Today we are a strategic partner of [HUB A], but within a couple of years, the architecture may change, and [HUB A] may decided to offer our solution themselves." However, the partnership manager stated that due to the good relationship with HUB A, s/he is confident that the partnership is sustainable.

Both MEDIA and PRINT aimed at establishing a closer link with HUB A. Both partners were able to benefit to some extent from HUB A's resources by investing in hub-specific knowledge creation and focusing on a singular partnership. Also, both partners tried to develop personal links to HUB A's employees, but were rather unsuccessful. As PRINT's head of software development framed it, "it's very anonymous and we don't have personal links to [HUB A]'s personnel." In a similar way, MEDIA's head of product development explained that MEDIA's people sometimes discuss technological and market-related issues with HUB A's employees. "But when it comes to decisions about future product releases, we don't get a lot of information." Consequently, the empirical analysis reveals only a moderate success of PIM's and MEDIA's partnerships with HUB A .

Taken together, the empirical findings suggest that organizational coupling moderates the link between actual complementary of hub's and spoke's resources and partnership success from the spokes' perspective.

> *Proposition 6: The higher the degree of the spoke's organizational coupling with a platform vendor, the stronger the positive influence of inter-firm resource complementarity on the partnership success from the spoke's perspective.*

While organizational coupling may increase the benefits resulting from complementary resource endowments, there are also direct and indirect costs associated with closer linkages that reduce partnership success. In the short run, these costs include the increased time and effort of informal coordination as opposed to formal coordination as well as the large amount of partner-specific investments that may be necessary. In the long run, as outlined above, a higher degree of organizational coupling may increase the likelihood of opportunistic behavior by the hub, jeopardizing the spokes' business model.

Also, spokes may face the problem that sociologists refer to as overembeddedness (Uzzi, 1997). By successfully relying on strong personal ties in the short term, spokes may miss the opportunity to develop their own resources and capabilities. If the personal network ceases to exist, for example due to job fluctuation, spokes may eventually be penalized.

In addition, the scenario that the spokes face resembles a prisoner's dilemma (Axelrod and Hamilton, 1981). If one spoke achieves a tighter coupling with a hub and thereby undercuts the standard coordination mechanisms, it may be beneficial for this spoke in the short run. If all spokes do so, however, the whole network and thus its participants may eventually lose ground in the system competition with other networks that coordinate relationships more efficiently.

Whether these costs are justified, that is, whether the benefits from the access to external resources outweigh the costs of organizational coupling, depends on the actual complementarity of the hub's resources. Thus, partnership success depends on the assessment of the degree of complementarity by the responsible spoke managers. If spoke organizations perceive this degree of complementarity to be higher than it actually is, the costs resulting from a close partnership may be higher than the benefits, resulting in an unsuccessful collaboration.

The examples above illustrate these insights. CAD established a high degree of organizational coupling through investments in partner-specific resources and the establishment of informal governance mechanisms. Although the efforts to do so and the resulting threat of opportunistic behavior are considerably high, the benefits resulting from the gained access to external resources and capabilities are higher than the resulting costs and risks. Put differently, the complementarity of HUB A's resources is not only perceived to be high, but indeed is.

Interestingly, despite the lower level of actual resource complementarity, both MEDIA and PRINT tried to establish a closer partnership with their larger partner by investing in hub-specific knowledge accumulation and assets as well as by trying to establish informal governance mechanisms. Yet, both MEDIA and PRINT were rather unsuccessful in doing so. MEDIA and PRINT may have misjudged resource complementarity and over-invested in hub-specific assets and informal coordination mechanisms, resulting in reduced partnership success.

In accordance with these observation and extant literature, the following proposition is put forth.

> *Proposition 7: The higher the degree of the spoke's organizational coupling with a platform vendor, the lower the partnership success from the spoke's perspective.*

4.3 Summary

The goal of this chapter was to build a mid-range theory that is able to explain the coordination and success of partnerships between platform vendors and complementors from the complementors' point of view. In order to do so, the study has built on both existing literature and a positivist, exploratory multiple-case study of 17 spoke organizations that have entered certified partnerships with two hub organizations.

Two theoretical models resulted from the findings (see Figure 4.1 and 4.2). The first explains the coordination of partnerships which is conceptualized through the degree of organizational coupling that spokes strive for. It is proposed that the more a hub organization possess technological, commercial, and social capital that is perceived to be complementary to a spoke's own resources, the more the spoke aims at a higher degree of organizational coupling by investing in hub-specific assets and relying on informal instead of formal governance (Proposition 1). This link between complementarity and coordination is proposed to be moderated by the availability of appropriate inter-organizational information systems. These systems may facilitate the access to the hub's resources without having to increase the degree of organizational coupling (Proposition 2).

In line with extant literature, the degree of organizational coupling, and particularly the investment in partner-specific assets, are proposed to increase the perceived threat of opportunistic behavior by the hub organization (Proposition 3). The hub may be reluctant to share resources with spokes or may compete with the spokes through capitalizing on knowledge spillover. In order to avoid or at least predict this opportunistic behavior, spokes are proposed to even increase the degree of organizational coupling (Proposition 4).

In accordance with existing work, the findings of the exploratory study suggest that partnerships with a platform vendor are more successful for spokes if the actual complementarity (as opposed to the complementarity perceived by spoke organizations) between resources and capabilities of hub and spoke is high (Proposition 5). Moreover, the degree of organizational coupling is suggested to influence the partnership success in two ways. First, it was found to moderate the link between complementarity and success in that a higher degree of organizational coupling may enable spokes to benefit from external resources to a greater extent (Proposition 6). Second, organizational coupling is proposed to be costly and may, therefore, reduce partnership success (Proposition 7).

These theoretical assertions are subsequently corroborated and refined empirically. The next chapter discusses in detail the design and findings of this refinement phase.

5 Empirical substantiation and theory refinement

As discussed in Chapter 3, this study follows a two-staged approach in order to answer the research question of how spokes coordinate the partnership with hubs and how the partnership can be successful from a spoke's point of view. Chapter 4 has presented in detail the findings of the first, exploratory phase. These results show that the way how spoke organizations coordinate the partnerships with hubs depends on the perceived complementarity between the resources and capabilities of hub and spoke (Figure 4.1). Moreover, the coordination mechanisms that spokes strive for were found to be influenced by the availability of IOS as well as the perceived threat of opportunistic behavior on part of the hub. The success of the partnerships from the spokes' perspective was in turn found to depend on the *actual* complementarity between hub and spoke resources as well as the degree of organizational coupling (Figure 4.2).

The goal of the second phase is to substantiate these findings by examining if the models built by means of the exploratory case studies hold when explaining the coordination and success of a wider set of partnerships. Moreover, the second round of empirical investigation aims at refining the identified constructs and theoretical links. In particular, by means of a second round of case studies that are driven by the gained theoretical insights, the study aims at shedding more light on the differences between perceived and actual resource complementarity.

Next, the analyzed case companies as well as the data collection and analysis procedure are presented in detail, based on the general discussion in Chapter 3. Subsequently, the empirical findings and the resulting refinements of the explanatory framework are discussed.

5.1 Data selection and analysis

In total, 11 case companies were studied in the refinement phase, five partners in HUB A's and six partners in HUB B's partnership network. A mixed approach was chosen with respect to the question of whether or not to re-approach the companies that had already been studied in the exploratory phase. In particular, HUB A's partners MACHINE, MEDIA, ARCHIVE, and PIM as well as PROJECT and WORKFLOW from HUB B's partnership network were first re-approached with the developed theoretical models in mind, while additional companies that had not been part of the first phase's data set were contacted in a second step.

The rationale for this mixed approach was that the re-approached case companies were either been faced with interesting developments regarding the partnership that the explanatory models should be able to explain, or provided particularly rich data, making them suitable for corroborating the developed theoretical framework. In particular, while the exploratory phase focused on discovering the links between the identified constructs, the refinement phase corroborates whether the resulting theoretical models are able to explain the behavior of a specific case company in a comprehensive and holistic way. In addition, the knowledge gained from the exploratory investigation enabled a theoretical replication logic by deliberately selecting companies that differ regarding the degree of organizational coupling and the partnership success (Yin, 2009).

For the explanatory models to be useful and applicable for explaining and predicting coordination and success in contexts outside of the original data set, it was considered indispensable to include other case companies in the empirical investigation. In other words, additional cases were included in order to avoid a selection bias and hence allow for an analytical generalization of the study's results. Table 5.1 gives a description of the core businesses of the case companies studied for the refinement phase.

Case company	Hub	Core business
MACHINE	A	Integration between the hub's system and various machines such as vending machines or intelligent refrigerators
MEDIA	A	Full-range supplier of IT systems and services for newspaper publishing companies
ARCHIVE	A	Integration between the hub's system and various archiving systems
PIM	A	Providing a product information management system for cross-media publishing
E-BUSINESS	A	Providing an e-business suite that comprises content and e-commerce management, document management, and collaboration tools
PROJECT	B	Development of applications based on the hub's groupware system, for example project and knowledge management systems
WORKFLOW	B	Providing e-business, groupware, and portals solutions
MANU-FACTURE	B	Providing a manufacturing execution system
ANALYSIS	B	Providing a web analysis tool
ONTOLOGY	B	Providing ontology-based knowledge management system
EXTEND	B	Extension of HUB B's platform in different contexts

Table 5.1: Analyzed case companies – refinement phase

Similar to the exploratory phase, data was collected through expert interviews as well as secondary material such as company websites. Again, executives or partnership managers were selected as interview partners whenever possible. Within the companies that had already been part of the exploratory phase, the same experts could be interviewed. In two cases (MACHINE and ARCHIVE) follow-up interviews were necessary for completing the interviews. In one case (PROJECT) two experts were consulted in order to obtain a comprehensive picture.

Case company	**Hub**	**Number of interviews**	**Interviewee(s)**
MACHINE	A	2	Founder and CEO
MEDIA	A	1	Head of product development
ARCHIVE	A	2	Partnership manager
PIM	A	1	Founder and CEO
E-BUSINESS	A	1	CEO
PROJECT	B	2	CEO Partnership manager
WORKFLOW	B	1	Sales director
MANU-FACTURE	B	1	Head of marketing
ANALYSIS	B	1	Head of marketing
ONTOLOGY	B	1	Partnership manager
EXTEND	B	1	Director
Total		14	

Table 5.2: Interviewees and number of interviews – refinement phase

Interviews were conducted both face-to-face as well as through telephone. As discussed in Chapter 3, telephone interviews are in line with the purpose of the refinement phase, since they enable a wider range of potential case companies.

Moreover, as a result of the corroborating nature of the study, the interview guideline – which is designed along the explanatory models developed in the exploratory phase – is more structured (see Appendix 1.2), reducing the need for personal, on-site visits. In total, the data set consists of 14 expert interviews in 11 companies. Table 5.2 provides an overview of the conducted interviews.

All interviews were tape-recorded and transcribed, resulting in more than 70,000 words and more than 150 pages of qualitative data. As a first step of the data analysis procedure, the interview transcripts were coded according to the constructs of the two theoretical frameworks as defined in Table 4.3 (Miles and Huberman, 1994). That is, brief labels (*perceived complementarity of technological, commercial,* and *social capital, IOS, hub-specific investments, informal governance, competition, reluctance to share resources, subjective* and *objective partnership success*) were assigned to the respective text passages using the qualitative data analysis tool NVivo. This procedure resulted in a table of 518 assigned statements. Table 5.3 offers indicators for the identified constructs, as drawn from the exploratory case studies and reflected in the interview guideline of the refinement phase as shown in Appendix 1.2 (Sherif et al., 2006).

Construct	**Indicators**
Technological capital	- Spokes report to access critical knowledge related to the platform - Spokes report that own innovations make use of platform innovations
Commercial capital	- Spokes report to benefit from the use of hub's marketing channels
Social capital	- Spokes report to use hub's brand name to signal reliability and trustworthiness
Inter-organizational information systems	- Spokes access critical knowledge via IOS offered by the hub - IOS substitute personal communication as a source of knowledge

Construct	Indicators
Relation-specific investments	- Spokes invest heavily in hub-specific knowledge accumulation - Spokes focus exclusively on the partnership with the respective hub - Spokes report that having alternative partnership at the same time would be unfeasible
Informal governance mechanisms	- Spokes aim at coordinating the partnership via informal contacts - Spokes deliberately try to establish a network of informal contacts within the hub organization
Competition	- Spokes report situations of competition with the hub - Spokes see knowledge spillover as a critical issue
Reluctance to share resources	- The access to the hub's technological, commercial, and social capital is below expectations - Spokes report situations in which the hub did not provide the necessary resources
Partnership success (subjective)	- Spokes consider the partnership to be successful - Spokes report that the original goals of the partnership have been fulfilled - Spokes do not report fundamental potential improvements of the partnership
Partnership success (objective)	- Revenue and number of employees increased since the partnership has been initiated - Spokes do not plan or consider a substitution of the partnership

Table 5.3: Indicators for the identified constructs

Next, case stories were written on each case separately. The case stories enabled an understanding of the relative importance of each dimension within the context of each case (Miles and Huberman, 1994; Patton, 2002). Through this qualitative data analysis procedure, it was possible to not only scrutinize the propositions developed in the exploratory phase, but also to refine the theoretical frameworks and, for example, gain an in-depth understanding of the nature of perceived and actual complementarity of resources within the context of each case.

In order to substantiate the initial qualitative assessment and clearly identify the impact variations between cases, a more fine-grained coding of the particular quotes was performed. For this purpose, the level of the constructs as indicated by a corresponding statement was examined for each of the 518 categorized interview statements (Miles and Huberman, 1994). Therefore, a scale from low via medium to high was used. Congruence between this evaluation and the qualitative findings for each case increased the confidence in the validity of the study's results.

Finally, the data was re-examined in order to gain a deeper understanding of the notion of complementarity of the partners' resources and capabilities. In line with previous findings, the empirical data suggests a link between complementarity of resources and capabilities as well as product-level complementarity between partners (Kude et al., 2012). Therefore, the level of product-level complementarity between hub and spoke was first determined for each case (Miles and Huberman, 1994). This assessment was based on the product description by the interview partners as well as on an analysis of the hubs' and the spokes' company websites.

For example, if the products of hub and spoke could be assigned to distinct layers in the software stack model (Figure 2.1), then the level of layer overlap was rated low, indicating a high level of product complementarity (Gao and Iyer, 2006; Milgrom and Roberts, 1995). The assessment of the layer overlap of the analyzed partnerships was then used to discover patterns regarding the interplay of external resources, opportunistic behavior, and partnership success. This examination was again followed by a qualitative in-depth analysis of the findings in the context of each case.

The following section provides the results of the study's refinement phase, first reporting the findings from each case in isolation. Subsequently, a cross-case analysis is presented, referring to the propositions devised in Chapter 4. The cross-case analysis was performed with the goal of refining the models according to the study's findings whenever indicated.

5.2 Result from single-case analysis

This section presents the results from each case of the refinement phase independent from each other. In order to do so, the case companies are introduced shortly, before the coordination and success of each partnership with the respective hub organization is discussed. After the corresponding section, the cases from each of the two partnership networks are summarized briefly. Tables with an assessment of the ten constructs included in the two models and corresponding evidence are presented for each case in Appendix 2.

5.2.1 Complementors in in HUB A's partnership network

The partnership coordination and success of the case companies that participate in HUB A's partnership network are presented subsequently. As described in Chapter 3, HUB A provides both a middleware platform for service-oriented architecture as well as enterprise applications. The partners of HUB A focus on various niches within this product portfolio. MEDIA, PIM, and E-BUSINESS fill gaps of HUB A's system on the application layer by providing additional functionality, while MACHINE and ARCHIVE act on the middleware layer by integrating HUB A's system with third-party systems.

5.2.1.1 MACHINE

MACHINE was founded in 2005 and became a partner of HUB A right after its foundation. The company offers software adapters that connect different types of machines and devices as well as software services in general with the enterprise software of HUB A. Customers of MACHINE include, among others, operators of vending machines and wind power stations. With MACHINE's solutions, customers can automatically transfer business data from the machines and devices (e.g., the amount of sold goods), to their enterprise software system. Given that small companies either do not have HUB A's system running or do not employ enough devices to justify investments into automated data transmission, the customers of MACHINE are usually large enterprises. While standardized software solutions are clearly the core business of MACHINE, the company also offers consulting services.

As already discovered in the exploratory phase, MACHINE perceives the complementarity between HUB A's and its own technological capital to be high. The CEO of MACHINE stressed that all of HUB A's products build on HUB A's platform, and therefore getting access to HUB A's knowledge and technology is crucial for MACHINE. In the second phase of interviews with the CEO, however, s/he acknowledged that getting access to this kind of knowledge is not an easy task.

The perceived complementarity of HUB A's social capital can be considered to be high. The CEO of MACHINE stressed that "the name and reputation of [HUB A] is very important for us. Customers wouldn't notice and know us without the certification of [HUB A]". In contrast, apart from the obvious advantage of having a large number of potential customers – those companies that run HUB A's system – the interviewee mentioned that a more intense collaboration regarding marketing and sales initiatives would be desirable.

The theoretical model devised in Figure 4.1 suggests that such a medium degree of perceived resource complementarity can be expected to result in a modest level of organizational coupling. Indeed, MACHINE has established and aims at intensifying informal and personal relationships and hence benefit from external resource, most notably through a technical advisory board that, among others, consists of former executives of HUB A. The CEO comments that the access to technological know-how is in many cases only possible through personal contacts that could be established throughout the last years. According to the interviewee, even though IOS are used by MACHINE's employees to obtain technological know-how, the information available through these systems is either too generic or too overwhelming. "Some kind of information won't be available through these systems. You have to call somebody you know and ask him, that's the only way." MACHINE heavily uses one of the IOS offered by HUB A as a marketing tool, explaining the lower importance of close cooperation regarding sales and marketing efforts.

MACHINE tries to keep hub-specific resources at a rather low level. Interestingly, in course of the several interviews conducted at MACHINE, the company tried to reduce the dependence on HUB A by diversifying its business and engage in more intense partnerships with other companies. Notably, these other partners are not enterprise software vendors like HUB A, but hardware vendors, like

HP. As a result, and in line with Proposition 3, this leads to a reduced threat of opportunistic behavior. "What we try to do is diversify our business in order to make us less vulnerable."

The partnership between MACHINE and HUB A provides solid results for MACHINE. After considerable growth throughout the last years, MACHINE now has around 25 employees and applies its core competency of integrating machinery and services with HUB A's platform to several, diverse areas. Interestingly, even though the CEO is aware that a similar partnership with another major hub organization is not feasible due to the necessary hub-specific investments, MACHINE still tries to intensify the business relationships with other partners.

It can be stated that HUB A indeed provides complementary resources and capabilities as perceived by the CEO. MACHINE integrates third-party hardware with HUB A's system, and is therefore in need of detailed information regarding technological issues and new developments of HUB A's software. Moreover, since customers of MACHINE are mostly large cooperations, the reputation of HUB A clearly provides a huge benefit for MACHINE. In contrast, given that the markets that MACHINE and HUB A address do not completely overlap, HUB A's commercial capital is of minor importance for MACHINE.

MACHINE, and particularly its CEO, are aware of the opportunities and limitations of external resources that HUB A provides, and invest to an appropriate extent in hub-specific resources as well as in informal governance. Therefore, the costs of the partnership as well as the resulting risks are limited. In particular, most of the personal contacts with HUB A's employees have been existing for a long time. However, one risk that may result is that if these contacts cease to exist, MACHINE could encounter problems to continue absorbing external technological know-how.

5.2.1.2 MEDIA

MEDIA provides complementary functionality specific to the media and newspaper industry. The company was founded as a spin-off out of the data centers of various media groups. Today, MEDIA is a full-range supplier of IT services for the media industry. Its core business is adjusting HUB A's system as well as developing complementary add-ons based on HUB A's platform, specifically addressing the idiosyncrasies and needs of the media industry.

While MACHINE's partnership with HUB A can be considered as rather successful, this is not the case for MEDIA. This is illustrated by the changes in the relationship between MEDIA and HUB A as reported by the interviewees at the two visits of MEDIA both during the exploratory as well as the refinement phase of this study. This will be outlined subsequently.

As a result of the specific industry structure in which MEDIA acts, the complementarity with HUB A's commercial and social capital is rather low, which has been acknowledged by the interview partners in both phases of this study. The interviewees report that MEDIA's market – the media industry in German-speaking countries – is very small and has even decreased throughout the last years due to a number of mergers and acquisitions of (potential) customer companies. Moreover, MEDIA has only one real competitor in the market. As a result of the fact that MEDIA is well-known in its market, the potential to find new customers with the help of HUB A's resources and capabilities is very limited. Moreover, the value of HUB A's reputation to convince new customers is low. As a result, MEDIA decided to not obtain HUB A's certification for the latest releases of its software products. "For the certification, we would have to pay ten to 15 thousand Euros, plus we would have to work on it for around ten days. We skip the certifications for some of our solutions, because the gains for us are very limited."

In contrast, the complementarity between MEDIA's and HUB A's technological capital had been perceived to be very high by the interview partners. MEDIA's solutions are exclusively based on HUB A's platform, resulting in a high need for technological know-how that is specific to HUB A's software. Even though MEDIA's employees use the inter-organizational knowledge management systems and data bases offered by HUB A to some extent, MEDIA had to invest heavily in hub-specific knowledge accumulation and in establishing informal relationships with relevant members of HUB A.

As a result and in line with this study's theoretical assertions, the threat of opportunistic behavior on part of HUB A is very high. In fact, HUB A offers a version of its enterprise software that is specific to the media industry, thus being in competition with MEDIA in some areas. While in the exploratory phase, the interviewees considered the partnership to be successful despite this potential threat, MEDIA's head of product development comments in the refinement phase that "some people within MEDIA now realize in a painful way how dependent we became on HUB A."

Specifically, HUB A stopped offering a module of its platform on which some of MEDIA's solutions are built upon. Moreover, MEDIA does not get reliable information on the product strategy of HUB A concerning the media industry. In line with Proposition 4, MEDIA tries to establish even better informal contacts in order to avoid product overlaps and get access to important information. Yet, the success is limited, as MEDIA's head of product development explained.

In summary, the actual complementarity between MEDIA's and HUB A's resources is rather low, resulting in a partnership that is unsatisfying for MEDIA. This is reinforced by the high costs and risks resulting from a high organizational coupling. Indeed, MEDIA considers to resign from the partnership with HUB A and instead build its complementary solutions on a different vendors platform – preferably one that offers only generic and no media-specific solutions, as the interviewee stressed. The head of product development concluded that "the partnership between MEDIA and HUB A is not the big love anymore that it used to be."

5.2.1.3 ARCHIVE

ARCHIVE has been offering complementary archiving functionality based on HUB A's enterprise application software for almost 20 years. ARCHIVE exclusively provides complementary solutions for HUB A's software system. As a result, ARCHIVE perceives the access to HUB A's technological capital as particularly beneficial.

Specifically, ARCHIVE benefits from HUB A's innovations in the field of data archiving, allowing the company to develop and market new additional software. ARCHIVE entered the partnership and started to develop complementary solutions when the first version of HUB A's enterprise software was on the market. The archiving functionality of this early version was very restricted (only four gigabytes of data could be filed), allowing ARCHIVE to successfully market its additional piece of software. Throughout the years, HUB A released several new versions of its enterprise software, which in turn triggered a process of coming up with own innovations within ARCHIVE. For instance, when HUB A had enlarged the amount of data that could be filed, ARCHIVE focused on offering solutions to improve archiving performance.

Although performance is still a key selling point, recent releases of HUB A's platform decreased the customers' need for additional performance-improving solutions, encouraging ARCHIVE to find a new niche. Thus, ARCHIVE came up with tools that help customers comply with statutory requirements related to archiving that are specific to certain industries or regions.

Moreover, the partnership manager of ARCHIVE explained that through the partnership with HUB A, ARCHIVE is able to address a broader market. Specifically, by making use of HUB A's marketing and sales network, ARCHIVE is enabled to sell its solutions on a global basis, which, according to the partnership manager, would otherwise not be possible for a small company like ARCHIVE. In addition, the gain in reputation that results from the partnership with HUB A is considered to be crucial by the partnership manager. "Being a partner of [HUB A] shows our customers that we have a healthy business relationship with [HUB A]. Customers know that for participating in [HUB A]'s partnership network, we have to fulfill certain requirements. Therefore, customers perceive us as a reliable software vendor." S/he added that "using [HUB A]'s logo on our homepage helps us a lot. That's what potential customers look for." Indeed, a look at ARCHIVE's website confirms that the partnership with HUB A is communicated widely and prominently.

The degree of organizational coupling in the sense of the theoretical framework developed above is very high. A certain amount of partner-specific investments are a direct consequence of ARCHIVE's exclusive focus on HUB A's platform. For example, through its close personal links to HUB A's employees, ARCHIVE is able to tap into the partner's commercial capital by having HUB A's staff recommend ARCHIVE's solutions. However, the partnership manager explained that ARCHIVE makes heavy use of IOS offered by HUB A in order to obtain technological know-how and to benefit from HUB A's marketing channel, reducing the need for partner-specific investments.

Interestingly, in line with Proposition 4, the reason for the high degree of organizational coupling is less the better access to the hub's resources and capabilities, but more a response to the threat of opportunistic behavior on part of HUB A. As discussed above, ARCHIVE benefits from innovations of HUB A in the field of archiving, since they allow ARCHIVE to come up with own innovations that make use of improvements of the overall platform. At the same time, however, ARCHIVE's business model is severely challenged by these architectural innovations of the hub.

ARCHIVE's partnership manager stated that "HUB A's innovativeness opens opportunities for [ARCHIVE] to develop new software based on these improvements." At the same time, s/he admitted that "[ARCHIVE] has to be careful. If [HUB A] develops new solutions in the field of archiving, this could overlap with our solutions and render them obsolete." By establishing personal relationships with key actors within HUB A, ARCHIVE tries to obtain information on HUB A's future products and potential niches. Thus, through informal governance, ARCHIVE is able to overcome the threat of obsolescence and actually benefit from architectural innovations.

The partnership manager of ARCHIVE described the partnership with HUB A as a "huge success." Indeed, ARCHIVE has been successfully selling complimentary archiving solutions for almost 20 years, continuously finding new niches. The great success of ARCHIVE's partnership with HUB A can be ascribed to the resource complementarity, but also to the high degree of organizational coupling between the partners that helps access resources and avoid obsolescence by opening new niches for ARCHIVE.

The complementarity between ARCHIVE's resources and capabilities and HUB A's technological, commercial and social capital can indeed be considered very high. ARCHIVE was found to benefit from HUB A's technological know-how and from the chance to innovate on a modular level based on HUB A's architectural innovations. Also, HUB A's commercial capital complements that of ARCHIVE, since ARCHIVE was found to greatly benefit from the recommendation of the provided archiving solutions by HUB A. In a similar way, ARCHIVE benefits from HUB A's reputation in the market.

ARCHIVE tied its business very closely to HUB A by investing in partner-specific knowledge accumulation and successfully establishing informal coordination mechanisms. Although the effort to do so is considerably high, the benefits resulting from the access to external resources clearly exceed the partnership costs. Therefore, ARCHIVE has been able to maintain a successful collaboration with HUB A. In other words, the resource complementarity is not only perceived to be high by ARCHIVE, but indeed is. As a downside, the dependence on the partnership with HUB A and on key relationships is extremely high.

5.2.1.4 PIM

As described in the exploratory part of this study, PIM develops a product information management solution that supports customers in managing large amounts of product data. Moreover, it enables a professional publishing via various outlets such as websites, product brochures, or catalogs. Re-examining the case of PIM promises to be particularly insightful because of two major changes in its partnership with HUB A. First, between the two rounds of interviews, HUB A acquired another software firm that offers a solution which overlaps with PIM's software, leading to a situation of competition between HUB A and PIM. Shortly after, HUB A exchanged the key managers within its master data management division, which were among the most important contact persons for PIM.

As pointed out above, the complementarity between HUB A's and PIM's resources is perceived to be particularly high regarding commercial and social capital. PIM's founder and CEO explained that there were two main reason for PIM to participate in a partnership with HUB A. On the one hand, through the partnership, PIM was able to make use of HUB A's distribution channel by convincing its partner's sales staff of the usefulness and value of its product information management solution. On the other, the interviewee points out that through tapping into HUB A's reputation "our visibility is top-notch."

While PIM decided to engage in a partnership with HUB A in order to benefit from its sales network and reputation, the access to technological know-how played a less important role according to the interviewee. While some technological knowledge about the platform's functioning was necessary to integrate the solutions, the interviewee explained that the ongoing need for knowledge about HUB A's system that goes beyond interface specifications is limited. In fact, PIM's system is not only compatible with HUB A's platform, but also with enterprise software systems from various other vendors.

PIM does not make use of any IOS offered by HUB A for accessing the partner's commercial and social capital. Instead, the main strategy of PIM was to establish a broad network of personal contacts within HUB A's organization, particularly with sales staff and managers within the master data management division of HUB A. In other words, PIM decided to engage in a high level of organizational coupling.

In conformance with the theoretical assertions, such a high degree of organizational coupling increased the perceived threat of opportunistic behavior on part of HUB A. Being aware of this potential threat, PIM even increased the degree of organizational coupling in order to ensure the continuing access to HUB A's sales network and to avoid that HUB A comes up with its own product information management solution. While this strategy had been rather successful until recently, the two events mentioned above dramatically changed the situation.

Although HUB A and PIM continue to be official partners, HUB A is reluctant to grant PIM access to its marketing and sales network and promote PIM's solution after having acquired a competitor of PIM in the field of product information management. Moreover, HUB A decided to exchange key actors in the sub-division with which PIM used to closely collaborate. Given that PIM had invested heavily in the establishment of these contacts, this is particularly harmful for PIM.

The theoretical model developed in the exploratory phase is able to explain the resulting behavior of PIM. PIM's response to this disruptive change in the partnership is twofold. In the current transition phase, PIM tries to revive the close collaboration with HUB A, particularly with its sales organization, with the goal of convincing HUB A that PIM's solution is better than the one HUB A has acquired. In other words, in line with Proposition 6, PIM aims at increasing the partnership success by ensuring the access to external resources and capabilities through organizational coupling. At the same time, however, PIM prepares for a situation that makes an exclusive cooperation impossible by actively looking for alternative partners.

5.2.1.5 E-BUSINESS

E-BUSINESS was founded in 2000 and became a partner of HUB A in the year 2004. As of today, E-BUSINESS has 16 employees in its German headquarters and two small sales offices in Japan and Australia. E-BUSINESS' product portfolio comprises content and e-commerce management, document management, as well as collaboration tools.

The case of E-BUSINESS illustrates very well the theorized link between perceived resource complementarity and the degree of organizational coupling. Concluding from the expert interview with E-BUSINESS' CEO, there is great potential for benefiting from technological know-how that resides within the hub organization. In particular, s/he stated that there is a strong need for knowledge about the integration of E-BUSINESS' solutions with those of HUB A. "As a small company you are potentially weak regarding development resources. A partnership with a large platform vendor can help overcome these problems."

E-BUSINESS' CEO perceived the complementarity with HUB A's commercial capital to be particularly high. S/he stated that "the partnership was interesting for us because we wanted to get access to [HUB A]'s sales unit." The interviewee explained that a lot of customers decided to purchase E-BUSINESS' solutions as a result of recommendations by HUB A's sales staff. E-BUSINESS' CEO stressed that the partner's marketing capabilities were particularly helpful in the start-up phase of the company when E-BUSINESS was lacking commercial capital.

Also, the CEO reported that E-BUSINESS benefits from HUB A's reputation. "Customers usually know that if a company is a partner of [HUB A], then the quality of the organization and the products have been assessed by [HUB A]." However, s/he added that "you don't sell your product just because it is certified."

The case study showed that the IOS offered by HUB A do not help E-BUSINESS obtain access to these resources and capabilities. The CEO commented that in the field of marketing and sales, communication is always via personal contacts. The interviewee also explained that in order to get access to technological know-how, appropriate formal communication channels would be helpful. However, "the documentation about the platform was very bad and didn't help us understand the system" (CEO).

In line with the explanatory model developed above, E-BUSINESS had to invest heavily in hub-specific resources and informal governance mechanisms in order to get access to HUB A's resources and capabilities. For instance, the CEO of E-BUSINESS explained that the initial and ongoing fees for certification of its solutions were substantial. Even more important, the CEO explained that in order "to make the system compatible with [HUB A]'s platform, we needed three full-time employees for accumulating know-how about the platform. You need to know the system before you can start developing." Also, E-BUSINESS tried to increase the degree of organizational coupling and invest in informal governance. "Of course, there is a lot of formal overhead, but the success or failure of a partnership is decided in the personal collaboration of people" (CEO). In the case of E-BUSINESS, this was found to be especially true for the area of marketing and sales. In addition, in order to facilitate the access to technological know-how, E-BUSINESS tried to establish personal contacts with developers of HUB A. However, according to the CEO, this is difficult because HUB A develops large parts of its software off-shore.

As predicted in the explanatory model, the high degree of organizational coupling resulted in a strong threat of opportunistic behavior by HUB A. The CEO said that there is always a threat that HUB A competes with E-BUSINESS in some areas. "It happened to us before that [HUB A] decided to develop similar functionality for a customer. If a project becomes strategic for [HUB A], then the partnership is over"(CEO). Also, the CEO reported that, at one point, HUB A decided to enter a partnership with one of E-BUSINESS' biggest competitors. Even though this plan was not realized eventually, the CEO said that "it was a critical situation. This could happen anytime." In addition, the CEO complained that it happened several times that HUB A ended the certification agreement without any forewarning, resulting in the need for E-BUSINESS to put huge effort into adjusting its products to the architecture of new releases and to pay fees for the re-certification.

Summing up, while the complementarity between HUB A's and E-BUSINESS' resources is high, the adverse implications resulting from the extensive investments in hub-specific resources and informal governance mechanisms exceed these benefits. This is acknowledged by the CEO. According to the interviewee, the partnership with HUB A generated a lot of revenue in the last five years. S/he stated that "it's not that we could not make profit with the partnership, but the return on investment is just not high enough."

As a consequence, E-BUSINESS decided to not re-certificate its solutions for new releases. Instead, the company adjusts its solutions ad-hoc for specific customers according to the platform they use. "We do not develop further our products for [HUB A]'s platform. By broadly offering our products independent from [HUB A], we have a higher return on investments" (CEO).

5.2.1.6 Summary

The analyzed case companies that participate in HUB A's partnership network have in common that they all show at least a medium degree of organizational coupling. Two reasons for this observation may be distinguished. First, all case companies perceive the complementarity between their own resources and capabilities and those of the hub to be rather high. In particular, the case companies participate in the partnership with HUB A to obtain in-depth knowledge about the functioning of HUB A's system.

Also, all analyzed case companies except MEDIA (due to the small market) perceive the ability to tap into HUB A's reputation to be particularly high. In contrast, the cases differ substantially regarding the perceived complementarity of the partner's commercial capital. Interestingly, the usefulness of IOS offered by HUB A is perceived to be rather low by the analyzed spokes, reinforcing the need for a high degree of coupling in order to access external resources.

The high degree of organizational coupling has different implications for the partners of HUB A. Some spokes (ARCHIVE and MACHINE) have been able to establish a rather successful partnership with HUB A. Others (MEDIA, PIM, and E-BUSINESS), were seriously challenged by the consequences of opportunistic behavior of the hub due to the high degree of organizational coupling. The cross-case analysis presented in Chapter 5.3 examines these interesting observations in more detail.

5.2.2 Complementors in HUB B's partnership network

In the following sections, the partnership coordination and success of the case companies that participate in HUB B's partnership network are presented. While HUB A provides both a middleware platform as well as enterprise applications, HUB B currently focuses on infrastructure and middleware solutions as well as implementation and consulting services. The partners of HUB B focus on various niches in HUB B's product portfolio.

The spoke organizations selected for the refinement phase offer solutions that are based on the platforms offered by HUB B. In addition, all case companies offer implementation and consulting services to varying extents.

5.2.2.1 PROJECT

PROJECT is a software firm that develops complementary applications based on HUB B's groupware system. The provided solutions include a project management system, a solution that enables the management of incidents and change requests, a system for the management of a company's product portfolio, a survey tool, as well as a system for the recording and approval of working hours. PROJECT was founded in 1998 and today has around 80 employees located in three different countries.

The complementarity between HUB B's and PROJECT's resources and capabilities is perceived to be rather high by PROJECT's managers. In particular, the interviewees explained that the hub's reputation is crucial in order to signal trustworthiness to potential customers. Moreover, even though the actual marketing support has been somewhat disappointing so far, PROJECT considers the potential of HUB B's marketing and sales support to be high. PROJECT's CEO stated that "it's one of our goals in the partnership to attract new customers with the help of [HUB B]." In addition, s/he stressed that "through the partnership we can access [HUB B]'s technological know-how. That's the big advantage."

Interestingly, however, PROJECT's employees that work with HUB B on an operational level consider the access to external technological know-how that is enabled through the partnership to be rather limited. For instance, PROJECT's partnership manager commented that "the access to know-how is not really the reason why we participate [in the partnership]. This kind of information you can just as well access without being a partner."

This is also reflected by the interviewees' attitude toward the information and knowledge management systems deployed by HUB B to coordinate its partnership network. In a nutshell, PROJECT does not use these IOS, because in these systems, PROJECT's employees only "find out that other people have the same problems. But that's not a solution" (CEO).

As a result of the relatively high degree of perceived complementarity and the low availability of appropriate IOS to access and make use of external resources, PROJECT ties its business closely to HUB B. The interviewees explained that because PROJECT is in the highest partnership level, the cost and efforts associated with the partnership are very high. Moreover, PROJECT's partnership manager explained that in order to actually benefit from the partnership, "we have built up a huge amount of know-how over the years regarding [HUB B]'s system. Having the same know-how for different systems would be impossible." In a similar way, PROJECT puts considerable effort into the establishment and maintenance of informal and personal relationships with HUB B.

In line with the theoretical assertions, the interviews showed that as a consequence of the high degree of organizational coupling, PROJECT faces a high threat of opportunism on part of HUB B. In particular, even though PROJECT participates in the partnership to benefit from HUB B's marketing capabilities, the actual marketing support has been rather low. As described above, PROJECT builds its applications on HUB B's groupware systems and the associated data base management system. However, according to HUB B's partnership manager, the groupware system has a rather low priority for HUB B and, thus, HUB B's efforts to promote the groupware platform and to keep it competitive is rather low. As a result, according to PROJECT's CEO, the number of products sold because of the partnership with HUB B is close to zero. As discussed above, the operational benefits resulting from the access to external know-how through the partnership are also rather low.

In addition to this reluctance to provide PROJECT with resources and capabilities, HUB B even enters into a situation of competition with its partner PROJECT. In this context, PROJECT's partnership manager complained that the company is forced to disclose a lot of information and feared that HUB B could take over PROJECT's business.

The success of PROJECT's partnership with HUB B is rather low. In accordance with the theory developed above, the main reason for this may be seen in the fact that the complementarity between HUB B's and PROJECTS resources and capabilities has been perceived to be higher by PROJECT than it actually is. In particular, HUB B and PROJECT focus on different markets. While HUB B's main business is in the field of infrastructure and middleware solutions as well as on providing consulting services, PROJECT focuses more on enterprise applications. For this reason, the benefit resulting from HUB B's commercial capital may be lower than PROJECT had expected when entering the partnership.

5.2.2.2 WORKFLOW

WORKFLOW is a software company that provides solutions for content management, supply chain management, e-commerce, groupware, and portals which are built upon HUB B's platforms. In total, WORKFLOW offers more than 40 complementary software modules. The firm's know-how and its solutions focus on process optimization and are used by customers from all over the world. WORKFLOW was co-founded by a former employee of HUB B and three other colleagues in 1992. Today, WORKFLOW employs around 60 professionals that are located in the German headquarters and two branch offices in Russia. WORKFLOW became an official partner of HUB B two years after being founded.

Asked about the main reasons why WORKFLOW decided to participate in a partnership with HUB B, the sales director stressed the access to external know-how and HUB B's capability to constantly innovate the platform that WORKFLOW's solutions are based upon. "The partnership is clearly about technological leadership. We have access to technological know-how and innovative products" (sales director). Moreover, according to WORKFLOW's sales director, the way how potential customers perceive and evaluate WORKFLOW and its products is improved through tapping into HUB B's reputation by using HUB B's logo for marketing purposes. The partnership with HUB B is mentioned and its logo is prominently visible on WORKFLOW's company website. In addition, the interviewee remarked that "marketing is definitely an important aspect." Taken together, it can be concluded from the empirical data that the complementarity between WORKFLOW's and HUB B's resources and capabilities is perceived to be relatively high by WORKFLOW.

During the first round of interviews, WORKFLOW's employees were using information and knowledge management systems offered by HUB B in order to get access to external know-how, but had already been somewhat unsatisfied about the information overload that is inherent in these systems. Since then, this disappointment has even increased. "The information systems change all the time. You don't find things anymore in the portal" (sales director).

As a consequence, in order to benefit from external resources and capabilities, WORKFLOW relies on informal contacts. "Usually we have our contacts within [HUB B] that tell us where to find things in the systems" (sales director). These informal contacts that WORKLFOW has been cultivating partly originate in the fact that one of the founders of WORKFLOW used to work for HUB B. Yet, the interviewee stressed that establishing and maintaining these contacts is an endeavor that requires considerable effort. For instance, the sales director described that it took himself several years to establish a personal network within HUB B.

In addition to these costs and efforts related to the cultivation of an informal partnership coordination, WORKFLOW generally invests into partner-specific resources and capabilities in order to benefit from the partnership. As a result, the interviewee reckoned that WORKFLOW would not be able to handle more than one partnership with a major platform vendor. "We have to employ one person that works only on the partnership management." At the same time, however, WORKFLOW is aware of the high degree of unilateral dependency that might result from over-investing in partner-specific resources. Indeed, in addition to its main partnership with HUB B, WORKFLOW participates in a business network in which various small and medium-sized IT firms join forces.

The empirical data shows that there is a considerable threat of opportunism on part of HUB B that results from WORKFLOW's organizational coupling. In particular, the sales director pointed out that "if our projects become very big, [HUB B] might decide to take over the business." WORKFLOW also had to deal with HUB B's reluctance to offer the necessary resources in the past. "It happened to us several times that we were using products from [HUB B] and then they decided to stop offering these products after we had invested several thousands of Euros. That was tough!"

WORKFLOW seems to be well aware of these potential threats of opportunism. "We have to be aware that the partner may change the partnership conditions from one day to the other. That has happened to us before" (sales director). This mindfulness when it comes to the risks and threats in a partnership with a powerful platform vendor together with a realistic evaluation of resource complementarity and adequate investments in partner-specific resources result in a rather successful partnership between WORKFLOW and HUB B. "It is a successful partnership because we have understood the rules of the game within [HUB B]'s partnership network. You have to accept these rules and design your strategy correspondingly" (sales director). This subjective assessment is strengthened when considering that WORKFLOW has been successfully developing complimentary solutions based on HUB B's platform for almost 20 years and that WORKFLOW's partnership with HUB B was intensified during this period. Moreover, WORKFLOW does currently not consider changing to an alternative platform vendor.

5.2.2.3 MANUFACTURE

MANUFACTURE was established in 2000 as a result of the spin-off of the enterprise software division of a larger IT firm. The core product of MANUFACTURE is a manufacturing execution system. The partnership with HUB B was established right after MANUFACTURE's foundation. The complementor employs around 50 professionals.

The complementarity between HUB B's and MANUFACTURE's resources is perceived to be particularly high regarding reputation and marketing aspects, as MANUFACTURE's head of marketing explained. Specifically, MANUFACTURE benefits from HUB B's standing in the market when approaching large companies on an international scale. The head of marketing stated that "[HUB B] has good contacts to the large companies. These companies know [HUB B], they know what they can expect. That is, we use [HUB B]'s reputation. [...] It is a huge advantage when we approach large companies. The big firms say: You are a tiny company of 50 people. Our risk is too high that you don't survive the next crisis, and then we have your software here. But if we go there as a partner of [HUB B], the perception is very different and the trust is much higher." An examination of MANUFACTURE's company website corroborates this perception. Although the communication of the partnership with HUB B is not presented as a key resource, HUB B's logo is used on MANUFACTURE's website and the partnership is communicated on a sub-page.

In addition, the head of marketing explained that making use of HUB B's international sales network is crucial for MANUFACTURE. Moreover, s/he added that "thanks to the partnership we get access to [HUB B]'s customer data base, we can use marketing material such as fliers and brochures, participate in trade fairs, and use [HUB B]'s facilities for workshops." Thus, the analysis of the empirical data shows that the complementarity of HUB B's commercial capital is perceived to be high.

The situation is different for the complementarity of HUB B's technological capital, which is perceived to be low by MANUFACTURE. The reason for this can be seen in the fact that MANUFACTURE's solutions for manufacturing management are designed in a very modular way, which even enables them to run on many different platforms. As a result, following the head of marketing, MANUFACTURE does not benefit significantly from HUB B's resources and capabilities to develop and innovate the underlying platform.

As a consequence of the high degree of perceived complementarity regarding marketing aspects, the partnership with HUB B is mainly focused on HUB B's services and sales devision and less on technological areas. In order to get access to HUB B's marketing and sales network, MANUFACTURE has cultivated a collaboration that is based on personal contacts in this area. Some of these contacts stem from long-lasting acquaintances. Interestingly, however, the most important one is a contact person within HUB B who is, among others, officially responsible for managing the partnership with MANUFACTURE. Thus, while the interviewee explained that IOS do not play an important role for getting access to knowledge and benefiting from complementary resources, the coordination of the partnership is still based on an institutionalized knowledge-sharing routine. While the personal relationships indicate a certain degree of organizational coupling, the investments in resources and capabilities that are specific to HUB B are rather low. The reason for this can be seen in the fact that MANUFACTURE's solutions are mostly platform-independent.

As predicted by this study's theoretical model, the moderate degree of organizational coupling results in a rather low threat of opportunistic behavior. MANUFACTURE's head of marketing is aware that when working with HUB B in a specific project, a certain degree of knowledge spillover is inevitable. Yet, due to the high degree of autonomy, this is not seen as problematic. In a similar way, the interviewee reported that there have been situations were HUB B was reluctant to share the needed resources. "When we want to address new markets together with [HUB B], it takes some time until [HUB B] is up and running." However, MANUFACTURE is aware about potential threats in the future. "We try to reduce risk and not be completely dependent on [HUB B]. Because out of the blue, [HUB B] might make a new strategic decision that changes the game" (head of marketing).

In total, MANUFACTURE evaluates the complementarity between HUB B's resources and capabilities and its own in a realistic way. In particular, working together with HUB B's services and sales division indeed enables MANUFACTURE to benefit from HUB B's commercial and social capital. Accordingly, the partnership between MANUFACTURE and HUB B can be called a success from MANUFACTURE's point of view. For instance, the company has grown from ten employees at the outset to almost 50 as of today. The interviewee agrees with this observation. "Sometimes working together with [HUB B] is a little bit cumbersome, but, in general, we have backed the right horse."

5.2.2.4 ANALYSIS

ANALYSIS was founded as a spin-off of a research institute 10 years ago and has around 40 employees as of today. The company offers software for the analysis and tracking of customer behavior on websites that enables an optimization of a client's Internet presence. The solutions developed by ANALYSIS are built on HUB B's middleware platforms for service-oriented architectures and information management. The partnership with HUB B was initiated eight years ago.

The partnership between ANALYSIS and HUB B is particularly interesting because it can be considered to be very successful from ANALYSIS' point of view, even though the degree of organizational coupling between ANALYSIS and HUB B is rather low. The reason for this is that ANALYSIS is able to access complementarity technological, commercial, and social capital at a rather low cost and effort, mainly through the institutionalized channels for information exchange offered by HUB B.

More specifically, the degree of complementary resources and capabilities is perceived to be moderate. With regard to marketing and sales support, the interviewee stated that "together with [HUB B], we try to approach new customers, especially in the insurance industry." Moreover, ANALYSIS benefits from HUB B's reputation in that "especially in the phase of client acquisition, [HUB B]'s name and reputation in the market really helps us" (head of marketing). Even though the interviewee noted that in some cases, being a partner of HUB B could also be a disadvantage when approaching customers, s/he is convinced that the benefits outweigh this risk. Moreover, ANALYSIS' head of marketing reported that getting access to external technological know-how is of lower importance because of the modular product design, s/he still recognized that "the partnership gives us the opportunity to access technological resources within [HUB B]."

In spite of this medium degree of perceived resource complementarity, the degree of organizational coupling that ANALYSIS strives for is rather low. In particular, apart from the regular costs and efforts for participating in HUB B's partnership network, ANALYSIS does not perform substantial partner-specific investments. In addition, ANALYSIS does coordinate the partnership via personal relationships, but mainly relies on the channel offered by HUB B through one of HUB B's employees that acts as the official contact person.

This observation could be interpreted as a disconfirmation of this study's Proposition 1 which holds that a higher degree of perceived resource complementarity leads to a higher degree of organizational coupling. However, the explanatory power of the model is strengthened when considering the fact that ANALYSIS makes heavy use of institutionalized modes for exchanging information and know-how. Specifically, ANALYSIS' employees use the information systems offered by HUB B on a regular basis to get access to technological know-how. As an example, the interviewee reported that "we use instant messaging to get software support from [HUB B]." In addition to these IOS offered by HUB B, ANALYSIS usually relies on the offical contact person assigned by HUB B to manage the partnership. As a result, ANALYSIS' employees know who to turn to when being in need of external resources and capabilities. Thus, the necessity of investing heavily in personal networks within HUB B significantly decreases.

In line with the theoretical model developed above, the low degree of organizational coupling results in a reduced threat of opportunistic behavior. Although ANALYSIS has to deal with some issues that result from the fact that HUB B is a large company and therefore reacts not as fast as a small firm like ANALYSIS, there has been no serious crisis throughout the partnership between ANALYSIS and HUB B. In general, the partnership is considered as being very trustful by ANALYSIS' head of marketing.

As a consequence of the low costs and risks inherent in the partnership with HUB B and the benefits resulting from the partnership – especially in terms of marketing and reputation gains – the partnership between ANALYSIS and HUB B can be considered to be very successful. Indeed, the partnership between ANALSIS and HUB B has evolved to higher partner levels over time. Moreover, ANALYSIS has been very successful in the course of the partnership, being able to grow substantially. These facts were also acknowledged by the interview partner, who is very satisfied with the partnership.

5.2.2.5 ONTOLOGY

ONTOLOGY was founded as a start-up company by members of a research institute in 1999. Today, ONTOLOGY employs around 50 professionals. The core business of ONTOLOGY are knowledge management systems. In particular, the company offers ontology-based systems for decision support and knowledge retrieval. Both products use HUB B's software platforms as a basis. The partnership between ONTOLOGY and HUB B was initiated four years ago.

The interview with ONTOLOGY's head of marketing revealed that the spoke perceives the complementarity of HUB B's technological capital to be rather low. While ONTOLOGY's solutions are exclusively based on HUB B's platforms, the systems are designed in a very modular way. As a consequence, the knowledge that is necessary to develop these solutions does not go beyond interface specifications.

In contrast, the interviewee perceives the potential benefits resulting from joining ONTOLOGY's and HUB B's commercial and social capital to be substantial. In particular, s/he stated that "one of the core benefits of the partnership with HUB B is that it gets us in touch with the right people within potential customer organizations." In a similar way, following the head of marketing's evaluation, the reputation benefits from engaging in a partnership with HUB B are very high. "Another advantage is that we can label our products as 'fitting with [HUB B]'s software'." Interestingly, however, the partnership with HUB B is only briefly mentioned on ONOTOLOGY's marketing material, such as its website, and not communicated as a key resource.

ONTOLOGY's head of marketing explained that the only inter-organizational information system s/he is aware of is a system that allows for getting in touch with HUB B via instant messaging in order to solve technological issues. Since the access to external technological know-how is of minor importance for ONTOLOGY, this system is not used on a regular base by ONTOLOGY's staff according to the interviewee.

Instead, ONTOLOGY relies on a network of personal contacts within HUB B in order to materialize the identified potential benefits resulting from resource complementarity, mostly regarding marketing and sales. To that effect, ONTOLOGY participates in meetings and events organized by HUB B in order to meet key individuals. While the degree of informal governance can be considered to be rather high, ONTOLOGY does not significantly invest in other resources or capabilities specific to HUB B.

Congruent with the theoretical assertions, this medium degree of organizational coupling results in a moderate level of threat of opportunism on part of HUB B. ONTOLOGY's head of marketing does not report any conflicts or situations of competition in the partnership with HUB B. S/he explained that "there is no risk of competition between us and [HUB B] because we are acting in a small niche." Interestingly, HUB B had acquired a Chinese competitor of ONTOLOGY some years ago, but "since then I haven't heard anything about it" (head of marketing).

While the risk that ONTOLOGY's solution might become obsolete because HUB B may include its functionality into its own platform is rather low, the interview revealed that there is indeed a certain threat of opportunistic behavior in that the partner might be reluctant to grant access to the complementary resources and capabilities. In particular, ONTOLOGY's head of marketing reported that "there are situations where [HUB B] does not support us like we wished or reacts more slowly then we expected." As proposed above, instead of lowering the degree of organizational coupling as a consequence of this threat, ONTOLOGY tries to engage in personal contacts mainly to avoid this reluctance to share resources. "Usually, we solve these issues through our network of personal contacts and through face-to-face meetings" (head of marketing).

In line with the explanatory framework developed in Chapter 4, ONTOLOGY's partnership with HUB B is seen as rather successful by ONTOLOGY's head of marketing. "The partnership with [HUB B] has always been of a high quality." Indeed, ONTOLOGY has performed well in the course of the partnership with HUB B, successfully selling its complementary solutions. Therefore, ONTOLOGY does not consider participating in partnerships with alternative platform vendors.

Yet, the access to complementary resources is rather limited in spite of considerably high efforts to establish and maintain a network of informal contacts. In a similar vein, ONTOLOGY has not intensified the partnership through advancing to a higher partnership level. A reason for this may be that the complementarity between ONTOLOGY's and HUB B's resources is actually lower than it is perceived by the spoke. In particular, ONTOLOGY acts in a market that is quite different from HUB B's, suggesting that the marketing gains for ONTOLOGY are rather limited. Moreover, instead of enabling a wider access to external resources, many of the personal contacts within HUB B are mostly used by ONTOLOGY in order to prevent HUB B from behaving opportunistically.

5.2.2.6 EXTEND

EXTEND was founded in 1999 and has 12 full-time employees. The partnership with HUB B was established right after being founded. The company extends the solutions offered by HUB B in several fields, such as production planning, logistics, and management accounting. Instead of changing the actual software, most of these extensions are rather adjustments of the software on a higher level.

The case of EXTEND is special in that the spoke maintains a partnership not only with HUB B, but also with another large platform vendor. This suggests a low degree of organizational coupling between EXTEND and HUB B. Indeed, the empirical examination revealed that EXTEND's investments and efforts specific to the partnership with HUB B are low. In particular, EXTEND does not offer comprehensive software solution and hence does not have the costs and efforts of a certification process. Similarly, EXTEND mostly relies on formal coordination mechanisms instead of engaging in informal coordination efforts. "We are not trying to establish a large network of contacts within [HUB B]" (director). Interestingly, while personal networks are of lower importance, the director stressed the importance of the good relationship with HUB B's manager responsible for the partnership with EXTEND. Hence, the partnership is coordinated through a personal contact, but in an institutionalized way.

In line with this study's theoretical assertions, the reason for this low degree of organizational coupling can be seen in the moderate complementarity of HUB B's and EXTEND's resources and capabilities as perceived by EXTEND. Indeed, the interview with EXTEND's director revealed that the complementarity of HUB B's and EXTEND's technological capital is perceived to be low. According to EXTEND's director, the reason for this is that for adjusting HUB B's solutions in various business contexts, the access to detailed technological know-how about the functioning of the system is of lower importance.

The situation is different for the perceived complementarity of HUB B's commercial and social capital. EXTEND's director explained that "even though we are a small partner, [HUB B] supports us a lot when it comes to marketing initiatives." HUB B supports EXTEND through joint appearances on trade fairs, financial support, and initiatives for product bundling. Similarly, the hub's social capital has played a role when EXTEND decided to partner with HUB B. "[HUB B]'s name and reputation is a huge asset for us." Interestingly, the partnership with HUB B is not communicated on EXTEND's website. Taken together, while the perceived complementarity of HUB B's technological complementarity is low, it is on a medium level for its commercial and social capital.

The interview revealed that a substantial part of the knowledge transfer – particularly regarding marketing and sales initiatives – is obtained through IOS deployed by HUB B. EXTEND's director stated that "we obtain a lot of information through [HUB B]'s information systems. But that's more a unidirectional information transfer than real communication." Also, the director mentioned that in the second partner network in which EXTEND participates, coordination is achieved more through IOS than it is the case for HUB B's partner network.

In summary, as a consequence of the moderate perceived resource complementarity together with the opportunity to obtain information through IOS offered by HUB B, the organizational coupling aimed at by EXTEND is low. As a result of this low degree of coupling, the threat of opportunistic behavior by HUB B is very low. The empirical examination does not reveal any threat of HUB B competing with EXTEND. HUB B was also found to not be particularly reluctant to share resources with EXTEND. The director of EXTEND mentioned that the company is dependent on HUB B, but does not see this as a critical issues. S/he added that "[HUB B] is a huge company, sometimes things take longer to be done." Yet, again, this is not seen as a critical issue.

The partnership with HUB B is advantageous for EXTEND, because it provides the spoke with access to external resources and capabilities, particularly regarding marketing and sales. The director explained that the expectations were rather low and added that considering these limited expectations, the partnership can be seen as a success. From a more objective point of view, EXTEND did not grow or advance to higher partnership levels since its foundation. Moreover, EXTEND's focus tends to be more on the second platform vendor with which the company maintains a partnership.

Summing up, the partnership with HUB B provides advantages to EXTEND at a rather low cost and with limited risks. However, it cannot be considered an overwhelming success. The reason for this might be that the complementarity between EXTEND's and HUB B's resources and capabilities is actually higher than perceived by EXTEND. For instance, the interviewee does not mention the partner's ability to innovate architectures. However, since EXTEND's business model is to adjust the solutions developed by HUB B, the innovative capability can be considered crucial for EXTEND. Through a higher degree of organizational coupling, EXTEND might be able to benefit more by getting access to information about technological issues, particular about new solutions. On the other hand, such a strategy of higher organizational coupling might be unfeasible when maintaining two partnerships with platform vendors and could result in the necessity to focus on one partnership and hence increase the dependency and the threat of opportunistic behavior.

5.2.2.7 Summary

The analyzed case companies within the partnership network of HUB B differ substantially, both in terms of the degree of organizational coupling, as well as regarding partnership success. Interestingly, the partnerships of MANUFACTURE, ANALYSIS, ONTOLOGY, and EXTEND are successful despite a low degree of organizational coupling. In contrast, PROJECT and WORKFLOW tied their businesses very closely to HUB B by investing in partner-specific resources and by establishing and maintaining personal contacts for an informal coordination of the partnership. While WORKFLOW benefits from a high degree of organizational coupling and has established a successful partnership with HUB B, PROJECT faces the negative implications that result from over-investing in partner-specific resources and personal networks.

One of the reasons why some of the spoke organizations manage to be successful in the partnership without a high degree of organizational coupling is the fact that they benefit from using the institutionalized coordination mechanisms offered by HUB B. Interestingly, these institutionalized coordination mechanisms do not only comprise inter-organizational information systems, but also include a dedicated partnership manager who is the main contact person for the spoke organizations. Through this personal but institutionalized channel, the successful spoke organizations obtain access to external resources and capabilities.

By means of a cross-case analysis, the following section discusses and explains commonalities and differences among spoke organizations and the implications for organizational coupling and partnership success.

5.3 Results from cross-case analysis

After having presented the analyzed spoke organizations in isolation, this section provides an aggregated discussion of the cases. The goal is to examine if the explanatory models are able to explain commonalities and differences among the cases and hence achieve analytical generalization. Also, the discussion sheds light on differences at a network level, that is, between the two analyzed hub-and-spoke networks.

In addition, as a result of the aggregated analysis, the models are refined and extended. In particular, the roles of perceived and actual complementarity between the hub's and spoke's resources and capabilities are studied in more detail. The cross-case analysis is structured according to the explanatory models. First, the influencing factors of the way how spokes coordinate the partnership are examined. Then, the determinants of partnership success are studied, paying particular attention to the role of perceived versus actual resource complementarity.

5.3.1 Coordination

5.3.1.1 Perceived complementarity and coordination

In line with the results of this study's exploratory phase, the single-case analysis confirmed that the complementarity of the hub's resources and capabilities as perceived by the spoke indeed plays an important role in deciding about the degree of organizational coupling with the hub. The cases clarify that spokes invest in partner-specific assets and informal governance mechanisms in order to actually benefit from the potential that they see in the complementarity of the partner's resources.

Previous literature proposed three groups of external resources and capabilities: technological, commercial, and social capital (Ahuja, 2000). Interestingly, this taxonomy of external resources and capabilities was found to be not applicable to the link between perceived resource complementarity and organizational coupling without further adjustments.

While being an important reason to participate in a partnership with a hub organization as theorized, the empirical data shows that the hub's reputation does not influence the degree of organizational coupling aimed at by spokes. Figure 5.1 compares the complementarity of the hub's social capital (i.e., the hub's reputation) as perceived by the analyzed spokes with the level of hub-specific investments and informal governance, that is the degree of organizational coupling.

The comparison suggests that the degree of organizational coupling is independent of the hub's reputation. In particular, all spoke organizations – except MEDIA which is well-known in its small group of potential customers – perceive the complementarity of the hub's reputation to be rather high. However, being a certified partner of the respective hub organization was found to be sufficient to actually benefit from the hub's reputation. Spokes do not communicate the intensity of the partnership to the customers, but simply use the hub's brand name and logo as a marketing tool to signal trustworthiness, compatibility, and reliability. In other words, in order to benefit from the hub's reputation, spokes only have to participate in the partnership. A higher degree of organizational coupling does not increase the benefits resulting from the hub's reputation.

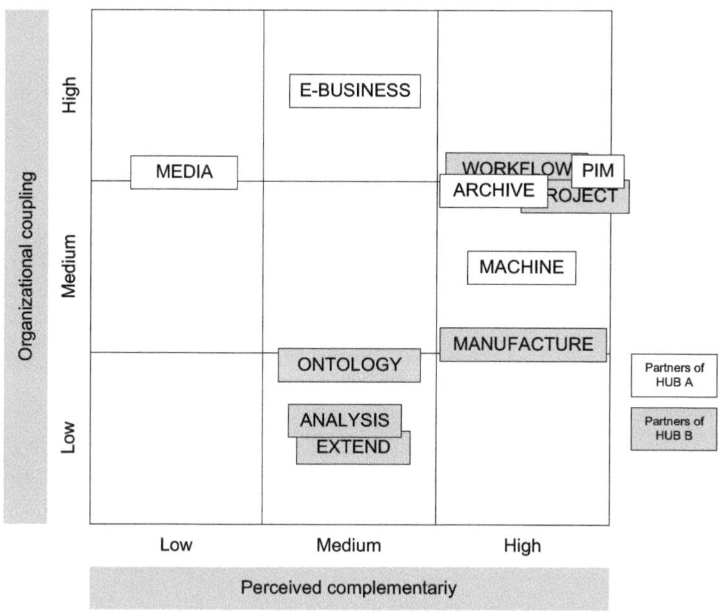

Figure 5.1: Perceived complementarity of hub's reputation and organizational coupling

While the hub's reputation does not influence the spokes' decision on a certain degree of organizational coupling, the empirical results show that the perceived complementarity of the hub's technological and commercial capital indeed increases the degree of organizational coupling aimed at by spokes. Figure 5.2 compares the average degree of complementarity of the hub's technological and commercial capital as perceived by the spokes with the the degree of organizational coupling aimed at by spokes. As suggested in Proposition 1 of the explanatory model developed above, a higher degree of perceived resource complementarity indeed leads to a higher degree of organizational coupling.

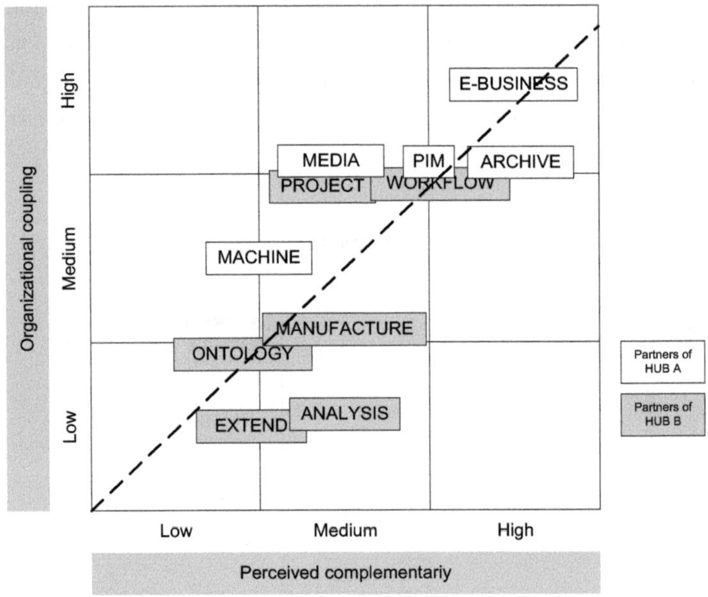

Figure 5.2: Perceived complementarity of technological, commercial capital and organizational coupling

The data analysis revealed that some spokes perceive the benefits resulting from the hub's ability to address broad markets to be high. These spokes were found to aim at a tight coupling with the partner, in particular by investing in informal contacts to the hub's marketing and sales department. In contrast, other complementors saw only minor advantages from joined marketing efforts. Consequently, these spokes invested less in hub-specific resources in the area of marketing.

The same was found to be true for the hub's technological capital. Interestingly, the empirical results show that a more fine-grained categorization is necessary in order to study the diverse reasons why spokes enter close and intense partnerships with a hub. In particular, spokes were found to not only benefit from the hub's capability to currently provide comprehensive, integrated systems. Instead, some interviewees also stressed the complementarity regarding the hub's future-oriented capability to innovate these systems.

The capabilities to provide an integrated system refer to the exploitation of the potential of an existing system that has been defined by the hub organization. Indeed, all spokes were found to depend on the existence of a comprehensive system in order to be able to market their own piece of software that provides niche functionality. Some interviewees stressed that their companies critically depend on the access to external knowledge about the functioning of the platform and its interfaces. To ensure the access to hub-specific technological knowledge and actually benefit from the hub's technological capital, these spokes were found to invest heavily in partner-specific knowledge accumulation and in establishing personal, informal channels to hub personnel. Other spokes that perceived the benefits resulting from external technological knowledge to be lower chose a lower degree of organizational coupling.

This rather short term-oriented "synchronic" capability differs from the long term capability to introduce incrementally or radically new systems. Such a future-oriented ability to innovate has been referred to as "diachronic" systems integration capabilities (Prencipe, 2004; Hagedoorn, 1993; Chesbrough and Teece, 1996).

Previous work argued that for industries which are characterized by a modular mode of operation, innovation at the component and at the system level can be distinguished (Henderson and Clark, 1990). While component innovations accrue within the boundaries of a module, system innovations are affecting the general structure by which the components are bound together to form a coherent system. A prominent and recent example for such an innovation at the system level can be seen in the emergence of SOA as a new system architecture.

System innovations require the capability to understand interdependencies between the different components as well as the functionality of the entire system

(Henderson and Clark, 1990). In other words, these system innovations are not confined to the narrowly circumscribed components in which the small companies specialize. The empirical results show that small spoke organizations face difficulties in developing innovations on the system level.

In contrast, in order to stay competitive in the systems competition with rival vendors, hub organizations have to continuously advance the overall system. It is important to stress that not only particular innovative products or services turn firms into attractive partners, but the capability to constantly invent new products and services and to bring them to market (Teece et al., 1997). Spokes were found to aim at providing a module of a comprehensive and innovative system that fulfills and will fulfill the changing customer requirements. This can be achieved through partnering with hub organizations.

The data suggests that those spokes that perceive the advantages resulting from the hub's ability to innovate architectures to be particularly high indeed aim at a higher degree of organizational coupling. Through increasing the degree of organizational coupling, spokes aim at accessing up-to-date knowledge about future products. In contrast, complementors which are indifferent toward the hub's innovativeness were found to aim at a relatively lower degree of coupling.

To sum up, the aggregated analysis of the case companies generally substantiates Proposition 1. However, the findings from the refinement phase suggest that while the hub's reputation does not play a role regarding the coordination of hub-and-spoke partnership, the hub's technological capital needs to be subdivided into the hub's synchronic and its diachronic technological capital in order to capture the link between perceived complementarity and organizational coupling in a comprehensive way. Taken together, the following propositions are put forth:

Proposition 1a: The higher the degree of complementarity of the hub's capability to provide integrated systems as perceived by the spoke, the higher is the spoke's organizational coupling with the hub.

Proposition 1b: The higher the degree of complementarity of the hub's capability to innovate system architecture as perceived by the spoke, the higher is the spoke's organizational coupling with the hub.

Proposition 1c: The higher the degree of complementarity of the hub's capability to provide access to broad markets as perceived by the spoke, the higher is the spoke's organizational coupling with the hub.

5.3.1.2 Knowledge-sharing routines

The single-case analysis showed that in some cases, the availability of an IOS that provides appropriate and high-quality information indeed reduces the need for a high degree of organizational coupling while still benefiting from external, complementary resources and capabilities. However, when analyzing all cases, a consistent pattern of a moderating effect does not emerge. Figure 5.3 compares the perceived complementarity of external technological and commercial capital with the degree of organizational coupling for three different levels of the availability of IOS. If the availability of IOS did moderate the proposed link as theorized above, then the slope of the linear trend (see dashed line) should decrease with increasing availability of appropriate IOS. In contrast, the graphs show that for all three levels, the slope of the linear trend is rather consistent, suggesting a refinement of the explanatory model.

When examining the empirical data in more detail, an interesting commonality among complementors that participate in the network of HUB B emerges. While some of HUB B's partner firms use IOS to obtain relevant information and some do not, all spokes that participate in HUB B's network mentioned that HUB B assigned an official partnership manager as a contact person. All interviewees explained that the personal contact to this partnership manager helps access complementary resources and capabilities that reside within the partner firm. In contrast, partners of HUB A did not mention the role of such an official partnership manager in accessing external resources and capabilities.

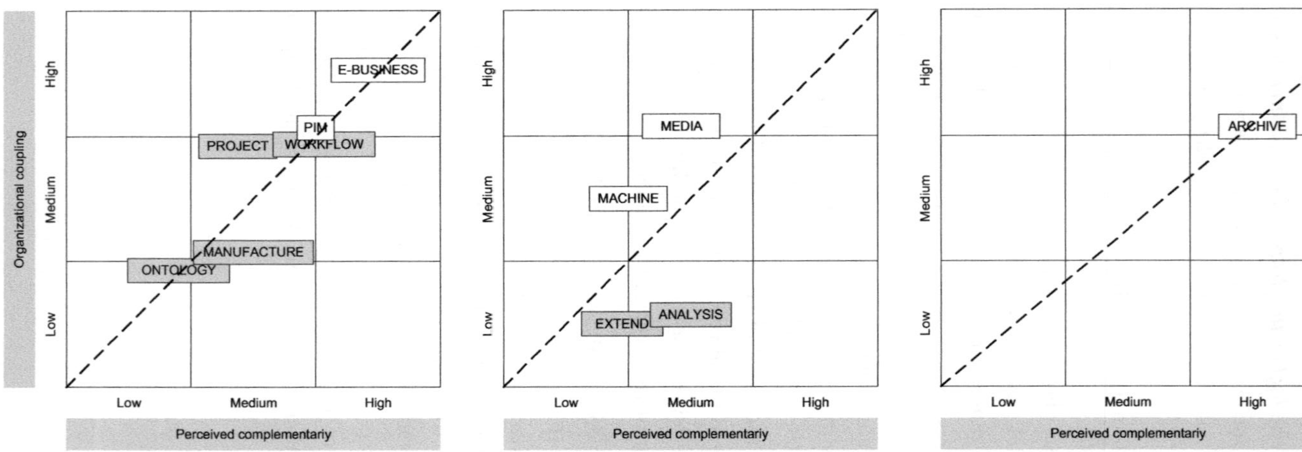

(a) Low level of availability of IOS (b) Medium level of availability of IOS (c) High level of availability of IOS

Figure 5.3: Perceived complementarity of technological, commercial capital and organizational coupling for different levels of availability of IOS

Previous literature has discussed the role of such "boundary spanners" (Sydow and Windeler, 2003) in the context of inter-firm arrangements in the enterprise software industry (Huber et al., 2010). It has been argued that with the help of these boundary spanning organizational units, hubs may be able to resolve the tension between formal and informal control that results from the asymmetry between hub and spokes. While on a macro level, hubs set the basic rules and structures for efficiently coordinating the network, personal trust is fostered on a micro-level through personal coordination (Huber et al., 2010). The empirical findings of this study support the result of previous work that through institutionalized personal coordination, the threat of opportunistic behavior by hubs as perceived by the spokes can be decreased (Huber et al., 2010). Interestingly, the impact of institutionalized personal coordination on the threat of opportunistic behavior was found to be indirect: By establishing boundary-spanning units, partners are enabled to access complementary resources and capabilities without the need for a high degree of organizational coupling, which in turn reduces the threat of opportunistic behavior.

In other words, the empirical data suggests that personal contacts to the official partnership manager may play a similar role as IOS. Thus, the explanatory model may explain the coordination of hub-and-spoke partnerships in a better way when considering this institutionalized personal information transfer. Hence, the model is refined in that the availability of both appropriate IOS and institutionalized personal coordination means are subsumed under the construct "inter-firm knowledge-sharing routines." In line with extant work, inter-firm knowledge-sharing routine can be defined as a regular pattern of inter-firm interactions that allows for transferring, recombining, and creating specialized knowledge (Dyer and Singh, 1998; Grant, 1996a). In other words, inter-firm knowledge-sharing routines are "institutionalized inter-firm processes that are purposefully designed to facilitate knowledge exchange between alliance partners" (Dyer and Singh, 1998).

It should be stressed that the institutionalized personal coordination mechanisms established by a hub organization conceptually differ from the personal coordination that spokes strive for when increasing the degree of organizational coupling. The institutionalized boundary-spanners can be perceived as a standardized communication channel as opposed to the ad-hoc communication that spokes were proposed to aim at if perceived complementarity is high. In other words, hubs and spokes aim at different forms of mutual adjustment which have been discussed in literature (Kieser and Walgenbach, 2007). Spokes that strive for a higher degree of organizational coupling try to establish a flexible case-by-case adjustment that does not follow specifically structured rules (Kieser and Walgenbach, 2007, p. 112).

Case company	**Inter-orgnizational information system**	**Institutionalized personal coordination**	**Knowledge-sharing routines**
MACHINE	Medium	Low	Low-Medium
MEDIA	Medium	Low	Low-Medium
ARCHIVE	High	Low	Medium
PIM	Low	Low	Low
E-BUSINESS	Low	Low	Low
PROJECT	Low	High	Medium
WORKFLOW	Low	High	Medium
MANU-FACTURE	Low	High	Medium
ANALYSIS	Medium	High	Medium-High
ONTOLOGY	Low	High	Medium
EXTEND	Medium	High	Medium-High

Table 5.4: Knowledge-sharing routines

In contrast, hubs may try to avoid such a coordination through a network of personal contacts by establishing an institutionalized interaction as a communication channel to "discuss and clarify any kind of problem that requires coordination" (Kieser and Walgenbach, 2007, p. 113, translated from German). In doing so, hubs may enable an effective knowledge-sharing routine that satisfies the spokes' request for personal coordination, while still being able to establish a large partnership network in a structured way and at reasonable costs.

Table 5.4 shows the level of availability of appropriate IOS as inferred from the single-case study (compare Appendix 2). In addition, the table shows the degree of institutionalized personal coordination that is different in the hub-and-spoke networks of HUB A (low degree of institutionalized personal coordination) and HUB B (high degree of institutionalized personal coordination). The last column of Table 5.4 shows the average of both constructs, that is the level of appropriate inter-firm knowledge-sharing routines.

Similar to Figure 5.3, Figure 5.4 compares the perceived complementarity of external resources and capabilities with the degree of organizational coupling for three different levels of the the new construct "knowledge-sharing routines", that is the aggregation of the availability of appropriate IOS and institutionalized personal coordination mechanisms.

The empirical data indeed suggests that this new construct moderates the link between perceived resource complementarity and the degree of organizational coupling. The higher the level of appropriate inter-firm knowledge-sharing routines is, the weaker is the impact of perceived resource complementarity on the degree of organizational coupling. This is illustrated by the linear trend line that has a decreasing slope if the level of inter-firm knowledge-sharing routines increases. Taken together, this leads to the following revised propositions:

> *Proposition 2a: The more appropriate inter-firm knowledge-sharing routines (IOS and institutionalized personal coordination) are in place, the weaker is the proposed positive link between the degree of perceived complementarity of the hub's capability to provide integrated systems and the degree of organizational coupling.*

> *Proposition 2b: The more appropriate inter-firm knowledge-sharing routines (IOS and institutionalized personal coordination) are in place, the weaker is the proposed positive link between the degree of perceived complementarity of the hub's capability to innovate system architecture and the degree of organizational coupling.*

> *Proposition 2c: The more appropriate inter-firm knowledge-sharing routines (IOS and institutionalized personal coordination) are in place, the weaker is the proposed positive link between the degree of perceived complementarity of the hub's capability to provide access to broad markets and the degree of organizational coupling.*

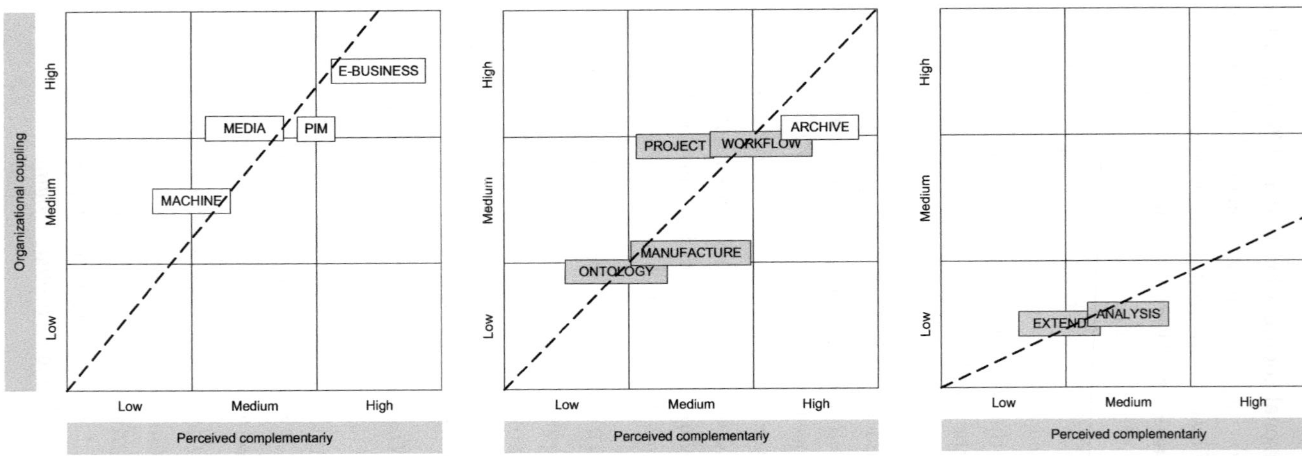

(a) Low and low-medium level of knowledge-sharing routines (b) Medium level of knowledge-sharing routines (c) Medium-high and high level of knowledge-sharing routines

Figure 5.4: Perceived complementarity of technological, commercial capital and organizational coupling for different levels of knowledge-sharing routines

5.3.1.3 Organizational coupling and opportunism

The stories of the single cases confirmed the finding from this study's exploratory phase that a higher degree of organizational coupling increases the perceived threat of opportunism, that is, the threat that the hub may decide to compete with its partner or be reluctant to share resources and capabilities.

This observation is in line with well-established results from previous literature (Williamson, 1981). Specifically, a high level of hub-specific investments results in a lock-in situation because complementors realize that these partner-specific investments would be lost in case of a termination of the partnership, for example if the complementor had to establish a similar partnership with another hub. This lock-in situation increases the threat of opportunistic behavior by the hub as perceived by the spokes.

Interestingly, as theorized above, instead of loosening the partnership when faced with a threat of opportunistic behavior, spokes were found to even increase the degree of organizational coupling with the hub. In order to avoid the hub from behaving opportunistically, the empirical data indeed suggests that the spokes tie their business even closer to their partner by establishing informal governance mechanisms. Specifically, spokes seek to obtain information about future extensions of the hub's product portfolio that potentially overlaps with the spokes offerings. Moreover, spokes try to re-assure the access to external resources through personal ties with hub employees. Figure 5.5 compares the degree of organizational coupling with the perceived threat of opportunistic behavior. The graph shows that the analyzed case companies are located on the diagonal, that is, the degree of organizational coupling and the perceived threat of opportunistic behavior are closely aligned. This observation supports Proposition 3 and 4 as suggested in the explanatory models.

5.3.2 Partnership success

5.3.2.1 Complementarity, layer overlap, and partnership success

The empirical results so far suggest that complementors may misjudge the potential benefits resulting from complementarity, that is, complementors may perceive a degree of complementarity between the partners' resources that deviates from

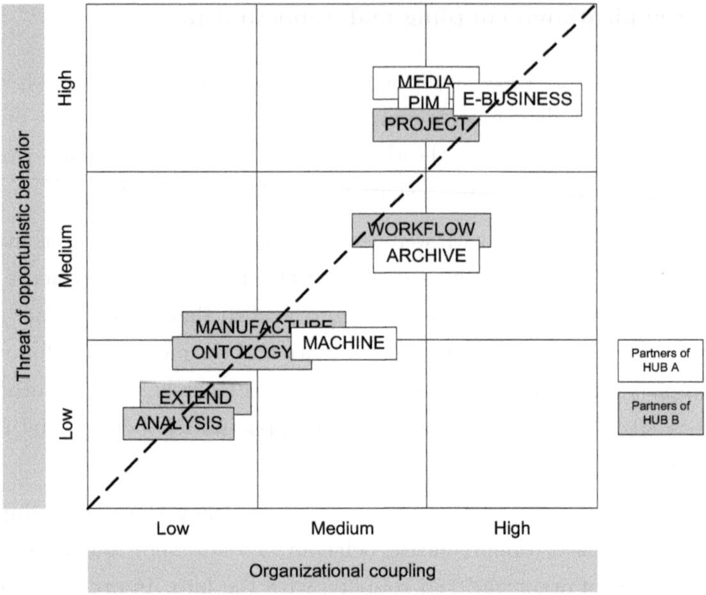

Figure 5.5: Degree of organizational coupling and perceived threat of opportunistic behavior

the actual degree of complementarity. The findings suggest that in order to establish successful hub-and-spoke partnerships, it is crucial for spokes not to over- or underestimate the complementarity of own resources and capabilities and those of the hub organizations. In particular, spokes that establish a level of organizational coupling that fits with the degree of resource complementarity seem to be especially successful. However, the question arises as to what determines the *actual* complementarity of resources and capabilities as opposed to the complementarity *perceived* by the spokes, that is how actual complementarity can be conceptualized.

In line with previous findings, the empirical results suggest that there is a link between complementarity on the product level and complementarity of resources and capabilities when explaining partnership success (Kude et al., 2012). The following section discusses the interplay of product-level and resource complementarity in the context of this study.

Layer overlap	Low	Medium	High
Case company	PROJECT WORKFLOW MANUFACTURE ANALYSIS ONTOLOGY EXTEND	MACHINE ARCHIVE	MEDIA PIM E-BUSINESS

Table 5.5: Layer overlap in the software stack between complementors and their respective partner

When examining the profiles of the analyzed spoke companies as shown in Table 5.1 in more detail, it becomes apparent that they vary substantially. While some spoke organizations provide middleware solutions, others focus on business applications. Comparing the spokes' and the hubs' position within the layers of the software stack (see Figure 2.1), it can be observed that the solutions of some spokes overlap to a greater extent with the core business of the respective hub than others, indicating a low level of product complementarity (Gao and Iyer, 2006; Milgrom and Roberts, 1995).

For example, MEDIA offers business applications for the media industry that are closely integrated with the enterprise applications of HUB A. Thus, layer overlap in the enterprise software stack between MEDIA and HUB A can be assumed to be high. As another example, ARCHIVE provides archiving solutions that complement HUB A's enterprise software. Specifically, it connects HUB A's platform to database systems and therefore acts on the middleware layer. Given that HUB A mainly focuses on the application layer, but also offers middleware solutions, a medium layer overlap between HUB A and ARCHIVE can be assumed. WORKFLOW provides application software based on HUB B's middleware platform. Since HUB B focuses on middleware solutions, layer overlap between WORKFLOW and HUB B is rather low. Table 5.5 shows the layer overlap between the analyzed spokes and the respective hub as inferred from the expert interviews and the companies' websites.

The empirical data suggests that the actual complementarity between the spoke's and hub's resources and capabilities depends on the degree of product-level complementarity between hub and spoke. Specifically, a re-examination of the data suggests an interaction effect between product-level complementarity and the hub's capability to provide integrated systems, its capability to innovate system architectures, as well as its capability to access broad markets.

Interestingly, the direction of the effect of layer overlap (i.e., product-level complementarity) on the link between hub capabilities and partnership success was found to be different for the three types of capabilities. The analysis of this study's qualitative data enables an exploration of theoretical links between constructs, but not a comparison of the strengths of these links. Therefore, the proposed interaction effects result from an in-depth analysis of qualitative data.

Since an empirical analysis of the hub organizations and their strengths with respect to different types of capabilities was not part of this study, the level of technological and commercial capital of the hub organization was assumed to be the same for the two hubs. By elaborating on the interaction effects between the layer overlap and the hub's technological and commercial capital, the following discussion provides a suggestion on how to theorize about the notion of actual complementarity (as opposed to the complementarity perceived by the spokes).

Hub's capability to provide integrated systems. The empirical analysis showed that the extent to which the hub's capability to provide integrated systems increases partnership success varied considerably among spokes. While some complementors benefited substantially from the hub's synchronic technological capital, the hub's capability to provide integrated systems played a minor role for other spokes.

A re-examination of the cases shows that those complementors that act on the same layer as the respective hub tended to benefit to a larger extent from the hub's capability to provide integrated systems, thus increasing partnership success. The reason for this can be seen in the fact that the products of companies that act on similar layers in the software stack tend to be designed in a less modular way than those acting on distinct layers. The products of partners on different layers are usually connected via standardized interfaces. This was not always the case for companies that act on the same layer in the software stack model, increasing the need for getting access to know-how about the functioning of the platform.

The products of ONTOLOGY and EXTEND interact with HUB B's platform only via highly standardized interfaces. While the availability of the comprehensive platform is of utmost importance for the spokes in order to sell their own complementary niche functionality, the access to technological know-how about the functioning of the platform was not found to influence partnership success. In contrast, MEDIA acts on the same layer as HUB A. As a consequence, the solutions of MEDIA and HUB A are highly intertwined, resulting in a high need for platform-specific know-how for the partnership to be successful.

Hub's capability to innovate system architectures. A re-examination of the cases in light of the discovered differences in layer overlap suggests that those partners whose products did not overlap with the hub's solution were able to especially benefit from the hub's capability to innovate system architectures. The reason for this can be seen in the fact that for spokes that act on a different layer than the hub, architectural innovations often provide the basis for own innovations on a modular level. In contrast, spokes that act on the same layer as their partner often aim at providing functionality that is missing in the hub's system and that might be addressed by architectural innovations.

For example, WORKFLOW and HUB B have a low degree of layer overlap because HUB B offers middleware solutions and WORKFLOW focuses on providing application functionality. Therefore, architectural innovations by the hub were found to be rather beneficial for WORKFLOW. Even though these innovations may result in additional effort for WORKFLOW because its e-business, groupware, and portal solutions may have to be adjusted to the idiosyncrasies of new releases of HUB B's platform, such platform innovations give WORKFLOW the chance to innovate on a modular level and come up with new products that attract customers.

However, even though all analyzed spokes acknowledged the hub's innovative capability, it did not strengthen the success of the partnership in those cases where layer overlap was high. For instance, the hub's system-level innovativeness was seen as less beneficial in the case of MEDIA, which acts on the same layer as HUB A (high layer overlap). MEDIA fills gaps in HUB A's product portfolio by providing additional functionalities specific to the media industry that are missing in HUB A's industry solution. Therefore, MEDIA does not benefit from architectural innovations that may close these gaps in HUB A's products.

Hub's capability to access broad markets. The empirical data also revealed that the level of product-level complementarity changed the extent to which the hub's commercial capital was beneficial for the analyzed spokes. For some spokes, the provided access to broad markets substantially increased partnership success, while for others it played a secondary role. The reason for this may be seen in the fact that if a spoke operates on the same layer as the respective hub, then the spoke is able to particularly make use of the hub's marketing channels. This is because both partners address very similar markets and target groups, such as similar procurement managers and users within potential customer organizations. In contrast, if the hub and spoke operate on different layers, then it is more difficult to align and combine marketing campaigns. Thus, the impact of the hub's commercial capital on partnership success is not as high as in the case of high layer overlap.

For example, PROJECT shows a rather low level of layer overlap with HUB B's middleware platform. Accordingly, the benefits obtained from HUB B's marketing activities were rather low, since they were directed to the middleware rather than to specific software applications such as the one offered by PROJECT. Interestingly, PROJECT initially perceived the complementarity of HUB B's commercial capital to be higher, but then realized that these expectations regarding marketing support were too high.

The picture was different for those spokes that show a higher degree of layer overlap with the respective hub, such as E-BUSINESS with HUB A. The e-business suite of E-BUSINESS is closely integrated with the enterprise software system of HUB A. In fact, as e-business functionality becomes more important for customers, HUB A actively informs customers that this functionality is available through its partner E-BUSINESS. E-BUSINESS was able to increase its sales in the company's start-up phase via its partnership with HUB A. According to the interviewee, this would not have been possible otherwise. Similarly, PIM was able to gain broad market access by tapping into the hub's distribution and sales network.

Summing up, the empirical results suggest that the hub's capabilities to provide integrated systems, to innovate these systems, to provide access to broad markets, as well as the hub's reputation increase the success of hub-and-spoke partnerships from the complementors' perspective. However, some of these links are moderated by the level of product complementarity. While a high level of layer overlap in the software stack model strengthens the positive effect of the hub's capabilities to provide integrated systems and to address broad markets on partnership success, it decreases the positive influence of the hub's capability to innovate system architectures on success. Taken together, the following revised propositions are put forth in order to refine the explanatory model.

> *Proposition 5a: The more a hub possesses the capability to provide integrated systems, the higher is the success of a spoke's partnership with this particular hub.*

> *Proposition 5b: The more a hub possesses the capability to innovate system architecture, the higher is the success of a spoke's partnership with this particular hub.*

> *Proposition 5b: The more a hub possesses the capability to provide access to broad markets, the higher is the success of a spoke's partnership with this particular hub.*

> *Proposition 5d: The better a hub's reputation in the market, the higher is the success of a spoke's partnership with this particular hub.*

> *Proposition 6a: The more the solutions of hub and spoke overlap in the software stack, the stronger is the positive influence of the hub's capability to provide integrated systems on partnership success from the spoke's perspective.*

> *Proposition 6b: The more the solutions of hub and spoke overlap in the software stack, the weaker is the positive influence of the hub's capability to innovate system architecture on partnership success from the spoke's perspective.*

> *Proposition 6c: The more the solutions of hub and spoke overlap in the software stack, the stronger is the positive influence of the hub's capability to provide access to broad markets on partnership success from the spoke's perspective.*

5.3.2.2 Organizational coupling and partnership success

The findings of the exploratory phase suggested that the influence of a higher degree of organizational coupling on the success of hub-and-spoke partnerships from the spokes' perspective is twofold. It was proposed that on the one hand, organizational coupling strengthens the link between resource complementarity and partnership success. On the other hand, the exploratory analysis suggested that due to the high cost and effort associated with a higher degree of organizational coupling as well as an increased threat of opportunistic behavior, partnership success is lowered.

As a result of this study's qualitative nature, a cross-case comparison of cases with respect to these two opposing theoretical links is unfeasible due to the lack of data about the strength of the relationships. Despite this characteristic of a qualitative, exploratory approach, the second phase of empirical analysis generally corroborated the findings. The case studies have shown that through investing in hub-specific resources and capabilities and informal governance mechanisms, the benefits resulting from the hub's technological and commercial capital, and thus the partnership success, increase substantially. For instance, the case study of ARCHIVE shows that via extensive hub-specific investments, ARCHIVE is able to gain access to important information, such as technological know-how about current and future products as well as the partner's future product portfolio. As a result, ARCHIVE's partnership with HUB A is very successful. In contrast, the case of EXTEND shows the negative consequences of under-investing in partner-specific resources. As discussed above, by investing more in resources and capabilities specific to HUB B, EXTEND may increase partnership success.

As discussed above, spokes are enabled to tap into the hub's reputation independent of the partnership intensity. Hence, the degree of organizational coupling does not influence the link between the hub's reputation and partnership success. Accordingly, the following propositions are put forth:

> *Proposition 6d: The higher the degree of a spoke's organizational coupling with a platform vendor, the stronger is the positive influence of the hub's capability to provide integrated systems on the partnership success from the spoke's perspective.*

Proposition 6e: The higher the degree of a spoke's organizational coupling with a platform vendor, the stronger the positive influence of the hub's capability to innovate system architecture on the partnership success from the spoke's perspective.

Proposition 6f: The higher the degree of a spoke's organizational coupling with a platform vendor, the stronger the positive influence of the hub's capability to provide access to broad markets on the partnership success from the spoke's perspective.

The case studies corroborate the finding that a high degree of organizational coupling also has adverse consequences for the success of a partnership. That is, the empirical results substantiate Proposition 7. For example, the case of WORKFLOW shows that a lot of time and effort may be necessary to establish informal governance mechanisms. In addition to the mere costs that directly result from a close cooperation, the empirical results show that – in line with previous research, particularly TCE – a high degree of organizational coupling indeed increases the threat of opportunistic behavior by the hub. In other words, partnership success is lowered by the costs that result from engaging in a close partnership with the hub organization.

In contrast, the case of ANALYSIS exemplifies that if a spoke organization is able to obtain access to external resources without extensive partner-specific investments and informal coordination mechanisms, the success of the partnership increases – simply because lower costs arise from partnering.

Interestingly, however, the findings show considerable differences regarding the intensity of this link. For instance, PIM, MEDIA, ARCHIVE and WORKFLOW have all tied their businesses closely to HUB A and invested heavily in hub-specific resources and capabilities. Yet, while the hub's innovativeness, that may lead to a situation of competition with HUB A in certain areas, was found to be an opportunity to come up with new innovations for ARCHIVE and WORKFLOW, this potential competition was found to be a tremendous threat by MEDIA and PIM. Also, the threat of the hub being reluctant to share resources was found to be higher in the cases of PIM and MEDIA than it was for ARCHIVE and WORKFLOW.

Analyzing these observations in more detail, it becomes apparent that the level of product-complementarity as described above also influences the extent to which organizational coupling decreases partnership success. In particular, the empirical data suggests that hub organizations are more likely to act opportunistically if the solutions of hub and spoke overlap in the software stack model. The following section will elaborate on this insight.

If the solutions of hub and spoke overlap in the software stack, it is more likely that the hub enters a situation of competition with that particular spoke. More specifically, if hub and spoke act on the same layer, platform innovations by the hub are more prone to render the spoke's solution obsolete because the innovated platform may include functionality that was previously lacking and that was the basis of the spoke's business model. This observation is exemplified by the cases PIM, MEDIA, ARCHIVE and WORKFLOW.

PIM has a high layer overlap with HUB A (see Table 5.5), since its product information management solution clearly overlaps with HUB A's core business on the application layer. PIM used to develop application functionality in a niche market that was different from that of HUB A. Thus, the application software of PIM went beyond HUB A's comprehensive enterprise software system. However, a company that was recently acquired by HUB A came up with a very similar solution, raising questions about the sustainability of the partnership and causing a serious threat to PIM's business model. The CEO of PIM commented "without doubt, this makes it very difficult for us to build up a real strategic partnership."

Similarly, the hub's system-level innovativeness was seen as problematic in the case of MEDIA, which acts on the same layer as HUB A (high layer overlap). MEDIA decided to provide complementary functionality specific to the media and newspaper industry even though HUB A offers a version of its enterprise software system that is tailored to the needs of the media industry itself. Although MEDIA has successfully been developing niche functionality for the media industry for more than 20 years, MEDIA struggles when decisions on the investment of developing new functionality have to be made. MEDIA's head of product development framed it in the following way: "There is always a high risk to invest in the development of new functionality because [HUB A] may decide to include it into its solution." As a consequence, there is a constant threat of obsolescence, because future releases of HUB A's enterprise system may wipe out the competitive advantage that MEDIA currently maintains in certain fields.

In contrast, if layer overlap is low, the positive impact of the hub's innovativeness is strengthened. For example, WORKFLOW and HUB B have a very low layer overlap because HUB B offers middleware solutions and WORKFLOW focuses on providing application functionality. Therefore, as discussed previously, architectural innovations by the hub were rather beneficial for WORKFLOW since such platform innovations give WORKFLOW the chance to innovate on a modular level and come up with new products that attract customers.

The solutions of ARCHIVE and HUB A have a medium level of overlap in the software stack (see Table 5.5). As a result, the hub's innovativeness was found to be a double-edged sword for ARCHIVE. This is also acknowledged by ARCHIVE's partnership manager, who stated on the one hand that "[HUB A]'s innovativeness opens opportunities for [ARCHIVE] to develop new software based on these improvements." On the other hand, s/he admitted that "[ARCHIVE] has to be careful. If [HUB A] develops new solutions in the field of archiving, this could overlap with our solutions and render them obsolete."

In addition to the threat of obsolescence, hub organizations were found to be more likely to be reluctant to share resources if the solutions of hub and spoke reside on the same layer in the software stack. The reason for this can be seen in the fact that hubs are unwilling to share knowledge with firms that may turn into competitors. This is well-illustrated by the case of MEDIA, which acts on the same layer as HUB A. Since both HUB A and MEDIA offer solutions for the media industry, HUB A could be expected to be unwilling to share information and knowledge with MEDIA's employees. Indeed, the case study showed that MEDIA struggled to obtain information about future developments of HUB A's platform.

Summing up, a re-examination of the cases in light of the discovered differences in product-level complementarity suggests that the link between the degree of organizational coupling and the success of hub-and-spoke partnerships is moderated by the degree of layer overlap in the software stack. In particular, if the solutions of hub and spoke overlap in the software stack model, the hub organization was found to be more likely to behave opportunistically in competing with the spoke and being reluctant to share resources. Since opportunistic behavior is more harmful in the case of a higher degree of organizational coupling, the following moderator effect is proposed.

> *Proposition 8: The more the solutions of hub and spoke overlap in the software stack, the stronger is the negative influence of the degree of organizational coupling of a spoke on the partnership success from the spoke's perspective.*

5.3.3 Summary

The cross-case analysis showed that generally, the complementarity of the hub's resources and capabilities as perceived by the spokes increase the degree of organizational coupling aimed at by these spokes, thus substantiating Proposition 1. However, two refinements were made based on the cross-case analysis. First, the empirical data revealed that while being an important partnership motive, the perceived complementarity of the hub's reputation did not increase organizational coupling. Second, it was found that when subdividing the hub's technological capital into the hub's synchronic capability to provide an integrated system as well as its diachronic capability to innovate these systems, the model is able to explain partnership behavior in a better way.

Similarly, the case studies revealed that the availability of IOS alone does not moderate the link between perceived complementarity and organizational coupling. Instead, the empirical data suggests that the availability of IOS together with institutionalized personal coordination mechanisms established by the hub is a moderator of the links suggested in Proposition 1a-1c. Hence, a new construct "knowledge-sharing routines" that comprises both IOS and institutionalized personal coordination mechanisms was introduced and suggested as a moderator in the revised propositions P2a-2c.

The link between the degree of organizational coupling and the perceived threat of opportunistic behavior was substantiated by the empirical data. Figure 5.6 shows the refined model that explains the coordination of hub-and-spoke partnerships from a spoke's perspective.

The empirical results also strengthened the original finding that there is a positive influence of the actual complementarity of the partners' resources and capabilities (as opposed to the perceived complementarity) on the partnership success from the spoke's perspective. The model was refined by including an interaction effect between the hub's technological and commercial capital and the complementarity of the solutions offered by hub and spoke – conceptualized as the overlap in the software stack model. Specifically, the degree of layer overlap was found to increase the positive impact of the hub's capability to provide integrated systems (Proposition 6a) and the hub's commercial capital (Proposition 6c) on partnership success. In contrast, the positive link between the hub's capability to innovate system architectures and the success of hub-and-spoke partnerships was found to become weaker with an increase in layer overlap across cases (Proposition 6b).

Moreover, the refinement phase showed that the degree of organizational coupling indeed moderates the link between the hub's technological and social capital and the partnership success (Proposition 6d-f). In contrast, the positive influence of the hub's reputation on partnership success was found to not be influenced by the degree of organizational coupling.

In addition, the refinement phase substantiated the proposed negative link between organizational coupling and partnership success (Proposition 7). Moreover, the explanatory model was refined by introducing a moderator effect. A higher level of layer overlap was proposed to strengthen the negative impact of organizational coupling on partnership success (Proposition 7b). Figure 5.7 shows the revised explanatory model that explains the success of hub-and-spoke partnerships from the spoke's perspective. The following chapter gives an in-depth discussion of these findings.

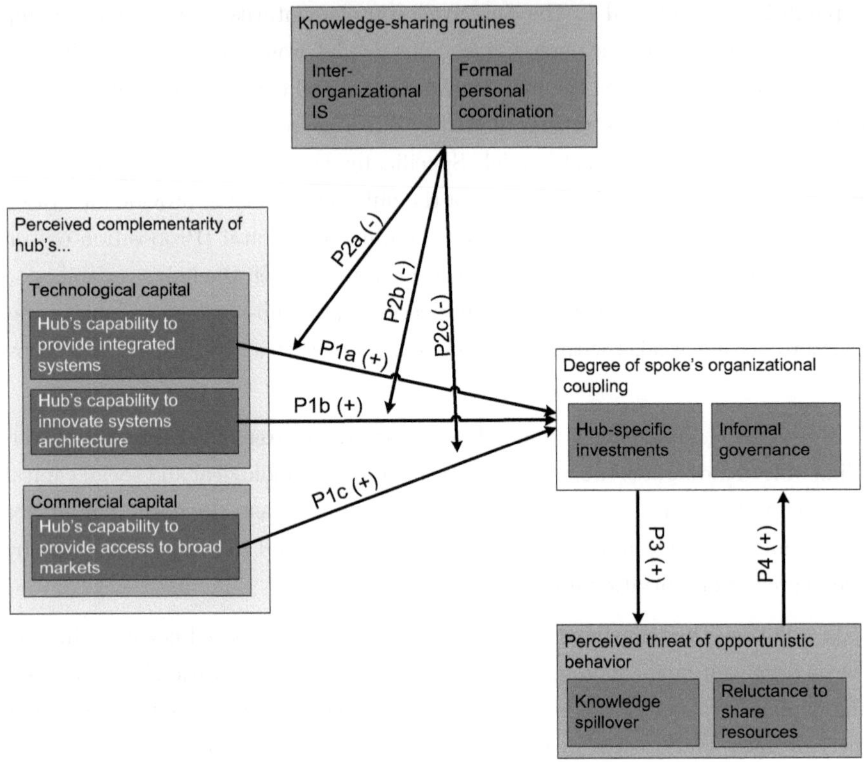

Figure 5.6: Revised model of spoke's organizational coupling

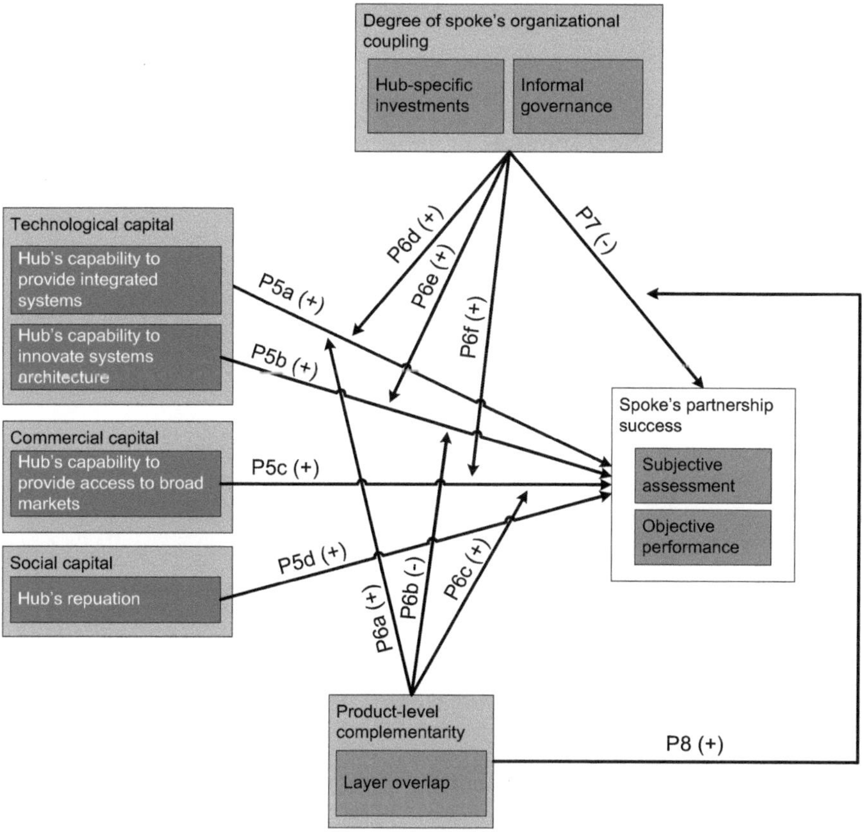

Figure 5.7: Revised model of spoke's partnership success

6 Discussion

This study was motivated by the intention to improve our understanding of how small complementor organizations in the enterprise software industry coordinate the partnership with a larger platform vendor and how these coordination mechanisms may improve partnership success from the complementors' point of view. Previous studies were able to explain the motivation of hubs and spokes respectively to enter partnership networks by analyzing resource complementarities (Huang et al., 2009; Kude et al., 2012; Arndt et al., 2009, 2008; Mathiassen and Vainio, 2007). In addition, the influence of the network structure and the type of link between the partners' products on partnership or network success has been discussed (Gao and Iyer, 2008; Chellappa and Saraf, 2010; Iyer et al., 2006).

This study is the first to examine the role of coordination when examining the link between resource complementarity and partnership success from the spoke organization's point of view. The study draws on theoretical contributions from reference disciplines, such as the RBV (Barney, 1986) and its derivatives (Amit and Schoemaker, 1993; Grant, 1996b; Eisenhardt and Schoonhoven, 1996), the relational view of competitive advantage (Dyer and Singh, 1998), and the RDT (Pfeffer and Salancik, 1978).

This study examines the role of coordination by introducing the degree of organizational coupling that spokes aim at. In doing so, the study makes important theoretical contributions and leads to several managerial implications. This chapter provides an in-depth discussion of these contributions to theory and practice. In addition, this chapter discusses the limitations of this study and provides suggestions for future research.

6.1 Theoretical implications

Based on the previous literature presented in chapter 2, this study offers a number of theoretical contributions, both in the field of IS as well as in adjacent disciplines

(Locke and Golden-Biddle, 1997; Corley and Gioia, 2011). Specifically, the study contributes by providing an understanding of the role of organizational coupling in explaining partnership success, by clarifying how and under which conditions the degree of organizational coupling that spokes aim at varies, and by explaining the moderating role of product-level complementarity when examining partnership success. The following sections elaborate on these contributions.

Understanding the role of organizational coupling in explaining partnership success. This study contributes to extant literature that has analyzed the link between complementarity and partnership success by examining the determinants and implications of organizational coupling. More specifically, it adds to previous work which found that a higher degree of resource complementarity increases partnership success (Gao and Iyer, 2006, 2008; Chellappa et al., 2010; Huang et al., 2009). While these studies provide important insights, the question of how and why complementarity increases partnership success has so far been neglected.

This study fills this gap by introducing coordination mechanisms that help partners get access to external, complementary resources and capabilities. In particular, this research took the perspective of organizations that act as complementors and found that by applying appropriate coordination mechanism, complementors can benefit to a larger extent from the hub's resources and capabilities. The coordination mechanisms applied by spokes were incorporated in an explanatory model as the degree of organizational coupling that these spokes aim at when partnering with a hub, that is the degree to which spokes invest in hub-specific resources and capabilities and aim at substituting formal governance mechanisms by informal ones.

The results show that the effect of organizational coupling on partnership success from the spoke's point of view is not a trivial one. On the one hand, spokes can improve the access to valuable external resources by increasing the degree of organizational coupling. That is, organizational coupling moderates the link between complementary resources and partnership success. On the other hand, organizational coupling also causes costs and effort and thus has a direct, negative effect on partnership success. In particular, the increased threat of opportunistic behavior that results from a higher degree of organizational coupling may countervail the benefits.

The study contributes to extant literature in that it shows that complementarity does not necessarily lead to partnership success. Instead, spokes may have to tie their business closer to the hub in order to benefit from resource complementarity. By considering this interaction effect between resource complementarity and organizational coupling, a spoke's partnership success can be explained in a better way.

By introducing the degree of organizational coupling as a factor that influcnces partnership success, this study contributes to theories drawn from adjacent disciplines, in particular the relational view (Dyer and Singh, 1998) and the RDT (Pfeffer and Salancik, 1978). The explanatory models developed in this study transfer the idea of competitive advantage that results from the close cooperation of organizational actors to the special case of asymmetric hub-and-spoke partnership networks. The relational view of competitive advantage holds that a high degree of organizational coupling of partners together with partners' complementary resource endowments results in the generation of relational rents (Dyer and Singh, 1998). This study corroborates these findings and adds to previous literature through providing a deeper understanding of how and why organizational coupling increases the benefits resulting from complementary resource endowments.

In addition, the study's findings add to the relational view in that they show that partner-specific investments can increase partnership success even if these investments are unilateral as it is the case in hub-and-spoke networks in the enterprise software industry. Given that hub organizations benefit from the network of spokes and usually not from a particular partner, the hub organization's investments were found to be network-specific instead of partner-specific. However, the hub's network-specific investments in knowledge-sharing routines enable the spokes to benefit from the hub's resources by investing reasonably in hub-specific resources and capabilities. Thus, both hub and spoke can benefit from the partnership networks, even though there may be no bilateral investments in partner-specific resources that generate relational rents as proposed by the relational view (Dyer and Singh, 1998).

This study contributes to the literature on the RDT (Pfeffer and Salancik, 1978), which suggests that constraint absorption, that is gaining partial control over external resources, is particularly unlikely if power asymmetry is high, as it is the case in a singular hub-and-spoke partnership (Casciaro and Piskorski, 2005). This study's findings clarify that in hub-and-spoke networks within the enterprise software industry, both hub and spokes are dependent on each other. However, while the spoke unilaterally depends on the hub organizations, the hub critically depends on the network of spokes to offer a wide range of niche functionality. Consequently, hubs were found to aim at constraint absorption to a certain extent by establishing knowledge-sharing routines with the goal of reducing the need for extensive hub-specific investments by its partners in order to maintain and extend its partnership networks.

Explaining varying degrees of organizational coupling. Previous research suggested that hub organization aim at coordinating the partnership network in a loosely-coupled way through standardization of interfaces and communication processes (Chesbrough and Teece, 1996; Kude et al., 2008). This study contributes to extant work on the coordination of separated activities – both in general (e.g., Malone and Crowston, 1994; Mintzberg, 1979; Thompson, 1967) as well as in the case of software development (e.g., Kraut and Streeter, 1995; Staudenmayer, 1997) – in that it provides an understanding of why some spokes strive for increasing the degree of organizational coupling, while others decide to rely on the standardized coordination mechanisms established by the hub organization.

This research is unique in that it distinguishes between the perceived and the actual degree of resource complementarity. The results show that the way how spokes coordinate the partnership with the hub organization, that is the degree of organizational coupling, is influenced by the complementarity of the hub's resources and capabilities as perceived by the spokes (as opposed to the actual degree of resource complementarity). Specifically, the empirical data revealed that if spokes perceive the complementarity of the hub's technological and commercial capital to be high, then these spokes invest more in hub-specific resources and informal governance mechanisms. Thus, they tie their business more closely to the hub.

In line with TCE (Williamson, 1981), a higher degree of organizational coupling reduces the spokes' possibilities to engage in a partnership with alternative hub organizations, thus increasing the threat of opportunistic behavior by the hub. Interestingly, instead of loosening the partnership with the hub and relying on market governance in the face of a high threat of opportunistic behavior, spokes were found to even increase organizational coupling in order to avoid opportunism by applying informal and relational governance (Zaheer and Venkatraman, 1995; Dyer and Singh, 1998). This observation can be traced back to the arguments of the RDT, since spoke organizations that are highly dependent on their larger partner were found to try to improve their position by aiming at informal governance mechanisms, that is by a higher degree of organizational coupling (Pfeffer and Salancik, 1978).

Hence, this study is among the first to be able to explain theoretically why and under which circumstances hub and spoke organizations within the enterprise software industry aim at opposing coordination mechanisms. By introducing the concept of knowledge-sharing routines in explaining varying degrees of organizational coupling, this study also offers means how hub organizations may overcome this tension of standardized versus partner-specific coordination. The study shows that knowledge-sharing routines as discussed in the literature (Dyer and Singh, 1998) comprise two different aspects in the context of hub-and-spoke networks in the software industry: IOS that facilitate knowledge transfer, as well as institutionalized personal governance mechanisms in the form of boundary spanners.

The findings of this study contribute to previous literature on network governance and trust by referring to the concept of institutionalized personal coordination of hub-and-spoke networks within the enterprise software industry (Sydow and Windeler, 1998). By installing boundary-spanning units, hub organization may resolve the aforementioned tension between the hub's preference for standardized coordination and the spokes' goal to establish a high degree of organizational coupling (Huber et al., 2010; Kude et al., 2008).

Moreover, the study provides guidance for a theory-informed design of IOS (Gregor, 2006; Hevner et al., 2004) that help spokes obtain access to important external resources and capabilities at a low cost. To that effect, an IOS that is designed guided by the theoretical insights of this study should not only grant access to resources that are actually complementary, but should take into account the perceptions of spoke organizations regarding valuable and important knowledge. That is, IOS should consider the difference between perceived (subjective) and actual (objective) information need (Heinrich et al., 2010; Wilson, 1999; Dervin and Nilan, 1986). Moreover, in order to avoid information overload, hub organizations should design IOS in a flexible way that enables an adjustment to the needs of the respective user. For example, IOS should focus on providing information about domains in which a certain spoke organization perceives the complementarity to be high, such as market and sales information or technological know-how.

The challenge of designing these systems is that in order to foster successful partnerships, hub organizations should also provide information in the domains where the actual complementarity of hub's and spoke's resources is high. The results of this study offer helpful guidance by providing an understanding of the types of resources and capabilities that different spokes perceive as being complementary and by distinguishing between perceived and actual complementarity.

By introducing the concept of perceived resource complementarity, this study also contributes to the literature on the motives of small and medium-sized enterprise software firms to participate in partnerships with platform vendors. In doing so, this study complements the exiting body of knowledge on the emergence of hub-and-spoke networks which has mostly focused on hub organizations (Lorenzoni and Baden-Fuller, 1995; Shapiro and Varian, 1999; Iansiti and Levien, 2004).

This study builds on previous work that examined specific partnership motives of firms in the enterprise software industry from a resource-oriented perspective (Mathiassen and Vainio, 2007; Huang et al., 2009). While previous research has focused on particular resources and capabilities as motivations to partner, this study considers multiple of these dimensions simultaneously. Based on the broader literature on inter-firm partnerships, four types of resources and capabilities of the hub have been identified that motivate spokes to partner with the hub: (1) the hub's ability to provide integrated systems, (2) the hub's ability to innovate systems, (3) the hub's commercial capital, and (4) the hub's reputation.

The hub's capabilities to provide and innovate systems as well as its commercial capital were found to not only motivate the spoke to participate in hub-and-spoke partnerships, but also to intensify the collaboration with a platform leader by aiming at a high degree of organizational coupling. In contrast, the hub's reputation was found not to influence partnership intensity, but only to motivate spokes to enter partnerships. By means of an in-depth, qualitative analysis, this study contributes to previous work by providing a deeper understanding of what these different types of resources and capabilities mean in the context of enterprise software development.

Explaining the moderating role of product-level complementarity. This study is among the first to simultaneously address the coordination and success of hub-and-spoke partnerships from the spokes' perspective. Specifically, it revealed that it is the actual degree of complementarity as opposed to the perceived degree of complementarity that influences partnership success.

The study provides an understanding of what constitutes the actual degree of complementarity between hub's and spoke's resources. In doing so, it contributes to existing knowledge by integrating two theoretical streams of literature that have been treated separately by previous research: the input-oriented contributions on external resources and dynamic capabilities as foundations for inter-organizational linkages on the one hand (Eisenhardt and Schoonhoven, 1996; Ahuja, 2000; Mathiassen and Vainio, 2007; Huang et al., 2009), and the output-oriented research on product-level complementarity including its effects on partnership formation and success on the other hand (Milgrom and Roberts, 1995; Grove, 1996; Bresnahan and Greenstein, 1999; Gao and Iyer, 2006, 2008; Chellappa and Saraf, 2010).

The empirical findings revealed a new and interesting interaction effect between the input- and output-oriented perspectives. The results indicate that out of the four identified types of hub resources and capabilities, only the hub's reputation is generally increasing partnership success. The impact of the other three types of resources and capabilities that hubs offer, that is, the hub's capability to provide an integrated enterprise software system, its capability to innovate these systems, as well as the hub's commercial capital, are contingent upon the level of complementarity that exists between the products offered by the partners.

By identifying an interaction effect between layer overlap in the software stack and the platform vendor's technological and commercial capital, the results contribute to explaining the so far inconclusive findings on the role of product-level complementarity in partnership arrangements (Gao and Iyer, 2006, 2008; Huang et al., 2009; Chellappa and Saraf, 2010). In particular, the findings suggest that instead of having a direct positive or negative effect on the success of a hub-and-spoke partnership from the spoke's perspective, product-level complementarity should be considered as a moderating factor regarding the effect of different types of external resources and capabilities on partnership success. In other words, the results contribute to existing literature on partnership success in that by combining the resource-based perspective on inter-firm arrangements and the notion of product-level complementarity, the explanatory power is higher than if both perspectives are applied in isolation.

If product complementarity is particularly low, that is, if layer overlap between the hub and spoke solution is particularly high, two opposing implications on partnership success result. On the one hand, the benefits from the hub's commercial capital and the hub's capability to provide an integrated system are particularly high for the spoke. On the other hand, however, the benefit from system-level innovations of the hub is decreased. In other words, the actual complementarity of the resources and capabilities of hub and spoke is determined by the hub's resources and capabilities on the one hand, and by the product characteristics of hub and spoke on the other hand. Partnership success from the spokes' perspective increases with an increasing fit between the solutions offered by hub and spoke and the hub's resources and capabilities. Thus, in analyzing the success of hub-and-spoke networks, it appears very fruitful to consider possible trade-offs between particular hub resources and capabilities resulting from different levels of product complementarity.

This study's results also contribute to the literature on partnership coordination (Malone and Crowston, 1994; Mintzberg, 1979; Thompson, 1967; Kraut and Streeter, 1995; Staudenmayer, 1997) and TCE (Williamson, 1981) by showing that product-level complementarity also moderates the direct, negative effect of organizational coupling on partnership success. Specifically, if hub and spoke act on the same layer, opportunistic behavior by the hub is particularly likely because system innovations of the hub may render the spokes' solutions obsolete, and thus jeopardize the spokes' original business model. This threat is reinforced because if hub and spoke have a high level of layer overlap, then the hub may absorb valuable knowledge throughout the partnership. Also, hubs may be more reluctant to share resources with spokes that reside on the same layer in the software stack as a result of the potential threat that the partner may turn into a serious competitor.

These results add to the relational view by clarifying that even if appropriate governance mechanisms are in place, partner-specific investments may still decrease relational rents if there is a high overlap of the solutions offered by partners. They also add to TCE by introducing product-level complementarity as a contingency factor to the link between asset specificity and transaction costs.

6.2 Managerial implications

The theoretical insights of this study lead to several managerial implications for different stakeholders. The study provides guidance for small and medium-sized complementor organizations in the enterprise software industry in successfully coordinating partnerships with large platform vendors. The results also help platform vendors establish a successful network of providers of complementary niche functionality. Moreover, the results of this study can be translated to hub-and-spoke networks outside the enterprise software industry. The following section discusses these implications for practice.

Implications for complementors in the enterprise software industry. This study's results have important implications for managers of complementor organizations in the enterprise software industry. First, this study's findings on the different implications of perceived versus actual complementarity of resources and capabilities have important consequences for spokes. Most notably, spokes benefit from the results of this study because it provides an understanding of what constitutes resource complementarity in hub-and-spoke networks in the enterprise software industry. Spokes should carefully evaluate the complementarity of the hub's technological, commercial and social capital with own resources and capabilities. In particular, spokes have to be aware that the degree of complementarity not only depends on the hub's resources and capabilities, but also on the question of how the hub's and spoke's products relate to each other.

More specifically, in order to be successful, it is inevitable for spokes to be aware that the complementarity of the hub's capability to provide integrated systems and its commercial capital is higher if hub and spoke act on the same layer in the software stack. In contrast, the complementarity of the hub's capability to innovate on a system level is particularly high if the spoke's solution complements the hub's platform on a separate layer.

In addition, complementor organizations can benefit from the findings of this study because it provides guidance on the vital question under which circumstances spokes should tie their business closely to the hub by investing in hub-specific assets and informal governance. The results of the study show that spokes should only increase the organizational coupling with a specific hub if complementarities are high. Also, spokes should carefully analyze if important resources may be available via knowledge-sharing routines, thus reducing the need for organizational coupling. By making use of the knowledge-sharing routines offered by a hub organization, spokes may be able to avoid the adverse implications of a high dependence on a particular hub. That is, they may be able to reduce partnership costs and the threat of opportunistic behavior by the hub.

In addition, this study provides complementor organizations with an understanding of the drivers of opportunistic behavior in hub-and-spoke networks in the enterprise software industry. More specifically, spoke organizations learn that not all of the hub's resources and capabilities are generally advantageous. In particular, if spokes operate on the same layer in the software stack as the hub, the spoke has to be aware of the risks arising from the hub's innovative capability to introduce new system architectures or business applications that may render the spoke's solutions obsolete. Moreover, spokes learn that in case of high layer overlap, hub organizations may be reluctant to share resources with a spoke in order to avoid loosing its competitive advantage in a particular market.

In the case of high layer overlap, the spoke is well advised to keep itself constantly up to date regarding the hub's planned innovations. Close inter-personal linkages to the personnel of the hub seem to be particularly important for this purpose. Another counterstrategy lies in the spoke's own innovativeness. If the spoke is able to constantly innovate, the risk of becoming obsolete is generally smaller, in particular if the spoke's innovations are aligned with those of the hub. In contrast, if a spoke's solution has the characteristics of a commodity with little innovative potential it may be more fruitful to complement the system of a hub that mainly acts on adjacent layers. As a consequence, benefits from the hub's capablity to provide integrated systems and its commercial capital are smaller. At the same time, however, the risk of obsolescence decreases.

Implications for platform vendors in the enterprise software industry. Large and well-established enterprise software vendors may also learn from the findings of this study. Platform vendors aim at fostering partnership networks with smaller niche players in order to benefit from network externalities and lower the costs and complexity of the overall systems. Knowing which capabilities the spokes aim at when participating in hub-and-spoke networks may help hub organizations to attract and select partners and manage the partnerships in a better way. Also, in order to foster sustainable inter-firm networks, hub organizations should reflect carefully whether it might be advantageous to explicitly focus on one layer of the enterprise software stack and leave adjacent layers to its partners.

Hubs should be aware of the spokes' general tendency towards a higher degree of coupling. Spokes were found to increase organizational coupling in order to benefit from resource complementarity. This tendency towards undermining the standardized coordination mechanisms established by the hub is even reinforced for two reasons. First, spokes may over-estimate the degree of complementarity. Second, due to the perceived threat of opportunistic behavior spokes were found to even increase the degree of organizational coupling.

To some extent, it may be beneficial for the hub organization if spokes invest in hub-specific assets because it increases network cohesiveness. Spokes that have invested heavily in a partnership with a certain hub were found to be locked into this particular partnership. However, a hub should not only aim at tying its current partners to the own platform in the short run, but also make sure that the partnership network and the provided software system are successful in the long run. That is, if the costs for partnering are too high, a hub's current partners may struggle and the hub may encounter difficulties in attracting new partners. In addition, by establishing "unofficial" informal governance mechanisms, spokes may undermine the efficiency and fairness of the overall network, which may eventually decrease the success of the network, and thus the success of the participating hub and spokes.

The results of this study provide guidance for hub organization in finding a balance between the need for efficient partnership management and the spokes' preference for relational governance. The study shows that by establishing appropriate knowledge-sharing routines, hub organizations may enable spokes to make use of the complementary resources in a loosely-coupled scenario, thus decreasing the degree of organizational coupling aimed at by spokes. In particular, hubs are advised to put effort in improving the IOS that spokes can use to access external knowledge. This study helps hub organizations reach this goal because it provides an understanding of what are the crucial design principles of such IOS. In particular, these IOS should provide relevant information in accordance with the perceived and actual complementarity of certain types of resources. In addition, hubs can improve communication and foster trust – and hence lower the perceived threat of opportunism – by installing organizational units that institutionalize personal coordination.

Implications for inter-organizational networks in other industries. The findings of this study are specific to the enterprise software industry but may partially be transferred to other industries and also provide valuable insights for organizations in hub-and-spoke networks outside the enterprise software sector.

Spoke organizations in the enterprise software industry usually do not exchange goods with the respective hub. Instead, they sell their solutions directly to the market, reinforcing the importance of obtaining access to the hub's commercial capital and its reputation.

While the hub's commercial and social capital may hence be of lower relevance in industries where complementors do engage in exchange relationships with platform vendors (like it is usually the case in the automotive sector), spoke organizations in these domains may still benefit from this study's results. In particular, the interaction effect between product-level complementarity and the hub's innovative capability may be important for these spoke companies in order to establish a successful partnership. In a similar way, the relationship between product-level complementarity and the threat of the hub behaving opportunistically is reinforced.

In addition, in industries that develop products or services that are less complex than enterprise software, the system integration know-how of the hub may be less important because a higher degree of modularity is more feasible. Moreover, tapping into the hub's reputation may be of lower importance because customers can more easily assess the quality of less complex products in advance, reducing the necessity of signaling reliability through a partnership. On the other hand, a partner's commercial capital and its innovative capabilities may still be important factors for spokes, reinforcing the importance of the discussed interaction effects.

6.3 Limitations and future research

This study has several limitations that have to be kept in mind when interpreting its results. This section discusses these limitations and provides suggestions on how they could be addressed in future studies. Moreover, this study provides ample opportunities for future research that will be discussed subsequently.

It should be kept in mind that the results of this research are based on a limited set of data. The data set consists of the partnership networks of two hubs. Although only a limited number of large hub organizations exist within the global enterprise software industry, peculiarities of other hubs may not be reflected by the data set. Future research may hence replicate the study in additional partnership networks in order to increase the generalizability of the findings.

Moreover, even though rigor was ensured through following a replicable process that is well-described and accepted in literature, the qualitative examination, the assessment of the level of the constructs for each case, as well as the evaluation of layer overlap may still be biased due to subjective ratings. In addition, despite the fact that increasing the number of cases and relying on a lower number of knowledgeable experts per case is consistent with the study's goals, this approach may entail the risk of a key informant bias (Kumar et al., 1993). Thus, a viable next step would be to corroborate the findings of this study by testing the developed explanatory model through a large-scale quantitative survey. That is, while this study focused on theory building, future research may aim at confirming the explanatory models that resulted from this research.

By identifying the moderating role of layer overlap, this study provides a first step in understanding the notion of actual versus perceived resource complementarity. Therefore, an interaction effect between product-level complementarity and the external resources and capabilities has been introduced. While modeling product-level complementarity as the degree of layer overlap in the software stack provided important insights for understanding the antecedents of partnership success, a more complex measure of product-level complementarity could increase the explanatory power of the model. Therefore, a fruitful avenue for future studies would be to move away from the rather generic stack model and analyze the product-level complementarity between the solutions offered by hubs and spokes in more detail, both in the enterprise software industry and in other sectors.

Specifically, it may be interesting to find out whether effects similar to the ones identified *between* layers (i.e., layer overlap) also exist *within* the layers of the stack. For instance, products may overlap in terms of the specificity of a software solution, that is, software solutions can be generic versus specific to certain context factors such as industries or customer types. In other words, a more fine-grained inspection of the differences and commonalities between groups of spoke organizations and their implications promises to be particularly insightful.

Moreover, future studies may gather longitudinal data on hub-and-spoke partnerships and examine how perceived complementarity changes over time, thus evaluating this study's conceptualization of perceived and actual complementarity.

For the goal of theory-building that this study pursued, measuring partnership success through subjective assessments of interview partners and high-level, objective indicators was considered a well-suited approach. This is especially because the common approach of measuring success via changes of share prices is unfeasible for small complementors that are usually not listed on stock markets. Therefore, finding a more direct measure of partnership success is another promising area of future research.

This study's results suggest that the degree of organizational coupling positively influences partnership success by increasing the benefits resulting from the partner's resources and capabilities. However, a higher degree of organizational coupling was also found to increase the costs of partnering and thus decrease partnership success. In a similar way, a higher level of layer overlap was found to strengthen the advantages resulting from the hub's capability to provide integrated systems and its commercial capital, but decrease the benefits arising from the hub's innovativeness and even increase the likelihood of opportunistic behavior. While these insights imply a number of theoretical and practical contributions, the findings are only a first step in explaining partnership success. Future studies may move beyond solely proposing directional effects and examine the strength of the identified theoretical links in order to better predict partnership success and thus derive managerial advice.

In addition, this study's implications are only partially generalizable to settings that differ from the assumptions outlined in Section 2.3. In particular, the power asymmetry in a singular hub-spoke relationship may be lower if the number of spokes in a network is low or if platform vendor and complementor are comparable in terms of resources, size, and revenue. While the assumptions of this study are well-justified because they are common in today's enterprise software industry, future research may relieve some of these assumptions and study the implications on the explanatory models. Specifically, it is interesting to examine in more detail the differences in power asymmetry across partnership networks with different characteristics.

In a similar way, future research may study the impact of technological progress (e.g., the development and market penetration of SOA and SaaS) on the power distribution between platform vendors and complementors. Even though the assumption that a seamless mixing and matching of software components is unfeasible seems to be well-justified due to the idiosyncrasies of enterprise software, architectural innovation may still increase the dependence of platform vendors on the availability of compatible niche functionality. Therefore, studying the dynamics of power asymmetry between hubs and spokes in more detail seems to be promising.

Introducing the availability of appropriate knowledge-sharing routines as a moderator of perceived resource complementarity and the aspired degree of organizational coupling provided valuable insights and increased the explanatory power of the theoretical model. In addition, this new moderator provides promising areas of future research. In particular, this study has referred to appropriate knowledge-sharing routines as communication channels that provide spokes with the relevant knowledge regarding technological and commercial capital. Future research may pick up this insight and analyze in more detail what determines the appropriate knowledge in terms of quality and quantity. Moreover, future studies may examine the determinants and implications of individuals' information behavior in the context of partnerships in the enterprise software industry. The interaction effect between product-level complementarity and external resources revealed in this study can provide a basis for researchers dealing with this question. Future research may also investigate how IOS can be improved in order to provide relevant knowledge and avoid information overload. For instance, the use of new media such as microblogging could be considered.

The refined explanatory model introduced the concept of an institutionalized organizational unit that acts as a boundary spanner and is responsible for a personal but institutionalized communication with a particular spoke. In doing so, this study has referred to the concept of trust in inter-firm arrangements. Recent work has begun to study the dynamics of trust in hub-and-spoke partnerships (Huber et al., 2010). Future research may follow this path and study the question of how past events influence trust and how trust emerges and declines over time. Hence, in contrast to the variance theory developed in this study, future research could aim at building a process theory of partnership formation (Mohr, 1982; Langley, 1999; Van de Ven, 1992).

This study revealed that spokes face the threat of their solution becoming obsolete as a result of system innovation by the hub, especially if there is a high degree of layer overlap. However, instead of including the functionality of the spoke's solution into its own product portfolio by developing comparable functionality, hub's may as well decide to acquire the spoke organization in order to avoid development costs. In fact, being acquired may even be in the interest of the shareholders of a spoke company in many cases. Future research may investigate in more detail what determines a hub's decision to acquire a partner instead of developing similar functionality. In particular, future studies may examine partnership dynamics and develop a process theory of what triggers the decision to copy a spoke's functionality or acquire a spoke organization. Such an inquiry seems to be particularly promising if it is combined with a more fine-grained analysis of product-level complementarity as suggested above.

7 Summary and conclusion

The goal of this study was to build a mid-range theory that explains how complementor organizations in the enterprise software industry coordinate the partnership with larger platform vendors and how coordination mechanisms influence partnership success. In order to do so, this study took a qualitative approach and conducted a multiple-case study of spoke organizations that participate in the partnership networks of two hubs.

After giving an introduction in the first chapter, the second chapter presented the study's theoretical foundations. Specifically, the enterprise software industry and the recent trend toward inter-organizational hub-and-spoke networks was introduced. Then, previous research both in IS and in adjacent disciplines was discussed. Based on this extant literature, a preliminary framework was deduced that guided the subsequent empirical research.

Chapter 3 gave an in-depth discussion on the research methodology of this study. The approach of conducting two rounds of positivist, qualitative case studies to explore and refine a theoretical model that answers the study's research questions was explained and justified. Chapter 4 and 5 presented the results of these two rounds of multiple-case studies. While the exploratory phase developed in Chapter 4 was structured along the theoretical links that emerged from the analysis of the empirical data, the refinement phase reported in Chapter 5 presented single cases in a comprehensive way to corroborate the explanatory power of the developed models. In addition, Chapter 5 elaborated on the results of a cross-case analysis that was conducted with the goal of refining the explanatory models.

Chapter 6 gave an in-depth discussion of the results of this study. First, theoretical contributions to the literature that the study drew on were discussed and elaborated. The next section discussed implications for stakeholders in practice, such as complementor organizations, platform vendors, and organizational actors outside the enterprise software industry. Finally, limitations and opportunities for future research were discussed.

This study aimed at answering three research question. First, it addressed the question of how small complementor organizations coordinate the partnership with their larger partner. Drawing on extant literature on the coordination of distributed work and on relational governance as well as on empirical evidence, the study showed that the coordination mechanisms applied by spoke organizations can be conceptualized by the degree of organizational coupling aimed at by spokes. Organizational coupling manifests itself through the level of hub-specific investments and through the reliance on informal governance mechanisms as opposed to formal ones. The degree of organizational coupling varied considerably across the analyzed cases. While some spokes aimed at a low level of organizational coupling and rather relied on the standardized and formal coordination mechanisms established by the hub, other spokes invested heavily in resources specific to the hub and tried to foster a network of informal contacts within the hub organization.

Second, this study posed the question of how variations in the way how complementors coordinate the partnership with their larger partner can be explained. The results show that the degree of organizational coupling increases with an increase in the complementarity of hub's and spoke's resources and capabilities as perceived by the spoke. Specifically, the higher the spoke's perception of the complementarity of the hub's technological and commercial capital, the higher is the degree of organizational coupling that spokes aim at. This link between perceived complementarity and organizational coupling was found to be moderated by the availability of appropriate knowledge-sharing routines. The more these appropriate knowledge-sharing routines are offered by the hub, the less does perceived complementarity induce spokes to increase the degree of organizational coupling. In addition, a high perceived threat of opportunistic behavior by the hub was found to increase the degree of organizational coupling because by establishing informal contacts, spokes try to prevent the hub from behaving opportunistically.

Third, the study had the goal to answer the question of how a particular complementor should coordinate its partnership with a hub in order to be successful. The study revealed that the success of hub-and-spoke partnerships from the spokes' perspective increases with a higher actual degree of complementarity of the hub's technological, commercial, and social capital as opposed to the degree of complementarity perceived by the spoke. The findings show that the actual complementarity depends on the hub's resources and capabilities, but also on product-level complementarity between the solutions offered by the partners. The partnership coordination applied by spokes was also found to influence partnership success. On the one hand, a higher degree of organizational coupling increases the benefits resulting from the hub's resources and capabilities. On the other hand, organizational coupling implies costs and effort for the spoke, thus reducing partnership success.

Appendix

1 Interview guidelines

1.1 Exploratory phase

1. Information regarding company and interview partner
   - Organization's main business area, historical development of the partnership?
   - Interviewee's position within organization, role regarding partnership?
2. Partnership formation
   - When was the partnership formed? What were the strategic goals associated with the decision to enter the cooperation?
   - Which formal criteria had to be met and which steps had to be taken in order to become a partner?
3. Partnership dynamics
   - Which strategic challenges or risks emerge throughout the partnership? Which are the reasons for these challenges and risks?
   - Has the nature of the partnership changed over time?
4. Operational aspects of the partnership
   - How is the procedure of cooperating with the partner in a specific project?
   - How are operational challenges managed?
5. Partnership success
   - Which impact has the partnership on the success of your business? Is partnership success evaluated systematically?
   - From your point of view, why is the partnership successful or not successful respectively?
   - In your opinion, how should/will the partnership develop over time and which steps have to be taken?

1.2 Refinement phase

1. Information regarding company and interview partner
   - Organization's main business area, historical development of the partnership?
   - Interviewee's position within organization, role regarding partnership?
2. Strategic goals of the partnership
   - What were the strategic goals and reasons to enter the cooperation?
   - What are the concrete advantages resulting from the partnership?
   - Which resources and capabilities of the partner are particularly useful and advantageous (technological know-how, market access, reputation gain,...)?
3. Partnership intensity
   - Which investments have to be performed in relation to the partnership?
   - To which extent is the business model focused on the partnership? Would it be possible to have a similar partnership with another partner?
   - How does the collaboration with the partner work (formal/standardized versus informal/personal)?
   - How is information transferred between the partners? Are information systems used for this purpose? What types of information is transferred via these information systems?
4. Partnership challenges
   - Does the access to the partner's resources and capabilities meet the original expectations?
   - Is there a risk of knowledge spillover that may be appropriated by the partner?
   - Is there a (partial) competition with the partner in some areas?
   - Are there other risks and challenges associated with the partnership?
   - How are these challenges of the partnership managed?
5. Partnership success
   - Can the partnership be called a success?
   - Have the original goals of the partnership been attained?
   - Which aspects of the partnership could be improved?
   - How did the company evolve in the course of the partnership regarding revenue, profit, number of employees, and others?
   - Is this development mainly caused by the success/failure of the partnership?
   - Is a substitution with an alternative partnership considered?

2 Assessment of constructs and evidence

2.1 MACHINE

Construct	Rating	Evidence
Perceived complementarity of hub's technological capital	Medium	- MACHINE's business model is focused on integrating HUB A's enterprise software with third-party hardware. Therefore, getting access to technological know-how that resides within HUB A is important for MACHINE
Perceived complementarity of hub's commercial capital	Low	- "It would be very desirable to intensify joint marketing initiatives, but I doubt that this is going to happen." (CEO)
Perceived complementarity of hub's social capital	High	- "The name and reputation of [HUB A] is very important for us. Customers wouldn't notice and know us without the certification of [HUB A]." (CEO)
Inter-organizational information systems	Medium	- "We use [HUB A's IOS for technological information], but sometimes there is even too much information. Plus, some kind of information won't be available through these systems. You have to call somebody you know and ask him, that's the only way." (CEO) - "For us, [HUB A's system for marketing purposes] is purely an advertising instrument. People find information on [MACHINE] if they look for it." (CEO)
Hub-specific investments	Medium	- "What we try to do is diversify our business in order to make us less vulnerable." (CEO)

Construct	Rating	Evidence
Informal governance	Medium	- “We have the contacts within [HUB A] we can ask about technological issues. But to obtain information about [HUB A]’s future strategy is not an easy task.” (CEO)
Competition	Low	- MACHINE and HUB A cover different markets.
Reluctance to share resources	Medium	- MACHINE struggles to obtain timely information about strategic decisions. - There is a risk that access to external resources expires if personal contacts cease to exist.
Success (subjective assessment)	Medium	- “The partnership is going well and will go on like this. At the same time, we try to establish similar partnerships with other firms.” (CEO) - “In the future, we will try to engage in partnerships with other vendors, in case a customer doesn’t run [HUB A]’s software.” (CEO) - “More marketing support on part of [HUB A] would be desirable.” (CEO)
Success (objective assessment)	Medium	- MACHINE is growing, both in terms of projects as well as regarding employees.

2.2 MEDIA

Construct	Rating	Evidence
Perceived complementarity of hub’s technological capital	High	- All solutions developed by MEDIA are based on HUB A’s platform. Therefore, MEDIA critically depends on external technological know-how.
Perceived complementarity of hub’s commercial capital	Low	- Low number of potential customers limits value of HUB A’s marketing and sales capabilities.

Construct	Rating	Evidence
Perceived complementarity of hub's social capital	Low	- MEDIA and its products and services are well-known among (potential) customers, reducing the need for using HUB A's reputation.
Inter-organizational information systems	Medium	- "We heavily use the information systems offered by [HUB A], because we need reliable information. However, a lot critical information is only available through personal contacts." (Head of product development)
Hub-specific investments	High	- "Some people within [MEDIA] now realize in a painful way how dependent we became on [HUB A]." (Head of product development)
Informal governance	Medium	- MEDIA tries to get access to technological know-how and strategic information through personal and informal contacts.
Competition	High	- HUB A itself offers a version of its software that is specific to the media industry. Therefore, HUB A and MEDIA are competitors in some areas.
Reluctance to share resources	High	- HUB A does not provide enough information about the future product landscape. - HUB A stopped offering parts of its system that were essential for MEDIA.
Success (subjective assessment)	Low	- "The partnership between [MEDIA] and [HUB A] is not the big love anymore that it used to be." (Head of product development)
Success (objective assessment)	Low	- MEDIA actively looks for other platform vendors to substitute HUB A. - Some of the latest releases of MEDIA's solutions were not re-certified.

2.3 ARCHIVE

Construct	Rating	Evidence
Perceived complementarity of hub's technological capital	High	- "Our solutions are very closely integrated with [HUB A]'s system. That means that we need information about technological issues from [HUB A], specifically if new releases of [HUB A]'s system come out." (Partnership manager)
Perceived complementarity of hub's commercial capital	High	- "The partnership with [HUB A] is a crucial marketing instrument." (Partnership manager)
Perceived complementarity of hub's social capital	High	- "Using [HUB A]'s logo on our homepage helps us a lot. That's what potential customers look for." (Partnership manager) - HUB A's logo is prominently used on ARCHIVE's website.
Inter-organizational information systems	High	- ARCHIVE heavily uses HUB A's IOS both for obtaining technological know-how as well as for accessing HUB A's marketing channel.
Hub-specific investments	Medium	- Investments in certification and marketing efforts that result from the exclusive focus on HUB A's system.
Informal governance	High	- "We have a very special contact to those employees of [HUB A] that work in the field of archiving. We have been putting a lot of effort in establishing these relationships." (Partnership manager)
Competition	High	- Since its foundation almost 20 years ago, ARCHIVE has constantly been faced with innovations of HUB A that overlap with its own products.
Reluctance to share resources	Low	- ARCHIVE does not face problems of limited access to external resources.

Construct	Rating	Evidence
Success (subjective assessment)	High	- “The partnership is a huge success.” (Partnership manager)
Success (objective assessment)	High	- ARCHIVE has been successfully selling its complementary software for almost 20 years, continuously finding new niches.

2.4 PIM

Construct	Rating	Evidence
Perceived complementarity of hub’s technological capital	Medium	- Some technological knowledge about the functioning of the hub’s platform was necessary to integrate the solutions. - According to PIM’s founder and CEO, the interfaces between HUB A’s and PIM’s solutions are highly standardized. - PIM’s solutions also works with other enterprise software systems.
Perceived complementarity of hub’s commercial capital	High	- The access to HUB A’s marketing and sales network used to bring great benefits to PIM and, according to its founder and CEO, still has the potential to do so.
Perceived complementarity of hub’s social capital	High	- “Our visibility and reputation is still top-notch and has even increased thanks to the official partnership with [HUB A].” (Founder and CEO)
Inter-organizational information systems	Low	- “By no means the personal interaction could possibly be substituted by any kind of inter-organizational information system.” (Founder and CEO)

Construct	Rating	Evidence
Hub-specific investments	Medium	- The interviewee mentions the very high costs of the certification and other partnership duties. - Because of the high standardization of the interfaces, the investments in resources and capabilities that are specific to HUB A are rather low. In fact, PIM's solution does not only run on HUB A's system, but on various enterprise software systems. - "In my opinion, a business model that is completely specific to one hub is very dangerous" (Founder and CEO)
Informal governance	High	- PIM puts a lot of effort into the establishment of informal relationships. - "We work very well with [HUB A] on an informal basis, there are regular personal meetings." (Founder and CEO) - "If our developers need some information, they just call somebody from [HUB A]. That's much faster than searching in an information system." (Founder and CEO)
Competition	High	- HUB A has acquired a company that provides a solution which competes with the ones offered from PIM.
Reluctance to share resources	High	- As a result of the recent acquisition, the marketing support has dramatically decreased.
Success (subjective assessment)	Medium	- "I would say that the partnership is successful, we are happy with it. It's not that it would bring the big breakthrough, it's more one aspect of many. Right now I would say that the partnership with [HUB A] is responsible for 15-20% of our revenue." (Founder and CEO)
Success (objective assessment)	Low	- PIM has invested into the partnership with HUB A, particularly into establishing informal relationships. However, the access to resources that used to be high, particularly regarding marketing and sales, is severely limited due to the recent acquisition made by HUB A.

2.5 E-BUSINESS

Construct	Rating	Evidence
Perceived complementarity of hub's technological capital	High	- The CEO reports that HUB A could potentially provide valuable technological know-how regarding the integration of the partners' products. - "As a small company you are potentially weak regarding development resources. A partnership with a large platform vendor can help overcome these problems." (CEO)
Perceived complementarity of hub's commercial capital	High	- "The partnership was interesting for us because we wanted to get access to [HUB A]'s sales unit." (CEO) - "A lot of customers we have result from [HUB A]'s promotion of our solution. They tell the customer: If you need this functionality, get it from [E-BUSINESS]." (CEO) - The CEO says that the marketing support from a hub organization can be particularly helpful in the start-up phase of a complementor organization.
Perceived complementarity of hub's social capital	Medium	- "Customers usually know that if a company is a partner of [HUB A], then the quality of the organization and the products have been assessed by [HUB A]." (CEO) - "You don't sell your product just because it is certified." (CEO)
Inter-organizational information systems	Low	- "The documentation about the platform was very bad and didn't help us understand the system." (CEO) - The CEO comments that in the field of marketing and sales, communication is always via personal contacts.

Construct	Rating	Evidence
Hub-specific investments	High	- "To make the system compatible with [HUB A]'s platform, we needed three full-time employees for accumulating know-how about the platform. You need to know the system before can start developing." (CEO) - "To keep the partnership running, we needed to invest up to 200.000 Euros a year." (CEO)
Informal governance	High	- "We try to communicate with [HUB A] on a personal level. The crucial part of the partnership with [HUB A] is the personal relationship to sales staff, and not the administrative part. Of course there is a lot of formal overhead, but the success or failure of a partnership is decided in the personal collaboration of people." (CEO) - E-BUSINESS tried to establish personal contacts with developers of HUB A to obtain a better access to technological know-how. However, according to the CEO, this is difficult because HUB A develops large parts of its software off-shore.
Competition	High	- "For [HUB A], our solution was considered a temporary gap in the product portfolio because they didn't offer this functionality at that time." (CEO) - "It happened to us before that [HUB A] decided to develop similar functionality for a customer. If a project becomes strategic for [HUB A], then the partnership is over." (CEO) - "At one point, [HUB A] planned to enter a partnership with one of our biggest competitors. At the end, it never happened, but it was a critical situation. This could happen anytime." (CEO)

Construct	Rating	Evidence
Reluctance to share resources	High	- "[HUB A] terminates the certification agreement without any forewarning, then we have to invest money again into re-certification." (CEO) - According to the CEO, HUB A sometimes terminates support contracts with customers. If a customer then decides for another platform, E-BUSINESS' solutions cannot be used anymore. - The CEO reports that new releases of HUB A's platform often result in a huge effort for adjusting E-BUSINESS' solutions to the new architecture. - Obtaining access to technological know-how is difficult for E-BUSINESS because, according to the CEO, most developers of HUB A are located off-shore.
Success (subjective assessment)	Medium	"It's not that we could not make profit with the partnership, but the return on investment is just not high enough." (CEO) - According to the CEO, the partnership with HUB A has generated 500.000 Euros of revenue in the last five years.
Success (objective assessment)	Low	- E-BUSINESS decided to not re-certificate its solutions for new releases and instead adjust the solution for specific customers according to the platform they use. - "We do not develop further our products for [HUB A]'s platform. By broadly offering our products independent from [HUB A], we have a higher return on investments." (CEO) - E-BUSINESS did not grow in terms of employees since the initiation of the partnership.

2.6 PROJECT

Construct	Rating	Evidence
Perceived complementarity of hub's technological capital	Medium	- "Through the partnership we can access [HUB B]'s technological know-how. That's the big advantage." (CEO) - "The access to know-how is not really the reason why we participate [in the partnership]. This kind of information you can just as well access without being a partner." (Partnership manager)
Perceived complementarity of hub's commercial capital	Medium	- "It's one of our goals in the partnership to attract new customers with the help of [HUB B]." (CEO)
Perceived complementarity of hub's social capital	High	- "When addressing new customers it's very important that we can say: 'We are a partner of [HUB B].' Customers know that we have the know-how because we are partners of [HUB B]." (Partnership manager)
Inter-organizational information systems	Low	- "The forums and systems offered by HUB B are not really helpful. It's faster if you google the problem." (Partnership manager) - "If we look for problems we have in these systems, we find out that other people have the same problems. But that's not a solution." (CEO)
Hub-specific investments	High	- According to the interviewees, the cost and effort for the partnership at the highest partnership level within the network of HUB B are very high. - "We have built up a huge amount of know-how over the years regarding [HUB B]'s system. Having the same know-how for different systems would be impossible." (Partnership manager)
Informal governance	Medium	- PROJECT puts considerable effort in the establishment of personal contacts with HUB B's personnel.

Construct	Rating	Evidence
Competition	High	- "I think it's not ok that we have to disclose everything. [HUB B] could just take over our business." (Partnership manager)
Reluctance to share resources	High	- HUB B's marketing support for PROJECT has been very limited. According to the interviewees, the number of products sold because of the partnership with HUB B is close to zero. - From PROJECT's perspective, HUB B does not promote enough its own groupware platform, which is the basis of PROJECT's system.
Success (subjective assessment)	Low	- "The question whether the partnership with [HUB B] is successful is a very difficult one. I can't really answer it." (Partnership manager) - "I think the partnership is not going too bad because of the software we can use."
Success (objective assessment)	Medium	- PROJECT is in the highest partner category within HUB B's partnership network. - The company has seen significant growth over the years regarding the number of employees. - "We are constantly looking for other enterprise software vendors as alternative partners. It is an option, but not right now." (Partnership manager)

2.7 WORKFLOW

Construct	Rating	Evidence
Perceived complementarity of hub's technological capital	High	- WORKFLOW's sales director stresses that his company benefits from the access to technological know-how and from new innovations on part of HUB B.

Construct	Rating	Evidence
Perceived complementarity of hub's commercial capital	Medium	- The interviewee mentions marketing benefits only once by saying that "marketing is definitely an important aspect."
Perceived complementarity of hub's social capital	High	- "The customer perception is much better because of our partnership with [HUB B]." (Sales director) - "We use [HUB B]'s logo to promote our software." (Sales director)
Inter-organizational information systems	Low	- "We have to use the information systems offered by [HUB B] for some aspects in the sense that we have to submit information." (Sales director) - "The information systems change all the time. You don't find things anymore in the portal and there is an information overflow. Usually we have our contacts within [HUB B] that tell us where to find things in the systems." (Sales director)
Hub-specific investments	Medium	- "Given that we are a small company, partnering with two platform vendors would not be feasible. The effort for the management of these kind of partnerships is too high." (Sales director) - WORKFLOW is aware of the threat arising from a high dependency on one single partner. Therefore, WORKFLOW tries to diversify by being part of another network of small and medium-sized IT firms and through not only focusing on complementary software, but also on consulting services that are not necessarily related to HUB B.
Informal governance	High	- WORKFLOW has always had good contacts to HUB B's employees given that one of its founders used to work for HUB B. - The sales director explains that a lot of effort is necessary to establish a good network within HUB B. "It took me several years. You know the names of the people, but it takes a long time until you actually work together." - WORKFLOW's sales director stresses the geographical proximity to one of HUB B's local headquarters and the visits on a regular base.

Construct	Rating	Evidence
Competition	Medium	- "if our projects become very big, [HUB B] might decide to take over the business." (Sales director)
Reluctance to share resources	Medium	- "It happened to us several times that we were using products from [HUB B] and then they decided to stop offering these products after we had invested several thousands of Euros. That was tough! But on the other hand, [HUB B] has a very good product roadmap." (Sales director) - "We have to be aware that the partner may change the partnership conditions from one day to the other. That has happened to us before." (Sales director)
Success (subjective assessment)	High	- "It is a successful partnership because we have understood the rules of the game within [HUB B]'s partnership network. You have to accept these rules and design your strategy correspondingly." (Sales director)
Success (objective assessment)	High	- WORKFLOW has been successfully developing complimentary solutions for almost 20 years. The partnership with HUB B was intensified during this period. - WORKFLOW does currently not consider changing to an alternative partner.

2.8 MANUFACTURE

Construct	Rating	Evidence
Perceived complementarity of hub's technological capital	Low	- MANUFACTURE perceives the technological complementarity to be low due to the high degree of modularity of the system. - Yet, MANUFACTURE critically depends on innovation and access to respective knowledge.

Construct	Rating	Evidence
Perceived complementarity of hub's commercial capital	High	- "One of the big advantages is [HUB B]'s international sales network." (Head of marketing) - "Thanks to the partnership we get access to [HUB B]'s customer data base, we can use marketing material like fliers and brochures, participate in trade fairs, and use [HUB B]'s facilities for workshops." (Head of marketing)
Perceived complementarity of hub's social capital	High	- "[HUB B] has good contacts to the large companies. These companies know [HUB B], they know what they can expect. That is, we use [HUB B]'s reputation." (Head of marketing) - "It is a huge advantage when we approach large companies. The big firms say: 'You are a tiny company of 50 people. Our risk is too high that you don't survive the next crisis, and then we have your software here.' But if we go there as a partner of [HUB B], the perception is very different and the trust is much higher." (Head of marketing) - MANUFACUTRE uses HUB B's logo on its website.
Inter-organizational information systems	Low	- The interviewee reports not to use any kind of IOS or inter-organizational knowledge management systems offered by HUB B.
Hub-specific investments	Low	- MANUFACTURE's production management solution are not platform-specific, that is, they run on many different systems. Indeed, event though the link to HUB B is MANUFACTURE's main partnership, the company maintains other partnerships with major platform vendors.
Informal governance	Medium	- MANUFACTURE coordinates the partnership with HUB B through personal contacts. Some of these stem from long-lasting acquaintances, but the most important one is an official contact person within HUB B who is, among others, responsible for the partnership with MANUFACTURE.
Competition	Low	- The interviewee mentions that when doing projects together, there is some inherent knowledge spill-over. However, this is not considered critical.

Construct	Rating	Evidence
Reluctance to share resources	Medium	- "When we want to address new markets together with [HUB B], it takes some time until [HUB B] is up and running." (Head of marketing) - "We try to reduce risk and not be completely dependent on [HUB B]. Because out of the blue, [HUB B] might make a new strategic decision that changes the game." (Head of marketing)
Success (subjective assessment)	Medium	- "Sometimes working together with [HUB B] is a little bit cumbersome, but, in general, we have backed the right horse." (Head of marketing)
Success (objective assessment)	High	- MANUFACTURE has been following a successful strategy. For instance, the company has grown from ten employees at the outset to almost 50 nowadays.

2.9 ANALYSIS

Construct	Rating	Evidence
Perceived complementarity of hub's technological capital	Medium	- "The partnership gives us the opportunity to access technological resources within [HUB B]." - ANALYIS builds its system upon HUB B's platforms in a modular way. Therefore, the access to technological know-how is perceived to be of moderate importance.
Perceived complementarity of hub's commercial capital	Medium	- "Together with [HUB B], we try to approach new customers, especially in the insurance industry." (Head of marketing) - "[HUB B] supports us financially, with marketing material, and by doing joint appearances on trade fairs." (Head of marketing)

Construct	Rating	Evidence
Perceived complementarity of hub's social capital	Medium	- "Especially in the phase of client acquisition, [HUB B]'s name and reputation in the market really heps us." (Head of marketing) - "Of course, it could also go the other way around. That customers say: 'You are a partner of IBM? Then we don't want to work with you'. But this situation is rare, the positive aspects dominate." (Head of marketing)
Inter-organizational information systems	Medium	- "We use instant messaging to get software support from [HUB B]." (Head of marketing)
Hub-specific investments	Low	- HUB B is ANALYSIS' main partner. Yet, apart from some effort in staying up-to-date about recent develops within HUB B, the partner-specific investments are low.
Informal governance	Low	- ANALYSIS coordinates the partnership via personal relationships, but mainly uses the formal channel offered by HUB B through an employee of HUB B that acts as the official contact person and manages the partnership.
Competition	Low	- There have been no serious crisis or other problems throughout the partnership between ANALYSIS and HUB B. - The partnership is considered as being trustful by the interviewee.
Reluctance to share resources	Low	- ANALYSIS has to deal with some issues that result from the fact that HUB B is a large company and therefore reacts more slowly than a small firm like ANALYSIS.
Success (subjective assessment)	High	- The interviewee considers the partnership with HUB B to be very successful.
Success (objective assessment)	High	- The partnership between ANALSIS and HUB B has evolved to higher partner levels over time. - ANALYSIS has been very successful in the course of the partnership, being able to grow substantially.

2.10 ONTOLOGY

Construct	Rating	Evidence
Perceived complementarity of hub's technological capital	Low	- ONTOLOGY's products are based on HUB B's middleware platforms. The knowledge that is necessary to do so does not go far beyond interface specifications.
Perceived complementarity of hub's commercial capital	Medium	- "One of the core benefits of the partnership with [HUB B] is that it gets us in touch with the right people within potential customer organizations." (Head of marketing)
Perceived complementarity of hub's social capital	Medium	- "Another advantage is that we can label our products as 'fitting with [HUB B]'." (Head of marketing) - The partnership is not communicated prominently on ONTOLOGY's website.
Inter-organizational information systems	Low	- The interview mentions the possibility to get technological support through IOS offered by HUB B. - ONTOLOGY's employees do not use these systems on a regular base.
Hub-specific investments	Low	- Apart from the regular costs and some reporting duties, ONTOLOGY does not perform any partner-specific investments.
Informal governance	Medium	- ONTOLOGY has established a wide network of contacts within HUB B. Also, ONTOLOGY's employees visit events organized by HUB B in order to meet contacts face-to-face.
Competition	Low	- The interviewee does not report any conflicts or situations of competition. - "There is no risk of competition between us and [HUB B] because we are acting in a small niche." (Head of marketing) - "If I remember correctly, [HUB B] had acquired a company in China that does something similar than we do, but since then I haven't heard anything about it." (Head of marketing)

Construct	Rating	Evidence
Reluctance to share resources	Medium	- "There are situations where [HUB B] does not support us like we wished or reacts slower then we expected." - "Usually, we solve these issues through our network of personal contacts and through face-to-face meetings." (Head of marketing)
Success (subjective assessment)	High	- "The partnership with [HUB B] has always been of a high quality."
Success (objective assessment)	Medium	- ONTOLOGY has not advanced to higher partnership levels. - The access to complementary resources is rather limited in spite of the considerably high efforts. - Alternative partners are not considered.

2.11 EXTEND

Construct	Rating	Evidence
Perceived complementarity of hub's technological capital	Low	- EXTEND does not develop comprehensive software solutions. Hence, the access to technological know-how is of lower importance.
Perceived complementarity of hub's commercial capital	Medium	- "Even though we are a small partner, [HUB B] supports us a lot when it comes to marketing initiatives." (Director) - HUB B supports EXTEND through joint appearances on trade fairs, provides financial support and product bundling.

Construct	Rating	Evidence
Perceived complementarity of hub's social capital	Medium	- "[HUB B]'s name and reputation is a huge asset for us." (Director) - The partnership with HUB B is not communicated on EXTEND's website.
Inter-organizational information systems	Medium	- "We obtain a lot of information through [HUB B]'s information systems. That is more a unidirectional information transfer than real communication." (Director) - The director mentions that the second partner network EXTEND participates in is coordinated through IOS to a larger extent.
Hub-specific investments	Low	- EXTEND has a second partnership with another large platform vendor. - Investments in the partnership are rather low due to the fact that EXTEND does not offer comprehensive software solution and hence does not have the costs and efforts of a certification process.
Informal governance	Low	- "We are not trying to establish a large network of contacts within [HUB B]." (Director) - The director stresses the importance of the good relationship with HUB B's manager responsible for the partnership with EXTEND. - The partnership is mostly coordinated via this contact person.
Competition	Low	- The interviewee does not mention any threat of HUB B competing with EXTEND.
Reluctance to share resources	Low	- The director of EXTEND mentions that his company is dependent on HUB B, but does not see this as a critical issues. - "[HUB B] is a huge company, sometimes things take longer to be done" (Director).
Success (subjective assessment)	Medium	- EXTENDS expectations regarding the partnership with HUB B are rather low. Considering this, the partnership is seen as a success.

Construct	Rating	Evidence
Success (objective assessment)	Medium	- The company did not grow or advance to higher partnership levels since its foundation. The focus tends to be more on the second platform vendor with which EXTEND maintains a partnership.

Bibliography

[Abdallah and Wadhwa 2009] ABDALLAH, F. ; WADHWA, A.: Collaborating with your rivals: Identifying sources of co-opetitive performance. In: *Druid Summer Conference* (2009)

[Adler 1995] ADLER, P.S.: Interdepartmental interdependence and coordination: The case of the design/manufacturing interface. In: *Organization Science* 6 (1995), No. 2, p. 147–167

[Adomavicius et al. 2007] ADOMAVICIUS, G. ; BOCKSTEDT, J.C. ; GUPTA, A. ; KAUFFMAN, R.J.: Technology roles and paths of influence in an ecosystem model of technology evolution. In: *Information Technology and Management* 8 (2007), No. 2, p. 185–202

[Adomavicius et al. 2008] ADOMAVICIUS, G. ; BOCKSTEDT, J.C. ; GUPTA, A. ; KAUFFMAN, R.J.: Making sense of technology trends in the information technology landscape: A design science approach. In: *Management Information Systems Quarterly* 32 (2008), No. 4, p. 779–809

[Ahuja 2000] AHUJA, G.: The duality of collaboration: inducements and opportunities in the formation of interfirm linkages. In: *Strategic management journal* 21 (2000), No. 3, p. 317–343

[Akerlof 1970] AKERLOF, G.A.: The market for "lemons": Quality uncertainty and the market mechanism. In: *The Quarterly Journal of Economics* 84 (1970), No. 3, p. 488–500

[Alavi and Carlson 1992] ALAVI, M. ; CARLSON, P.: A review of MIS research and disciplinary development. In: *Journal of Management Information Systems* 8 (1992), No. 4, p. 45–62

[Alvaro et al. 2005] ALVARO, A. ; DE ALMEIDA, E. S. ; DE LEMOS MEIRA, S. R.: Software component certification: A survey. In: *31st EUROMICRO*

Conference on Software Engineering and Advanced Applications (2005), p. 106–113

[Amit and Schoemaker 1993] AMIT, R. ; SCHOEMAKER, P.J.H.: Strategic assets and organizational rent. In: *Strategic Management Journal* 14 (1993), No. 1, p. 33–46

[Ansoff 1965] ANSOFF, H.I.: *Corporate strategy.* New York, NY : McGraw-Hill, 1965

[Arndt et al. 2008] ARNDT, J.M. ; KUDE, T. ; DIBBERN, J.: The emergence of partnership networks in the enterprise application development industry: A global corporation perspective. In: *Advances in Information Systems Research, Education and Practice* b (2008), p. 77–88

[Arndt et al. 2009] ARNDT, J.M. ; KUDE, T. ; DIBBERN, J. ; HEINZL, A.: The emergence of partnership networks in the enterprise application software industry - An SME perspective. In: *PRIMIUM - Process Innovation for Enterprise Software* (2009), p. 179–194

[Astley and Fombrun 1983] ASTLEY, W. G. ; FOMBRUN, C. J.: Collective strategy: Social ecology of organizational environments. In: *The Academy of Management Review* 8 (1983), No. 4, p. 576–587

[Axelrod and Hamilton 1981] AXELROD, R. ; HAMILTON, W.D.: The evolution of cooperation. In: *Science* 211 (1981), No. 4489, p. 1390–1396

[Bain 1956] BAIN, J. S.: *Barriers to new competition: Their character and consequences in manufacturing industries.* Cambridge, MA : Harvard University Press, 1956

[Bala and Venkatesh 2007] BALA, H. ; VENKATESH, V.: Assimilation of interorganizational business process standards. In: *Information Systems Research* 18 (2007), No. 3, p. 340–343

[Baldwin and Clark 1997] BALDWIN, C.Y. ; CLARK, K.B.: Managing in an age of modularity. In: *Harvard Business Review* 75 (1997), No. 5, p. 84–93

[Baldwin and Clark 2000] BALDWIN, C.Y. ; CLARK, K.B.: *Design rules: The Power Of Modularity.* Cambridge, MA : MIT Press, 2000

[Barney 1986] BARNEY, J.B.: Strategic factor markets: Expectations, luck, and business strategy. In: *Management Science* 32 (1986), No. 10, p. 1231–1241

[Barney 1991] BARNEY, J.B.: Firm resources and sustained competitive advantage. In: *Journal of Management* 17 (1991), No. 1, p. 99–120

[Barrett and Konsynski 1982] BARRETT, S. ; KONSYNSKI, B.: Inter-organization information sharing systems. In: *Management Information Systems Quarterly* 6, Special Issue (1982), p. 93–105

[Baum et al. 2000] BAUM, J.A.C. ; CALABRESE, T. ; SILVERMAN, B.S.: Don't go it alone: Alliance network composition and startups' performance in Canadian biotechnology. In: *Strategic Management Journal* 21 (2000), No. 3, p. 267–294

[Baumol 2002] BAUMOL, W.J.: *The free-market innovation machine - Analyzing the growth miracle of capitalism.* Princeton, NJ : Princeton University Press, 2002

[Beck et al. 2008] BECK, N. ; BRÜDERL, J. ; WOYWODE, M.: Momentum or deceleration? Theoretical and methodological reflections on the analysis of organizational change. In: *The Academy of Management Journal* 51 (2008), No. 3, p. 413–435

[Benbasat et al. 1987] BENBASAT, I. ; GOLDSTEIN, D.K. ; MEAD, M.: The case research strategy in studies of Information Systems. In: *Management Information Systems Quarterly* 11 (1987), No. 3, p. 369–386

[Bengtsson and Kock 1999] BENGTSSON, M. ; KOCK, S.: Cooperation and competition in relationships between competitors in business networks. In: *Journal of Business & Industrial Marketing* 14 (1999), No. 3, p. 178–194

[Berle and Means 1932] BERLE, A.A. ; MEANS, G.C.: *The Modern Corporation and Private Property.* New York, NY : Macmillan, 1932

[Bharadwaj et al. 2007] BHARADWAJ, S. ; BHARADWAJ, A. ; BENDOLY, E.: The performance effects of complementarities between information systems, marketing, manufacturing, and supply chain processes. In: *Information Systems Research* 18 (2007), No. 4, p. 437–453

[Black and Boal 1994] BLACK, J. A. ; BOAL, K. B.: Strategic resources: Traits, configurations and paths to sustainable competitive advantage. In: *Strategic Management Journal* 15, Special Issue on Strategy: Search for New Paradigms (1994), p. 131–148

[Boehm et al. 1978] BOEHM, B.W. ; BROWN, J.R. ; KASPAR, H. ; LIPOW, M. ; MACLEOD, G.J. ; MERRIT, M.J.: *Characteristics of software quality.* Amsterdam, Netherlands : North-Holland, 1978

[Brandenburger and Nalebuff 1996] BRANDENBURGER, A. ; NALEBUFF, B.: *Co-opetition.* New York, NY : Doubleday, 1996

[Brehm et al. 2000] BREHM, L. ; HEINZL, A. ; MARKUS, M.L.: Tailoring ERP systems: A spectrum of choices and their implications. In: *Proceedings of the 34th Hawaii International Conference on Systems Science* (2000)

[Brehm and Markus 2000] BREHM, L. ; MARKUS, M ..: The divided software life cycle of ERP packages. In: *Proceedings of the First Global Information Technology Management World Conference*, 2000, p. 43–46

[Bresnahan and Greenstein 1999] BRESNAHAN, T.F. ; GREENSTEIN, S.: Technological competition and the structure of the computer industry. In: *The Journal of Industrial Economics* 47 (1999), No. 1, p. 1–40

[Brews and Tucci 2004] BREWS, P.J. ; TUCCI, C.L.: Exploring the structural effects of internetworking. In: *Strategic Management Journal* 25 (2004), No. 5, p. 429–451

[Brooks 1987] BROOKS, F.P.: No silver bullet: Essence and accidents of software engineering. In: *IEEE computer* 20 (1987), No. 4, p. 10–19

[Brunsson 2000] BRUNSSON, N.: Organizations, markets and standardization. In: BRUNSSON, N. (Ed.) ; JACOBSSON, B. (Ed.): *A World of Standards.* Oxford, UK : Oxford University Press, 2000, p. 21–39

[Brusoni 2005] BRUSONI, S.: The limits to specialization: Problem solving and coordination in'modular networks'. In: *Organization Studies* 26 (2005), No. 12, p. 1885–1907

[Brusoni and Prencipe 2001] BRUSONI, S. ; PRENCIPE, A.: Managing knowledge in loosely coupled networks: Exploring the links between product and knowledge dynamics. In: *Journal of Management Studies* 38 (2001), No. 7, p. 1019–1035

[Brusoni et al. 2001] BRUSONI, S. ; PRENCIPE, A. ; PAVITT, K.: Knowledge specialization, organizational coupling, and the boundaries of the firm: Why do firms know more than they make. In: *Administrative Science Quarterly* 46 (2001), No. 4, p. 597–621

[Brynjolfsson et al. 1994] BRYNJOLFSSON, E. ; MALONE, T.W. ; GURBAXANI, V. ; KAMBIL, A.: Does information technology lead to smaller firms? In: *Management Science* 40 (1994), No. 12, p. 1628–1644

[Buck-Emden and Galimow 1996] BUCK-EMDEN, R. ; GALIMOW, J.: *Sap R\3 System: A client/server technology.* Boston, MA : Addison-Wesley Longman, 1996

[Burton-Jones and Gallivan 2007] BURTON-JONES, A. ; GALLIVAN, M.J.: Toward a deeper understanding of system usage in organizations: A multilevel perspective. In: *Management Information Systems Quarterly* 31 (2007), No. 4, p. 657–679

[Buxmann et al. 2008] BUXMANN, P. ; DIEFENBACH, H. ; HESS, T.: *Die Softwareindustrie: Ökonomische Prinzipien, Strategien, Perspektiven.* Berlin, Germany : Springer Verlag, 2008

[Campbell-Kelly 1995] CAMPBELL-KELLY, M.: Development and structure of the international software industry, 1950-1990. In: *Business and Economic History* 24 (1995), No. 2, p. 73–110

[Campbell-Kelly 2003] CAMPBELL-KELLY, M.: *From airline reservation to sonic the hedgehog: A history of the software industry.* Cambridge, MA : The MIT Press, 2003

[Casciaro and Piskorski 2005] CASCIARO, T. ; PISKORSKI, M.J.: Power imbalance, mutual dependence, and constraint absorption: A closer look at resource dependence theory. In: *Administrative Science Quarterly* 50 (2005), No. 2, p. 167–199

[Cash and Konsynski 1985] CASH, J.I. ; KONSYNSKI, B.R.: IS redraws competitive boundaries. In: *Harvard Business Review* 63 (1985), No. 2, p. 134–142

[Cavaye 1996] CAVAYE, A.L.M.: Case study research: A multi-faceted research approach for IS. In: *Information Systems Journal* 6 (1996), No. 3, p. 227–242

[Chellappa and Saraf 2010] CHELLAPPA, R.K. ; SARAF, N.: Alliances, rivalry and firm performance in enterprise systems software markets: A social network approach. In: *Information Systems Research* 21 (2010), No. 4, p. 849–871

[Chellappa et al. 2010] CHELLAPPA, R.K. ; SARAF, N. ; SAMBAMURTHY, V.: Competing in crowded markets: The dynamics of competition in the enterprise systems software industry. In: *Information Systems Review* 21 (2010), No. 3, p. 614–630

[Chesbrough and Teece 1996] CHESBROUGH, H.W. ; TEECE, D.J.: When is virtual virtuous? Organizing for innovation. In: *Harvard Business Review* 74 (1996), No. 1, p. 65–73

[Claro et al. 2003] CLARO, D.P. ; HAGELAAR, G. ; OMTA, O.: The determinants of relational governance and performance: How to manage business relationships? In: *Industrial Marketing Management* 32 (2003), No. 8, p. 703–716

[Coase 1937] COASE, R.H.: The Nature of the Firm. In: *Economica* 4 (1937), No. 16, p. 386–405

[Cohen and Levinthal 1990] COHEN, W.M. ; LEVINTHAL, D.A.: Absorptive capacity: A new perspective on learning and innovation. In: *Administrative Science Quarterly* 35 (1990), No. 1, p. 128–152

[Colombo et al. 2006] COLOMBO, M.G. ; GRILLI, L. ; PIVA, E.: In search of complementary assets: The determinants of alliance formation of high-tech start-ups. In: *Research Policy* 35 (2006), No. 8, p. 1166–1199

[Conner 1991] CONNER, K.R.: A historical comparison of resource-based theory and five schools of thought within industrial organization economics: Do we have a new theory of the firm? In: *Journal of Management* 17 (1991), No. 1, p. 121–154

[Conway 1968] CONWAY, M.E.: How do committees invent? In: *Datamation* 14 (1968), No. 4, p. 28–31

[Cool and Henderson 1998] COOL, K. ; HENDERSON, J.: Power and firm profitability in supply chains: French manufacturing industry in 1993. In: *Strategic Management Journal* 19 (1998), No. 10, p. 909–926

[Corley and Gioia 2011] CORLEY, K.G. ; GIOIA, D.A.: Building theory about theory building: What constitutes a theoretical contribution? In: *The Academy of Management Review* 36 (2011), No. 1, p. 12–32

[Cournot 1838] COURNOT, A.A.: *Recherches sur les principcs mathématiques de la théorie dcs richesses.* Paris, France : Hachette, 1838

[Coviello and Munro 1997] COVIELLO, N. ; MUNRO, H.: Network relationships and the internationalisation process of small software firms. In: *International Business Review* 6 (1997), No. 4, p. 361–386

[Crabtree and Miller 1992] CRABTREE, B.F. ; MILLER, W.L.: A template approach to text analysis: Developing and using codebooks. In: CRABTREE, B.F. (Ed.) ; MILLER, W.L. (Ed.): *Doing Qualitative Research.* Newbury Park, CA : Sage Publications, 1992, p. 93–109

[Creswell 1998] CRESWELL, J.W.: *Qualitative inquiry and research design - Chosing among five traditions.* Thousand Oaks, CA : Sage Publications, 1998

[Curley and Pyburn 1982] CURLEY, K.F. ; PYBURN, P.J.: "Intellectual" technologies: The key to improving white-collar productivity. In: *Sloan Management Review* 24 (1982), No. 1, p. 31–39

[Curtis 1989] CURTIS, B.: Modeling coordination from field experiments. In: *Proceedings of the Conference on Organizational Computing, Coordination and Collaboration: Theories and Technologies for Computer-Supported Work*, 1989

[Cusumano 2004] CUSUMANO, M.A.: *The business of software: What every manager, programmer and entrepreneur must know to succeed in good times and bad.* New York, NY : The Free Press, 2004

[Cyert and March 1992] CYERT, R.M. ; MARCH, J.G.: *A behavioral theory of the firm.* 2nd edition. Cambridge, MA : Blackwell, 1992

[Daft 1995] DAFT, R.L.: *Organization theory and design.* St. Paul, MN : West Publishing, 1995

[Damsgaard and Truex 2000] DAMSGAARD, J. ; TRUEX, D.: Binary trading relations and the limits of EDI standards: The procrustean bed of standards. In: *European Journal of Information Systems* 9 (2000), No. 3, p. 173–188

[Das and Teng 2000a] DAS, T. K. ; TENG, B.-S.: A resource-based theory of strategic alliances. In: *Journal of Management* 26 (2000), No. 1, p. 31–61

[Das and Teng 2000b] DAS, T.K. ; TENG, B.-S.: Instabilities of strategic alliances: an internal tensions perspective. In: *Organization Science* 11 (2000), No. 1, p. 77–101

[D'Aunno and Zuckerman 1987] D'AUNNO, T.A. ; ZUCKERMAN, H.S.: A life-cycle model of organizational federations: The case of hospitals. In: *Academy of Management Review* 12 (1987), No. 3, p. 534–545

[Davenport 1998] DAVENPORT, T.H.: Putting the enterprise into the enterprise system. In: *Harvard Business Review* 76 (1998), No. 4, p. 121–131

[Davenport and Brooks 2004] DAVENPORT, T.H. ; BROOKS, J.D.: Enterprise systems and the supply chain. In: *Journal of Enterprise Information Management* 17 (2004), No. 1, p. 8–19

[DeMarco and Lister 1987] DEMARCO, T. ; LISTER, T.R.: *Peopleware.* New York, NY : Dorset House, 1987

[Dervin and Nilan 1986] DERVIN, B. ; NILAN, M.: Information needs and uses. In: *Annual Review of Information Science and Technology* 21 (1986), p. 3–33. – ISSN 0066–4200

[Dexter and Nault 2006] DEXTER, A.S. ; NAULT, B.R.: Membership and incentives in network alliances. In: *IEEE Transactions on Engineering Management* 53 (2006), No. 2, p. 250–262

[Diao and Ma 2008] DIAO, L. ; MA, Y.: The evaluation of investment in inter-organizational information system. In: *Proceedings of the 4th International Conference on Wireless Communications, Networking and Mobile Computing* (2008)

[Dibbern 2004] DIBBERN, J.: *The Sourcing of Application Software Services: Empirical Evidence of Cultural, Industry and Functional Differences.* Berlin, Germany : Springer Verlag, 2004

[Dibbern et al. 2008] DIBBERN, J. ; WINKLER, J. ; HEINZL, A.: Explaining variations in client extra costs between software projects offshored to India. In: *Management Information Systems Quarterly* 32 (2008), No. 2, p. 333–366

[Dierickx and Cool 1989] DIERICKX, I. ; COOL, K.: Asset stock accumulation and sustainability of competitive advantage. In: *Management Science* 35 (1989), No. 12, p. 1504–1511

[DiMaggio and Powell 1983] DIMAGGIO, P.J. ; POWELL, W.W.: The iron cage revisited: Institutional isomorphism and collective rationality in organizational fields. In: *American Socilogical Review* 48 (1983), No. 2, p. 147–160

[Dosi 1988] DOSI, G.: Sources, procedures, and microeconomic effects of innovation. In: *Journal of Economic Literature* 26 (1988), No. 3, p. 1120–1171

[Drucker 1994] DRUCKER, P.F.: *Innovation and entrepreneurship.* Revised Reprint. Oxford, UK : Butterworth Heinemann, 1994

[Dube and Pare 2003] DUBE, L. ; PARE, G.: Rigor in information systems positivist case study research: Current practices, trends, and recommendations. In: *Management Information Systems Quarterly* 27 (2003), No. 4, p. 597–635

[Duschek 2004] DUSCHEK, S.: Inter-firm resources and sustained competitive advantage. In: *Management Revue* 15 (2004), No. 1, p. 53–73

[Dyer 1997] DYER, J.H.: Effective interfirm collaboration: How firms minimize transaction costs and maximize transaction value. In: *Strategic Management Journal* 18 (1997), No. 7, p. 535–556

[Dyer et al. 2004] DYER, J.H. ; KALE, P. ; SINGH, H.: When to ally and when to acquire. In: *Harvard Business Review* 82 (2004), No. 7, p. 109–115

[Dyer and Singh 1998] DYER, J.H. ; SINGH, H.: The relational view: Cooperative strategy and sources of interorganizational competitive advantage. In: *Academy of Management Review* 23 (1998), No. 4, p. 660–679

[Eisenhardt 1989] EISENHARDT, K.M.: Building theories from case study research. In: *Academy of Management Review* 14 (1989), No. 4, p. 532–550

[Eisenhardt and Graebner 2007] EISENHARDT, K.M. ; GRAEBNER, M.E.: Theory building from cases: Opportunities and challenges. In: *Academy of management journal* 50 (2007), No. 1, p. 25–32

[Eisenhardt and Schoonhoven 1996] EISENHARDT, K.M. ; SCHOONHOVEN, C.B.: Resource-based view of strategic alliance formation: Strategic and social effects in entrepreneurial firms. In: *Organization Science* 7 (1996), No. 2, p. 136–150

[Emerson 1962] EMERSON, R.M.: Power-dependence relations. In: *American Sociological Review* 27 (1962), No. 1, p. 31–41

[Erl 2005] ERL, T.: *Service-oriented architecture: Concepts, technology, and design.* Saddle River, NJ : Prentice Hall, 2005

[Ethiraj et al. 2005] ETHIRAJ, S.K. ; KALE, P. ; KRISHNAN, M.S. ; SINGH, J.V.: Where do capabilities come from and how do they matter? A study in the software services industry. In: *Strategic Management Journal* 26 (2005), No. 1, p. 25–45

[Evan 1966] EVAN, W.E.: The organization-set: Toward a theory of interorganizational relations. In: THOMPSON, J. D. (Ed.): *Approaches to Organizational Design.* Pittsburgh, PA : University of Pittsgurgh Press, 1966, p. 173–192

[Evans et al. 2006] EVANS, D.S. ; HAGIU, A. ; SCHMALENSEE, R.: *Invisible engines: How software platforms drive innovation and transform industries.* Cambridge, MA : The MIT Press, 2006

[Faraj and Sproull 2000] FARAJ, S. ; SPROULL, L.: Coordinating expertise in software development teams. In: *Management Science* 46 (2000), No. 12, p. 1554–1568

[Farrell et al. 1998] FARRELL, J. ; MONROE, H.K. ; SALONER, G.: The vertical organization of industry: System competition versus component competition. In: *Journal of Economics and Management Strategy* 7 (1998), No. 2, p. 143–182

[Friedman 1999] FRIEDMAN, M.: *Reconsidering logical positivism.* Cambridge, UK : Cambridge University Press, 1999

[Gao and Iyer 2006] GAO, L.S. ; IYER, B.: Analyzing complementarities using software stacks for software industry acquisitions. In: *Journal of Management Information Systems* 23 (2006), No. 2, p. 119–147

[Gao and Iyer 2008] GAO, L.S. ; IYER, B.: Partnerships between software firms: Is there value from complementarities? In: *Proceedings of the 41st Annual Hawaii International Conference on System Sciences* (2008)

[Garud and Kumaraswamy 1993] GARUD, R. ; KUMARASWAMY, A.: Changing competitive dynamics in network industries: An exploration of Sun Microsystems' open systems strategy. In: *Strategic Management Journal* 14 (1993), No. 5, p. 351–369

[Gawer and Cusumano 2002] GAWER, A. ; CUSUMANO, M.A.: *Platform leadership.* Cambridge, MA : Harvard Business School Press, 2002

[Gawer and Henderson 2007] GAWER, A. ; HENDERSON, R.: Platform owner entry and innovation in complementary markets: Evidence from Intel. In: *Journal of Economics & Management Strategy* 16 (2007), No. 1, p. 1–34

[Gibbert et al. 2008] GIBBERT, M. ; RUIGROK, W. ; WICKI, B.: What passes as a rigorous case study? In: *Strategic Management Journal* 29 (2008), No. 13, p. 1465–1474

[Golden-Biddle and Locke 2007] GOLDEN-BIDDLE, K. ; LOCKE, K.: *Composing qualitative research.* Thousand Oaks, CA : Sage Publications, 2007

[Gomes-Casseres 1996] GOMES-CASSERES, B.: *The alliance revolution: The new shape of business rivalry.* Cambridge, MA : Harvard University Press, 1996

[Gosain et al. 2004] GOSAIN, S. ; MALHOTRA, A. ; EL SAWY, O.A.: Coordinating for flexibility in e-business supply chains. In: *Journal of Management Information Systems* 21 (2004), No. 3, p. 7–45

[Granovetter 1985] GRANOVETTER, M.: Economic action and social structure: The problem of embeddedness. In: *American Journal of Sociology* 91 (1985), No. 3, p. 481–510

[Grant 1991] GRANT, R.M.: The resource-based theory of competitive advantage: Implications for strategy. In: *California Management Review* 33 (1991), Spring, p. 114–136

[Grant 1996a] GRANT, R.M.: Prospering in dynamically-competitive environments: Organizational capability as knowledge integration. In: *Organization Science* 7 (1996), No. 4, p. 375–387

[Grant 1996b] GRANT, R.M.: Toward a knowledge-based theory of the firm. In: *Strategic Management Journal* 17, Winter Special Issue (1996), p. 109–122

[Gregor 2006] GREGOR, S.: The nature of theory in information systems. In: *Management Information Systems Quarterly* 30 (2006), No. 3, p. 611–642

[Gregor and Johnston 2001] GREGOR, S. ; JOHNSTON, R.: Theory of interorganizational systems: Industry structure and processes of change. In: *Proceedings of the 34th Hawaii International Conference on System Sciences* (2001)

[Griffith 1999] GRIFFITH, T.L.: Technology features as triggers for sensemaking. In: *Academy of Management Review* 24 (1999), No. 3, p. 472–488

[Grint and Woolgar 1997] GRINT, K. ; WOOLGAR, S.: *The machine at work: Technology, work, and organization.* Cambridge, MA : Polity Press, 1997

[Grove 1996] GROVE, A. S.: *Only the Paranoid Survive.* New York, NY : Doubleday, 1996

[Gulati 1995] GULATI, R.: Social structure and alliance formation patterns: A longitudinal analysis. In: *Administrative science quarterly* 40 (1995), No. 4, p. 619–652

[Gulati 1999] GULATI, R.: Network location and learning: The influence of network resources and firm capabilities on alliance formation. In: *Strategic management journal* 20 (1999), No. 5, p. 397–420

[Gulati and Singh 1998] GULATI, R. ; SINGH, H.: The architecture of cooperation: Managing coordination costs and appropriation concerns in strategic alliances. In: *Administrative Science Quarterly* 43 (1998), No. 4, p. 781–814

[Gulati and Sytch 2007] GULATI, R. ; SYTCH, M.: Dependence asymmetry and joint dependence in interorganizational relationships: Effects of embeddedness on a manufacturer's performance in procurement relationships. In: *Administrative Science Quarterly* 52 (2007), No. 1, p. 32–69

[Hagedoorn 1993] HAGEDOORN, J.: Understanding the rationale of strategic technology partnering: Interorganizational modes of cooperation and sectoral differences. In: *Strategic management journal* 14 (1993), No. 5, p. 371–385

[Haigh 2002] HAIGH, T.: Software in the 1960s as concept, service, and product. In: *IEEE Annals of the History of Computing* 24 (2002), No. 1, p. 5–13

[Hamel 1991] HAMEL, G.: Competition for competence and inter-partner learning within international strategic alliances. In: *Strategic Management Journal* 12, Special Issue on Global Strategy (1991), p. 83 – 103

[Hansen and Wernerfelt 1989] HANSEN, G.S. ; WERNERFELT, B.: Determinants of firm performance: The relative importance of economic and organizational factors. In: *Strategic Management Journal* 10 (1989), No. 5, p. 399–411

[Harland et al. 2001] HARLAND, C.M. ; LAMMING, R.C. ; ZHENG, J. ; JOHNSEN, T.E.: A taxonomy of supply networks. In: *Journal of Supply Chain Management* 37 (2001), No. 4, p. 21–27

[Harpaz and Meshoulam 1997] HARPAZ, I. ; MESHOULAM, I.: Intraorganizational power in high technology organizations. In: *Journal of High Technology Management Research* 8 (1997), No. 1, p. 107–128

[Harrigan 1988] HARRIGAN, K.R.: Joint ventures and competitive strategy. In: *Strategic Management Journal* 9 (1988), No. 2, p. 141–158

[Hart and Moore 1988] HART, O. ; MOORE, J.: Incomplete contracts and renegotiation. In: *Econometrica* 56 (1988), No. 4, p. 755–785

[Heinrich et al. 2010] HEINRICH, L.J. ; HEINZL, A. ; RIEDL, R.: *Wirtschaftsinformatik: Einführung und Grundlegung*. Berlin, Germany : Springer, 2010

[Heinzl 1996] HEINZL, A.: *Die Evolution der Betrieblichen DV-Abteilung: Eine Lebenszyklustheoretische Analyse*. Heidelberg, Germany : Physica Verlag, 1996

[Heinzl and Oberweis 2007] HEINZL, A. ; OBERWEIS, A.: Industrialisierung der Softwareentwicklung. In: *Wirtschaftsinformatik* 49 (2007), No. 3, p. 157–158

[Henderson and Clark 1990] HENDERSON, R.M. ; CLARK, K.B.: Architectural innovation: The reconfiguration of existing product technologies and the failure of established firms. In: *Administrative Science Quarterly* 35 (1990), No. 1, p. 9–30

[Hevner et al. 2004] HEVNER, A.R. ; MARCH, S.T. ; PARK, J. ; RAM, S.: Design science in information systems research. In: *Management Information Systems Quarterly* 28 (2004), No. 1, p. 75–105

[Hill 1990] HILL, C.W.L.: Cooperation, opportunism, and the invisible hand: Implications for transaction cost theory. In: *Academy of Management Review* 15 (1990), No. 3, p. 500–513

[Hirschheim 1985] HIRSCHHEIM, R.: Information systems epistemology: An historical perspective. In: MUMFORD, E. (Ed.) ; HIRSCHHEIM, R. (Ed.) ; FITZGERALD, G. (Ed.) ; WOOD-HARPER, T. (Ed.): *Research Methods in IS*. Amsterdam, Netherlands : North-Holland, 1985, p. 13–35

[Hitt 1999] HITT, L.M.: Information technology and firm boundaries: Evidence from panel data. In: *Information Systems Research* 10 (1999), No. 2, p. 134–149

[Hitt and Brynjolfsson 1997] HITT, L.M. ; BRYNJOLFSSON, E.: Information technology and internal firm organization: An exploratory analysis. In: *Journal of Management Information Systems* 14 (1997), No. 2, p. 81–101

[Hitt et al. 2002] HITT, L.M. ; WU, DJ ; ZHOU, X.: Investment in enterprise resource planning: Business impact and productivity measures. In: *Journal of Management Information Systems* 19 (2002), No. 1, p. 71–98

[Hoetker 2006] HOETKER, G.: Do modular products lead to modular organizations? In: *Strategic Management Journal* 27 (2006), No. 6, p. 501–518

[Hong 2002] HONG, I.B.: A new framework for interorganizational systems based on the linkage of participants' roles. In: *Information & Management* 39 (2002), No. 4, p. 261–270

[Huang et al. 2009] Huang, P. ; Ceccagnoli, M. ; Forman, C. ; Wu, DJ: When do ISVs join a platform ecosystem? Evidence from the enterprise software industry. In: *Proceedings of the International Conference on Information Systems* (2009)

[Huber et al. 2010] Huber, T. ; Kude, T. ; Dibbern, J.: Resolving tensions in hub-and-spoke networks of the enterprise application software industry - An exploratory case study. In: *Americas Conference on Information Systems* (2010)

[Hutchby 2001a] Hutchby, I.: *Conversation and technology: From the telephone to the Internet.* Cambridge, MA : Polity Press, 2001

[Hutchby 2001b] Hutchby, I.: Technologies, texts and affordances. In: *Sociology* 35 (2001), No. 2, p. 441–456

[Iansiti and Levien 2004] Iansiti, M. ; Levien, R.: *The Keystone Advantage.* Cambridge, MA : Harvard Business School Press, 2004

[Inkpen and Beamish 1997] Inkpen, A.C. ; Beamish, P.W.: Knowledge, bargaining power, and the instability of international joint ventures. In: *Academy of management review* 22 (1997), No. 1, p. 177–202

[Ireland et al. 2002] Ireland, R.D. ; Hitt, M.A. ; Vaidyanath, D.: Alliance management as a source of competitive advantage. In: *Journal of Management* 28 (2002), No. 3, p. 413–446

[Iyer et al. 2006] Iyer, B. ; Lee, C.H. ; Venkatraman, N.: Managing in a "small world ecosystem": Some lessons from the software sector. In: *California Management Review* 48 (2006), No. 3, p. 28–47

[Jarillo 1988] Jarillo, J.C.: On Strategic Networks. In: *Strategic Management Journal* 9 (1988), No. 1, p. 31–41

[Jensen 2003] Jensen, M.: The role of network resources in market entry: Commercial banks' entry into investment banking, 1991 – 1997. In: *Administrative Science Quarterly* 48 (2003), No. 3, p. 466–497

[Kale et al. 2001] KALE, P. ; DYER, J. ; SINGH, H.: Value creation and success in strategic alliances: Alliancing skills and the role of alliance structure and systems. In: *European Management Journal* 19 (2001), No. 5, p. 463–471

[Katz 1953] KATZ, D.: Field studies. In: FESTINGER, L. (Ed.) ; KATZ, D. (Ed.): *Research methods in the organizational science.* New York, NY : The Dryden Press, 1953, p. 56–97

[Katz and Shapiro 1985] KATZ, M.L. ; SHAPIRO, C.: Network externalities, competition, and compatibility. In: *The American Economic Review* 75 (1985), No. 3, p. 424–440

[Kerlinger and Lee 2000] KERLINGER, F.N. ; LEE, H.B.: *Foundations of behavioral research.* 4th edition. Fort Worth, TX : Harcourt College Publishers, 2000

[Khanna et al. 1998] KHANNA, T. ; GULATI, R. ; NOHRIA, N.: The dynamics of learning alliances: Competition, cooperation, and relative scope. In: *Strategic Management Journal* 19 (1998), No. 3, p. 193–210

[Kieser and Walgenbach 2007] KIESER, A. ; WALGENBACH, P.: *Organisation.* 6th edition. Stuttgart, Germany : Schäffer-Poeschel, 2007

[Kraut and Streeter 1995] KRAUT, R.E. ; STREETER, L.A.: Coordination in software development. In: *Communications of the ACM* 38 (1995), No. 3, p. 69–81

[Kude and Dibbern 2009] KUDE, T. ; DIBBERN, J.: Tight versus loose organizational coupling within inter-firm networks in the enterprise software industry–The perspective of complementors. In: *Proceedings of the Americas Conference on Information Systems* (2009)

[Kude et al. 2008] KUDE, T. ; DIBBERN, J. ; HEINZL, A.: Complementarity, relation-specific investment, and opportunism: Explaining asymmetric governance modes in hub-and-spoke networks within the enterprise application software industry. In: *Proceedings of JAIS Theory Development Workshop* (2008)

[Kude et al. 2012] KUDE, T. ; DIBBERN, J. ; HEINZL, A.: Why do complementors participate? An empirical analysis of the emergence of partnership networks in the enterprise application software industry. In: *IEEE Transaction on Engineering Management* (2012), forthcoming

[Kumar et al. 1993] KUMAR, N. ; STERN, L.W. ; ANDERSON, J.C.: Conducting interorganizational research using key informants. In: *Academy of ;anagement Journal* 36 (1993), No. 6, p. 1633–1651

[Langley 1999] LANGLEY, A.: Strategies for theorizing from process data. In: *Academy of Management Review* 24 (1999), No. 4, p. 691–710

[Langlois 2002] LANGLOIS, R.: Modularity in technology and organization. In: *Journal of Economic Behavior and Organization* 49 (2002), No. 1, p. 19–37

[Lavie 2006] LAVIE, D.: The competitive advantage of interconnected firms: An extension of the resource-based view. In: *The Academy of Management Review* 31 (2006), No. 3, p. 638–658

[Lavie 2007] LAVIE, D.: Alliance portfolios and firm performance: A study of value creation and appropriation in the US software industry. In: *Strategic Management Journal* 28 (2007), No. 12, p. 1187–1212

[Lee 1989] LEE, A.S.: A scientific methodology for MIS case studies. In: *MIS quarterly* 13 (1989), No. 1, p. 33–50

[Lee 1999] LEE, A.S.: Researching MIS. In: CURRIE, W.L. (Ed.) ; GALLIERS, R.D. (Ed.): *Rethinking management information systems: An interdisciplinary perspective.* Cambridge, MA : Oxford University Press, 1999, p. 7–27

[Lee et al. 2001] LEE, C. ; LEE, K. ; PENNINGS, J.M.: Internal capabilities, external networks, and performance: A study on technology-based ventures. In: *Strategic Management Journal* 22 (2001), No. 6/7, p. 615–640

[Lertpittayapoom et al. 2007] LERTPITTAYAPOOM, N. ; PAUL, S. ; MYKYTYN JR., P.: A theoretical perspective on effective interorganizational knowledge. In: *40th Annual Hawaii International Conference on System Sciences*, 2007

[Licht et al. 2009] LICHT, G. ; MURRAY, G. ; WOYWODE, M.: Timing of international market entry of UK and German high-tech start-ups. In: *Zeitrschrift für Betriebswirtschaft* 1, Special Issue on International Entrepreneurship (2009)

[Liebowitz and Margolis 1995] LIEBOWITZ, S.J. ; MARGOLIS, S.E.: Path dependence, lock-in, and history. In: *Journal of Law, Economics, and Organization* 11 (1995), No. 1, p. 205–226

[Liebowitz and Margolis 1999] LIEBOWITZ, S.J. ; MARGOLIS, S.E.: *Winners, Losers & Microsoft*. Independent Institute, 1999. – Oakland, CA S.

[Liu and Chen 2008] LIU, L. ; CHEN, Y.: IOS and supply chain process innovation. In: *IEEE International Conference on Service Operations and Logistics, and Informatics*, 2008

[Locke and Golden-Biddle 1997] LOCKE, K. ; GOLDEN-BIDDLE, K.: Constructing opportunities for contribution: Structuring intertextual coherence and "problematizing" in organizational studies. In: *Academy of Management Journal* 40 (1997), No. 5, p. 1023–1062

[Lorenzoni and Baden-Fuller 1995] LORENZONI, G. ; BADEN-FULLER, C.: Creating a strategic center to manage a web of partners. In: *California Management Review* 37 (1995), Spring, p. 146–163

[Lorenzoni and Lipparini 1999] LORENZONI, G. ; LIPPARINI, A.: The leveraging of interfirm relationships as a distinctive organizational capability: A longitudinal study. In: *Strategic Management Journal* 20 (1999), No. 4, p. 317–338

[Lu and Beamish 2001] LU, J.W. ; BEAMISH, P.W.: The internationalization and performance of SMEs. In: *Strategic Management Journal* 22 (2001), No. 6/7, p. 565–586

[Mabert et al. 2001] MABERT, V.A. ; SONI, A. ; VENKATARAMANAN, M.A.: Enterprise resource planning: Common myths versus evolving reality. In: *Business Horizons* 44 (2001), No. 3, p. 69–76

[Malhotra and El Sawy 2005] MALHOTRA, A. ; EL SAWY, O.A.: Absorptive capacity configurations in supply chains: Gearing for partner-enabled market knowledge creation. In: *Management Information Systems Quarterly* 29 (2005), No. 1, p. 145–187

[Malhotra et al. 2007] MALHOTRA, A. ; GOSAIN, S. ; EL SAWY, O.A: Leveraging standard electronic business interfaces to enable adaptive supply chain partnerships. In: *Information Systems Research* 18 (2007), No. 3, p. 260–279

[Malone 1988] MALONE, T.W: What is coordination theory? In: *Proceedings of the National Science Foundation Coordination Theory Workshop* (1988)

[Malone and Crowston 1990] MALONE, T.W. ; CROWSTON, K.: What is coordination theory and how can it help design cooperative work systems? In: *Proceedings of the ACM conference on computer-supported cooperative work*, 1990

[Malone and Crowston 1994] MALONE, T.W. ; CROWSTON, K.: The interdisciplinary study of coordination. In: *ACM Computing Surveys* 26 (1994), No. 1, p. 87–119

[March and Simon 1958] MARCH, J.G. ; SIMON, H.A.: *Organizations*. New York, NY : John Wiley and Sons, 1958

[Mariti and Smiley 1983] MARITI, P. ; SMILEY, R.H.: Co-operative agreements and the organization of industry. In: *The Journal of Industrial Economics* 31 (1983), No. 4, p. 437–451

[Markovsky et al. 1988] MARKOVSKY, B. ; WILLER, D. ; PATTON, T.: Power relations in exchange networks. In: *American Sociological Review* 53 (1988), No. 2, p. 220–236

[Markus and Silver 2008] MARKUS, M.L. ; SILVER, M.S.: A foundation for the study of IT effects: A new look at DeSanctis and Poole's concepts of structural features and spirit. In: *Journal of the Association for Information Systems* 9 (2008), No. 10/11, p. 609–632

[Markus and Tanis 2000] MARKUS, M.L. ; TANIS, C.: The enterprise systems experience – From adoption to success. In: ZMUD, R.W. (Ed.): *Framing the domains of IT research: Glimpsing the future through the past*. Cincinnati, OH : Pinnaflex Educational Resources, 2000, p. 173–207

[Marshall 2009] MARSHALL, A.: *Principles of Economics.* 8th editions. New York, NY : Cosimo, 2009. – ISBN 1605208027

[Mata et al. 1995] MATA, F. ; FUERST, W. ; BARNEY, J.: Information technology and sustained competitive advantage: A resource-based analysis. In: *Management Information Systems Quarterly* 19 (1995), No. 1, p. 487–506

[Mathiassen and Vainio 2007] MATHIASSEN, L. ; VAINIO, A.M.: Dynamic capabilities in small software firms: A sense-and-respond approach. In: *IEEE Transactions on Engineering Management* 54 (2007), No. 3, p. 522–538

[McGrath 1981] MCGRATH, J.E.: Dilemmatics: The study of research choices and dilemmas. In: *American Behavioral Scientist* 25 (1981), No. 2, p. 179–210

[Medcof 2001] MEDCOF, J.W.: Resource-based strategy and managerial power in networks of internationally dispersed technology units. In: *Strategic Management Journal* 22 (2001), No. 11, p. 999–1012

[Mertens 2005] MERTENS, P.: *Integrierte Informationsverarbeitung 1.* 15th edition. Wiesbaden, Germany : Gabler, 2005

[Merton 1968] MERTON, R.K.: *Social theory and social structure.* Free Pr, 1968

[Messerschmitt and Szyperski 2003] MESSERSCHMITT, D.G. ; SZYPERSKI, C.: *Software ecosystem - Understanding an indispensable technology and industry.* Cambridge, MA : The MIT Press, 2003

[Meyer and Rowan 1977] MEYER, J.W. ; ROWAN, B.: Institutionalized organizations: Formal structure as myth and ceremony. In: *American Journal of Sociology* 83 (1977), No. 2, p. 340–363. – ISSN 0002–9602

[Mikkola and Gassmann 2003] MIKKOLA, J.H. ; GASSMANN, O.: Managing modularity of product architectures: Toward an integrated theory. In: *IEEE Transactions on Engineering Management* 50 (2003), No. 2, p. 204–218

[Miles and Huberman 1994] MILES, M.B. ; HUBERMAN, A.M.: *Qualitative Data Analysis.* 2nd edition. Thousand Oaks, CA : Sage Publications, 1994

[Miles et al. 2005] Miles, R.E. ; Miles, G. ; Snow, C.C.: *Collaborative entrepreneurship - How communities of networked firms use continuous innovation to create economic wealth.* Stanford, CA : Stanford Business Books, 2005

[Miles and Snow 1986] Miles, R.E. ; Snow, C.C.: Organizations: New concepts for new forms. In: *California Management Review* 28 (1986), Spring, p. 62–73

[Milgrom and Roberts 1995] Milgrom, P. ; Roberts, J.: Complementarities and fit: Strategy, structure and organizational change in manufacturing. In: *Journal of Accounting and Economics* 19 (1995), No. 2-3, p. 179–208

[Mintzberg 1979] Mintzberg, H.: *The Structuring of Organizations.* Englewood Cliffs, NJ : Prentice-Hall, 1979

[Mitchell 1989] Mitchell, W.: Whether and when? Probability and timing of incumbents' entry into emerging industrial subfields. In: *Administrative Science Quarterly* 34 (1989), No. 2, p. 208–230

[Moen et al. 2004] Moen, Ø. ; Gavlen, M. ; Endresen, I.: Internationalization of small, computer software firms. In: *European Journal of Marketing* 38 (2004), No. 9/10, p. 1236–1251

[Mohr and Spekman 1994] Mohr, J. ; Spekman, R.: Characteristics of partnership success: Partnership attributes, communication behavior, and conflict resolution techniques. In: *Strategic Management Journal* 15 (1994), p. 135–152

[Mohr 1982] Mohr, L. B.: *Explaining Organizational Behavior.* San Francisco, CA : Jossey-Bass, 1982

[Morris and Ferguson 1993] Morris, C.R. ; Ferguson, C.H.: How architecture wins technology wars. In: *Harvard Business Review* 71 (1993), No. 2, p. 86–96

[Myers and Avison 1997] Myers, M.D. ; Avison, D.E.: Qualitative research in information systems. In: *Management Information Systems Quarterly* 21 (1997), No. 2, p. 241–242

[Nelson 1970] Nelson, P.: Information and consumer behavior. In: *Journal of Political Economy* 78 (1970), No. 2, p. 311–329

[Nohria and Eccles 1992] NOHRIA, N. ; ECCLES, R.G.: *Networks and organizations: Structure, form, and action.* Boston, MA : Harvard Business School Press, 1992

[Nonaka 1994] NONAKA, I.: A dynamic theory of organizational knowledge creation. In: *Organization science* 5 (1994), No. 1, p. 14–37

[Nonaka and Takeuchi 1995] NONAKA, I. ; TAKEUCHI, H.: *The knowledge-creating company: How Japanese companies create the dynamics of innovation.* Cambridge, MA : Oxford University Press, 1995

[NSF-IRIS 1989] NSF-IRIS: A report by the NSF-IRIS review panel for research on coordination theory and technology. In: *NSF Forms & Publications Unit* (1989)

[Oliver 1990] OLIVER, C.: Determinants of interorganizational relationships: Integration and future directions. In: *Academy of management review* 15 (1990), No. 2, p. 241–265

[Orlikowski and Baroudi 1991] ORLIKOWSKI, W.J. ; BAROUDI, J.J.: Studying information technology in organizations: Research approaches and assumptions. In: *Information Systems Research* 2 (1991), No. 1, p. 1–28

[Orlikowski and Gash 1994] ORLIKOWSKI, W.J. ; GASH, D.C.: Technological frames: Making sense of information technology in organizations. In: *ACM Transactions on Information Systems* 12 (1994), No. 2, p. 174–207

[Orton and Weick 1990] ORTON, J.D. ; WEICK, K.E.: Loosely coupled systems: A reconceptualization. In: *Academy of Management Review* 15 (1990), No. 2, p. 203–223

[Ozcan and Eisenhardt 2009] OZCAN, P. ; EISENHARDT, K.M.: Origin of alliance portfolios: Entrepreneurs, network strategies, and firm performance. In: *The Academy of Management Journal* 52 (2009), No. 2, p. 246–279

[Papazoglou and Georgakopoulos 2003] PAPAZOGLOU, M.P. ; GEORGAKOPOULOS, D.: Service-oriented computing. In: *Communications of the ACM* 46 (2003), No. 10, p. 25–28

[Pare 2004] PARE, G.: Investigating information systems with positivist case study research. In: *Communications of the AIS* 13 (2004), No. 1, p. 233–264

[Parker and Van Alstyne 2008] PARKER, G. ; VAN ALSTYNE, M.: Managing platform ecosystems. In: *Proceedings of the International Conference on Information Systems* (2008)

[Pathak et al. 2007] PATHAK, S.D. ; DILTS, D.M. ; BISWAS, G.: On the evolutionary dynamics of supply network topologies. In: *IEEE Transactions on Engineering Management* 54 (2007), No. 4, p. 662–672

[Patton 2002] PATTON, M.Q.: *Qualitative research and evaluation methods.* 3rd edition. Thousand Oaks, CA : Sage Publications, 2002

[Penrose 1959] PENROSE, E.T.: *The theory of the growth of the firm.* London, UK : Blackwell, 1959

[Pentland 1992] PENTLAND, B.T.: Organizing moves in software support hot lines. In: *Administrative Science Quarterly* 37 (1992), No. 4, p. 527–548

[Peteraf 1993] PETERAF, M.A.: The cornerstones of competitive advantage: A resource-based view. In: *Strategic Management Journal* 14 (1993), No. 3, p. 179–191

[Pfeffer 1981] PFEFFER, J.: *Power in organizations.* London, UK : Pitman, 1981

[Pfeffer and Salancik 1978] PFEFFER, J. ; SALANCIK, G.R.: *The external control of organizations: A resource dependence perspective.* New York, NY : Harper Row, 1978

[Poppo and Zenger 1998] POPPO, L. ; ZENGER, T.: Testing alternative theories of the firm: Transaction cost, knowledge-based, and measurement explanations for make-or-buy decisions in information services. In: *Strategic Management Journal* 19 (1998), No. 9, p. 853–877

[Porter 1985] PORTER, M.E.: *Competitive Advantage.* New York, NY : Free Press, 1985

[Prahalad and Hamel 1990] PRAHALAD, C.K. ; HAMEL, G.: The core competence of the corperation. In: *Harvard Business Review* 68 (1990), No. 3, p. 79–91

[Premkumar 2000] PREMKUMAR, G.P.: Interorganization systems and supply chain management: An information processing perspective. In: *Information Systems Management* 17 (2000), No. 3, p. 1–14

[Prencipe 2004] PRENCIPE, A.: Corporate strategy and systems integration capabilities: Managing networks in complex systems industries. In: PRENCIPE, A. (Ed.) ; DAVIES, A. (Ed.) ; HOBDAY, M. (Ed.): *The business of systems integration*. Cambridge, MA : Oxford University Press, 2004, p. 114–131

[Rao and Klein 1994] RAO, P.M. ; KLEIN, J.A.: Growing importance of marketing strategies for the software industry. In: *Industrial Marketing Management* 23 (1994), No. 1, p. 29–37

[Reber 1989] REBER, A.S.: Implicit learning and tacit knowledge. In: *Journal of Experimental Psychology* 118 (1989), No. 3, p. 219–235

[Ren et al. 2008] REN, M. ; AO, X. ; WANG, H.: Service oriented architecture for inter-organizational IT resources sharing system. In: *Proceedings of the IEEE International Conference on Automation and Logistics* (2008)

[Rettig 2007] RETTIG, C.: The trouble with enterprise software. In: *MIT Sloan Management Review* 49 (2007), No. 1, p. 21–27

[Richardson 1972] RICHARDSON, G.B.: The organisation of industry. In: *The Economic Journal* 82 (1972), No. 327, p. 883–896

[Ring and Van de Ven 1992] RING, P.S. ; VAN DE VEN, A.H.: Structuring cooperative relationships between organizations. In: *Strategic Management Journal* 13 (1992), No. 7, p. 483–498

[Ro et al. 2007] RO, Y.K. ; LIKER, J.K. ; FIXSON, S.K.: Modularity as a strategy for supply chain coordination: The case of US auto. In: *IEEE Transactions on Engineering Management* 54 (2007), No. 1, p. 172–189

[Robey et al. 2002] ROBEY, D. ; ROSS, J.W. ; BOUDREAU, M.C.: Learning to implement enterprise systems: An exploratory study of the dialectics of change. In: *Journal of Management Information Systems* 19 (2002), No. 1, p. 17–46

[Robillard 1999] ROBILLARD, P.N.: The role of knowledge in software development. In: *Communications of the ACM* 42 (1999), No. 1, p. 87–92

[Rochet and Tirole 2003] ROCHET, J.C. ; TIROLE, J.: Platform competition in two-sided markets. In: *Journal of the European Economic Association* 1 (2003), No. 4, p. 990–1029

[Rothaermel 2001] ROTHAERMEL, F. T.: Incumbent's advantage through exploiting complementary assets via interfirm cooperation. In: *Strategic Management Journal* 22 (2001), No. 6/7, p. 687–699

[Ruokonen et al. 2008] RUOKONEN, M. ; NUMMELA, N. ; PUUMALAINEN, K. ; SAARENKETO, S.: Market orientation and internationalisation in small software firms. In: *European Journal of Marketing* 42 (2008), No. 11/12, p. 1294–1315

[Sääksjärvi et al. 2005] SÄÄKSJÄRVI, M. ; LASSILA, A. ; NORDSTRÖM, H.: Evaluating the software as a service business model: From CPU time-sharing to online innovation sharing. In: *Proceedings of the IADIS International Conference e-Society* (2005)

[Sahaym et al. 2007] SAHAYM, A. ; STEENSMA, H.K. ; SCHILLING, M.A.: The influence of information technology on the use of loosely coupled organizational forms: An industry-level analysis. In: *Organization Science* 18 (2007), No. 5, p. 865–880

[Salvador 2007] SALVADOR, F.: Toward a product system modularity construct: Literature review and reconceptualization. In: *IEEE Transactions on Engineering Management* 54 (2007), No. 2, p. 219–240

[Sanchez and Mahoney 1996] SANCHEZ, R. ; MAHONEY, J.T.: Modularity, Flexibility, and Knowledge Management in Product and Organizational Design. In: *Strategic Management Journal* 17, Special Issue: Knowledge and the Firm (1996), p. 63–76

[Sanders and Boivie 2004] SANDERS, W.G. ; BOIVIE, S.: Sorting things out: Valuation of new firms in uncertain markets. In: *Strategic Management Journal* 25 (2004), No. 2, p. 167–186

[Saraf et al. 2007] SARAF, N. ; LANGDON, C.S. ; GOSAIN, S.: IS application capabilities and relational value in interfirm partnerships. In: *Information Systems Research* 18 (2007), No. 3, p. 320–339

[Scandura and Williams 2000] SCANDURA, T.A. ; WILLIAMS, E.A.: Research methodology in management: Current practices, trends, and implications for future research. In: *Academy of Management Journal* 43 (2000), No. 6, p. 1248–1264

[Scheer and Habermann 2000] SCHEER, A.W. ; HABERMANN, F.: Enterprise resource planning: Making ERP a success. In: *Communications of the ACM* 43 (2000), No. 4, p. 57–61

[Schilling and Steensma 2001] SCHILLING, M.A. ; STEENSMA, H.K.: The use of modular organizational forms: An industry-level analysis. In: *Academy of Management Journal* 44 (2001), No. 6, p. 1149–1168

[Schilling 2000] SCHILLING, M.A.: Toward a general modular systems theory and its application to interfirm product modularity. In: *Academy of Management Review* 25 (2000), No. 2, p. 312–334

[Schmidt and Simonee 1996] SCHMIDT, K. ; SIMONEE, C.: Coordination mechanisms: Towards a conceptual foundation of CSCW systems design. In: *Computer Supported Cooperative Work* 5 (1996), No. 2, p. 155–200

[Schumpeter 1934] SCHUMPETER, J.A.: *The Theory of Economic Development.* Cambridge, MA : Harvard University Press, 1934

[Scott and Vessey 2002] SCOTT, J.E. ; VESSEY, I.: Managing risks in enterprise systems implementations. In: *Communications of the ACM* 45 (2002), No. 4, p. 74–81

[Seth and Thomas 1994] SETH, A. ; THOMAS, H.: Theories of the firm: Implications for strategy research. In: *Journal of Management Studies* 31 (1994), No. 2, p. 165–192

[Shang and Seddon 2000] SHANG, S. ; SEDDON, P.B.: A comprehensive framework for classifying the benefits of ERP systems. In: *Proceedings of the Americas Conference on Information Systems* (2000)

[Shapiro and Varian 1999] SHAPIRO, C. ; VARIAN, H.R.: *Information rules - A strategic guide to the network economy.* Cambridge, MA : Harvard Business School Press, 1999

[Sherif et al. 2006] SHERIF, K. ; ZMUD, R.W. ; BROWNE, G.J.: Managing peer-to-peer conflicts in disruptive information technology innovations: The case of software reuse. In: *Management Information Systems Quarterly* 30 (2006), No. 2, p. 339–356

[Shin 2006] SHIN, I.: Adoption of enterprise application software and firm performance. In: *Small Business Economics* 26 (2006), No. 3, p. 241–256

[Siggelkow 2007] SIGGELKOW, N.: Persuasion with case studies. In: *Academy of Management Journal* 50 (2007), No. 1, p. 20–24

[Simon 1962] SIMON, H. A.: The Architecture of Complexity. In: *Proceedings of the American Philosophical Society* 106 (1962), No. 6, p. 467–482

[Simon 1947] SIMON, H.A.: *Administrative behavior: A study of decision-making processes in administrative organizations.* New York, NY : Macmillan, 1947

[Simon 1957] SIMON, H.A.: *Models of man.* New York, NY : Wiley, 1957

[Snow et al. 1992] SNOW, C.C. ; MILES, R.E. ; COLEMAN, H.J.: Managing 21st century network organizations. In: *Organizational Dynamics* 20 (1992), No. 3, p. 4–20

[Sosa et al. 2004] SOSA, M.E. ; EPPINGER, S.D. ; ROWLES, C.M.: The misalignment of product architecture and organizational structure in complex product development. In: *Management Science* 12 (2004), No. 50, p. 1674–1689

[Spender 1996] SPENDER, J.C.: Making knowledge the basis of a dynamic theory of the firm. In: *Strategic management journal* 17 (1996), No. 2, p. 45–62

[Stafford and Wallnau 2001] STAFFORD, J. ; WALLNAU, K.: Is third party certification necessary? In: *Proceedings of the 4th ICSE Workshop on Component-Based Software Engineering* (2001)

[Stake 2006] STAKE, R.E.: *Multiple case study analysis.* New York, NY : The Guilford Press, 2006

[Stal 2002] STAL, M.: Web services: Beyond component-based computing. In: *Communications of the ACM* 45 (2002), No. 10, p. 71–76

[Staudenmayer 1997] STAUDENMAYER, N.A.: *Interdependency: Conceptual, empirical, & practical issues.* Cambridge, MA : International Center for Research on the Management of Technology, Sloan School of Management, MIT, 1997

[Stone 1978] STONE, E.: *Research Methods in Organizational Behavior.* Santa Monica, CA : Goodyear Publishing, 1978

[Straub et al. 2004] STRAUB, D. ; BOUDREAU, M.C. ; GEFEN, D.: Validation guidelines for IS positivist research. In: *Communications of the AIS* 13 (2004), No. 24, p. 380–427

[Subramani and Venkatraman 2003] SUBRAMANI, M.R. ; VENKATRAMAN, N.: Safeguarding investments in asymmetric interorganizational relationships: Theory and evidence. In: *Academy of Management Journal* 46 (2003), No. 1, p. 46–62

[Sydow and Windeler 1998] SYDOW, J. ; WINDELER, A.: Organizing and evaluating interfirm networks: A structurationist perspective on network processes and effectiveness. In: *Organization Science* 9 (1998), No. 3, p. 265–284

[Sydow and Windeler 2003] SYDOW, J. ; WINDELER, A.: Knowledge, trust, and control: Managing tensions and contradictions in a regional network of service firms. In: *International Studies of Management and Organization* 33 (2003), No. 2, p. 69–100. – ISSN 0020–8825

[Teece 1986] TEECE, D.J.: Profiting from technological innovation: Implications for integration, collaboration, licensing and public policy. In: *Research policy* 15 (1986), No. 6, p. 285–305

[Teece et al. 1997] TEECE, D.J. ; PISANO, G. ; SHUEN, A.: Dynamic capabilities and strategic management. In: *Strategic Management Journal* 18 (1997), No. 7, p. 509–533

[Thompson 1967] THOMPSON, J.D.: *Organizations in Action.* New York, NY : McGraw-Hill, 1967

[Thorelli 1986] THORELLI, H.B.: Networks: Between markets and hierarchies. In: *Strategic Management Journal* 7 (1986), No. 1, p. 37–51

[Tiwana 2008a] TIWANA, A.: Does interfirm modularity complement ignorance? A field study of software outsourcing alliances. In: *Strategic Management Journal* 29 (2008), No. 11, p. 1241–1252

[Tiwana 2008b] TIWANA, A.: Does technological modularity substitute for control? A study of alliance performance in software outsourcing. In: *Strategic Management Journal* 29 (2008), No. 7, p. 769–780

[Tiwana et al. 2010] TIWANA, A. ; KONSYNSKI, B. ; BUSH, A.A.: Platform Evolution: Coevolution of Platform Architecture, Governance, and Environmental Dynamics. In: *Information Systems Research* 21 (2010), No. 4, p. 675–687

[Tushman 1977] TUSHMAN, M.L.: A political approach to organizations: A review and rationale. In: *The Academy of Management Review* 2 (1977), No. 2, p. 206–216

[Ulrich and Barney 1984] ULRICH, D. ; BARNEY, J.B.: Perspectives in organizations: Resource dependence, efficiency, and population. In: *The Academy of Management Review* 9 (1984), No. 3, p. 471–481

[Uzzi 1997] UZZI, B.: Social structure and competition in interfirm networks: The paradox of embeddedness. In: *Administrative Science Quarterly* 42 (1997), No. 1, p. 35–67

[Van de Ven 1992] VAN DE VEN, A.H.: Suggestion for studying strategy process: A research note. In: *Strategic Management Journal* 13, Special Issue (1992), p. 169–191

[Van de Ven et al. 1976] VAN DE VEN, A.H. ; DELBECQ, A.L. ; KOENIG, R.: Determinants of coordination modes within organizations. In: *American Sociological Review* 41 (1976), No. 2, p. 322–338

[Van de Ven et al. 1979] VAN DE VEN, A.H. ; WALKER, G. ; LISTON, J.: Coordination patterns within an interorganizational network. In: *Human Relations* 32 (1979), No. 1, p. 19–36

[Van Everdingen et al. 2000] VAN EVERDINGEN, Y. ; VAN HILLEGERSBERG, J. ; WAARTS, E.: Enterprise resource planning: ERP adoption by European midsize companies. In: *Communications of the ACM* 43 (2000), No. 4, p. 27–31

[Varis et al. 2005] VARIS, J. ; KUIVALAINEN, O. ; SAARENKETO, S.: Partner selection for international marketing and distribution in corporate new ventures. In: *Journal of international entrepreneurship* 3 (2005), No. 1, p. 19–36

[Venkatraman 1989] VENKATRAMAN, N.: The concept of fit in strategy research: Towards verbal and statistical correspondence. In: *Academy of Management Review* 14 (1989), No. 3, p. 423–444

[Vessey et al. 2002] VESSEY, I. ; RAMESH, V. ; GLASS, R.L.: Research in information systems: An empirical study of diversity in the discipline and its journals. In: *Journal of Management Information Systems* 19 (2002), No. 2, p. 129–174

[Vinje and Paemen 2006] VINJE, T. ; PAEMEN, D.: Transatlantic issues in the European merger review of Oracle/PeopleSoft: Harmonious dissonance. In: MARSDEN, P. (Ed.): *Handbook of research in trans-Atlantic antitrust,*. Northamption, MA : Edward Elgar Publishing, 2006, p. 16

[Vitharana et al. 2003] VITHARANA, P. ; ZAHEDI, F. ; JAIN, H.: Design, retrieval and assembly in component-based software development. In: *Communications of the ACM* 46 (2003), No. 11, p. 97–103

[von Bertalanffy 1968] VON BERTALANFFY, L.: *General Systems Theory.* New York, NY : Braziller, 1968

[von Bertalanffy 1950] VON BERTALANFFY, L.w: An outline of general system theory. In: *The British Journal for the Philosophy of Science* 1 (1950), No. 2, p. 134–165

[Wade and Hulland 2004] WADE, M. ; HULLAND, J.: The resource-based view and information systems research: Review, extension, and suggestions for future research. In: *Management Information Systems Quarterly* 28 (2004), No. 1, p. 107–142

[Wand et al. 1999] WAND, Y. ; STOREY, V.C. ; WEBER, R.: An ontological analysis of the relationship construct in conceptual modeling. In: *ACM Transactions on Database Systems* 24 (1999), No. 4, p. 449–528

[Watts 2004] WATTS, D.J.: *Six degrees: The science of a connected age.* New York, NY : WW Norton & Company, 2004

[Wernerfelt 1984] WERNERFELT, B.: A resource-based view of the firm. In: *Strategic Management Journal* 5 (1984), No. 2, p. 171–180

[Wigand et al. 2003] WIGAND, R.T. ; MERTENS, P. ; BODENDORF, F. ; KÖNIG, W. ; PICOT, A. ; SCHUMANN, M.: *Introduction to business information systems.* Berlin, Germany : Springer, 2003

[Williamson 1975] WILLIAMSON, O.E.: *Markets and hierarchies: Analysis and antitrust implications.* New York, NY : Free Press, 1975

[Williamson 1979] WILLIAMSON, O.E.: Transaction-cost economics: The governance of contractual relations. In: *Journal of Law and Economics* 22 (1979), No. 2, p. 233–261

[Williamson 1981] WILLIAMSON, O.E.: The economics of organization: The transaction cost approach. In: *American Journal of Sociology* 87 (1981), No. 3, p. 548–577

[Williamson 1985] WILLIAMSON, O.E.: *The economic institutions of capitalism.* New York, NY : Free Press, 1985

[Williamson 1990] WILLIAMSON, O.E.: Transaction Cost Economics. In: SCHMALENSEE, R. (Ed.) ; WILLIG, R.D. (Ed.): *Handbook of Industrial Organization.* Dordrecht, Netherlands : Springer, 1990, p. 135–182

[Wilson 1999] WILSON, T.D.: Models in information behaviour research. In: *Journal of Documentation* 55 (1999), No. 3, p. 249–270

[Winkler et al. 2009] WINKLER, J. ; DIBBERN, J. ; HEINZL, A.: The impact of software product and service characteristics on international distribution arrangement for software solutions. In: *Proceedings of the International Conference on Information Systems* (2009)

[Yamagishi et al. 1988] YAMAGISHI, T. ; GILLMORE, M.R. ; COOK, K.S.: Network connections and the distribution of power in exchange networks. In: *American Journal of Sociology* 93 (1988), No. 4, p. 833–851

[Yamaguchi 1996] YAMAGUCHI, K.: Power in networks of substitutable and complementary exchange relations: A rational-choice model and an analysis of power centralization. In: *American Sociological Review* 61 (1996), No. 2, p. 308–332

[Yen et al. 2002] YEN, D.C. ; CHOU, D.C. ; CHANG, J.: A synergic analysis for web-based enterprise resources planning systems. In: *Computer Standards & Interfaces* 24 (2002), No. 4, p. 337–346

[Yin 2009] YIN, R.K.: *Case Study Research: Design and methods.* 4th edition. Thousand Oaks, CA : Sage Publications, 2009

[Yli-Renko et al. 2001] YLI-RENKO, H. ; AUTIO, E. ; SAPIENZA, H.J.: Social capital, knowledge acquisition, and knowledge exploitation in young technology-based firms. In: *Strategic Management Journal* 22 (2001), No. 6-7, p. 587–613

[Zaheer and Venkatraman 1995] ZAHEER, A. ; VENKATRAMAN, N.: Relational governance as an interorganizational strategy: An empirical test of the role of trust in economic exchange. In: *Strategic Management Journal* 16 (1995), No. 5, p. 373 – 392

[Zajac and Olsen 1993] ZAJAC, E.J. ; OLSEN, C.P.: From transaction cost to transactional calue analysis: Implications for the study of interorganizational strategies. In: *Journal of Management Studies* 30 (1993), No. 1, p. 131–145

[Zenger and Hesterly 1997] ZENGER, T.R. ; HESTERLY, W.S.: The disaggregation of corporations: Selective intervention, high-powered incentives, and molecular units. In: *Organization Science* 8 (1997), No. 3, p. 209–222

ENTSCHEIDUNGSUNTERSTÜTZUNG FÜR ÖKONOMISCHE PROBLEME

Herausgegeben von Christian Becker, Wolfgang Gaul, Armin Heinzl, Martin Schader und Daniel Veit

Band 1 Ingo Böckenholt: Mehrdimensionale Skalierung qualitativer Daten. Ein Instrument zur Unterstützung von Marketingentscheidungen. 1989.

Band 2 Jürgen Joseph: Arbeitswissenschaftliche Aspekte der betrieblichen Einführung neuer Technologien am Beispiel von Computer Aided Design (CAD). Felduntersuchung zur Ermittlung arbeitswissenschaftlicher Empfehlungen für die Einführung neuer Technologien. 1990.

Band 3 Eva Schönfelder: Entwicklung eines Verfahrens zur Bewertung von Schichtsystemen nach arbeitswissenschaftlichen Kriterien. 1992.

Band 4 Michael Bargl: Akzeptanz und Effizienz computergestützter Dispositionssysteme in der Transportwirtschaft. Empirische Studien zur Implementierungsforschung von Entscheidungsunterstützungssystemen am Beispiel computergestützter Tourenplanungssysteme. 1994.

Band 5 Reinhold Decker: Analyse und Simulation des Kaufverhaltens auf Konsumgütermärkten. Konzeption eines modell- und wissensorientierten Systems zur Auswertung von Paneldaten. 1994.

Band 6 Wolfgang Gaul / Martin Schader (Hrsg.): Wissensbasierte Marketing-Datenanalyse. Das WIMDAS-Projekt. 1994.

Band 7 Daniel Baier: Konzipierung und Realisierung einer Unterstützung des kombinierten Einsatzes von Methoden bei der Positionierungsanalyse. 1994.

Band 8 Ulrich Lutz: Preispolitik im internationalen Marketing und westeuropäische Integration. 1994.

Band 9 Kirsten Petersen: Design eines Courseware-Entwicklungssystems für den computerunterstützten universitären Unterricht. CULLIS-Teilprojekt I. 1996.

Band 10 Stefan Neumann: Einsatz von Interactive Video im computerunterstützten universitären Unterricht. CULLIS Teilprojekt II. 1996.

Band 11 Eberhard Aust: Simultane Conjointanalyse, Benefitsegmentierung, Produktlinien- und Preisgestaltung. 1996.

Band 12 Peter Heydebreck: Technologische Verflechtung. Ein Instrument zum Erreichen von Produkt- und Prozeßinnovationserfolg. 1996.

Band 13 Michael Pesch: Effiziente Verkaufsplanung im Investitionsgütermarketing. 1997.

Band 14 Frank Wartenberg: Entscheidungsunterstützung im persönlichen Verkauf. 1997.

Band 15 Thomas Lechler: Erfolgsfaktoren des Projektmanagements. 1997.

Band 16 Alexandre Saad: Anbahnung und Erfolg von europäischen kooperativen F&E-Projekten. Eine empirische Analyse anhand von ESPRIT-Projekten. 1998.

Band 17 Michael Löffler: Integrierte Preisoptimierung. 1999.

Band 18 Frank Säuberlich: KDD und Data Mining als Hilfsmittel zur Entscheidungsunterstützung. 2000.

Ab Band 19 erscheint die Reihe unter dem Titel 'Informationstechnologie und Ökonomie'.

Band 19 Rainer Kiel: Dialog-gesteuerte Regelsysteme. Definition, Eigenschaften und Anwendungen. 2001.

Band 20 Axel Korthaus: Komponentenbasierte Entwicklung computergestützter betrieblicher Informationssysteme. 2001.

Band 21 Markus Aleksy: Entwicklung einer komponentenbasierten Architektur zur Implementierung paralleler Anwendungen mittels CORBA. Mit Beispielen aus den Wirtschaftswissenschaften. 2003.

Band 22 Michael Zapf: Flexible Kundeninteraktionsprozesse im Communication Center. 2003.

Band 23 Yvonne Staack: Kundenbindung im eBusiness. Eine kausalanalytische Untersuchung der Determinanten, Dimensionen und Verhaltenskonsequenzen der Kundenbindung im Online-Shopping und Online-Brokerage. 2004.

Band 24 Lars Schmidt-Thieme: Assoziationsregel-Algorithmen für Daten mit komplexer Strutkur. Mit Anwendungen im Web Mining. 2003.

Band 25 Stefan Hocke: Flexibilitätsmanagement in der Logistik. Systemtheoretische Fundierung und Simulation logistischer Gestaltungsparameter. 2004.

Band 26 Viktor Jung: Markteintrittsgestaltung neugegründeter Unternehmen. Situationsspezifische und erfolgsbezogene Analyse. 2004.

Band 27 Lars Brehm: Postimplementierungsphase von ERP-Systemen in Unternehmen. Organisatorische Gestaltung und kritische Erfolgsfaktoren. 2004.

Band 28 Ralf Gitzel: Model-Driven Software Development Using a Metamodel-Based Extension Mechanism for UML. 2006.

Band 29 Bernd Stauß: Optimale Gestaltung von Auswahlmenüs und deren Verwendung im Variantenmanagement. 2006.

Band 30 Nils Schumacher: EDI via XML. Potentiale und Strategien für global orientierte kleine und mittlere Unternehmen. 2007.

Band 31 Christian Cuske: Quantifizierung operationeller Technologierisiken bei Kreditinstituten. Eine Ontologie-zentrierte Vorgehensweise im Spannungsfeld bankinterner und aufsichtsrechtlicher Sichtweise. 2007.

Band 32 Matthias Merz: Konzeptioneller Entwurf und prototypische Implementierung einer Sicherheitsarchitektur für die Java Data Objects-Spezifikation. 2008.

Band 33 Tobias Hildenbrand: Improving Traceability in Distributed Collaborative Software Development. A Design Science Approach. 2008.

Band 34 Karen H.L. Tso-Sutter: Towards Metadata-Aware Algorithms for Recommender Systems. 2010.

Band 35 Thomas Schoberth: Eine Längsschnittstudie der Kommunikationsaktivität in virtuellen Gemeinschaften. 2010.

Band 36 Nima Mazloumi: Entwurf eines Refernzmodells und Frameworks zur Erstellung hybrider Lehr- und Lernszenarien. Mit Fallbeispielen aus der Betriebswirtschaftslehre und der Wirtschaftsinformatik. 2010.

Band 37 Anja Zöller: Effizienzanalyse grundlegender Gestaltungsgrößen der OP-Organisation. 2010.

Band 38 Jessica Katharina Winkler: International Entry Mode Choices of Software Firms. An Analysis of Product-Specific Determinants. 2009.

Band 39 Martin J. Lafleur: *Loyalty Profiling.* Erfolgsdimensionen und Modellansätze eines effizienten und effektiven Customer Relationship Management. 2010.

Band 40 Ingo Ott: Effizientes Prozessmanagement im öffentlichen Dienst. 2010.

Band 41 Stefan Seedorf: Ontologie-gestützte Entwicklung komponentenbasierter Anwendungssysteme. Ein wissensbasiertes Informationssystem zur Unterstützung der Entwicklung und Wartung von Geschäftskomponenten (KompIS). 2010.

Band 42 Dominic Gastes: Erhebungsprozesse und Konsistenzanforderungen im Analytic Hierarchy Process (AHP). 2011.

Band 43 *erscheint in Kürze*

Band 44 Olaf Thiele: Informationsvisualisierungen auf mobilen Endgeräten zur Unterstützung des betrieblichen Datenmanagements. 2011.

Band 45 Krisztian Antal Buza: Fusion Methods for Time-Series Classification. 2011.

Band 46 Thomas Kude: The Coordination of Inter-Organizational Networks in the Enterprise Software Industry. The Perspective of Complementors. 2012.

www.peterlang.de